THE
PEN AND INK
DRAWING GUIDE

HOW TO CREATE INTRICATE FINELINE ARTWORKS

GIOVANA GHIZZI VESCOVI

rockynook

The Pen and Ink Drawing Guide
How to Create Intricate Fineline Artworks
Giovana Ghizzi Vescovi

Editor: Kelly Reed
Project manager: Lisa Brazieal
Marketing coordinator: Katie Walker
Copyeditor: Shawn Laflamme
Cover design: Amy DeGrote
Interior design: Amy DeGrote
Composition: Kim Scott/Bumpy Design
Cover Illustration: Giovana Ghizzi Vescovi

ISBN: 979-8-88814-160-1
1st Edition (1st printing, August 2024)
© 2024 Giovana Ghizzi Vescovi
All images © Giovana Ghizzi Vescovi unless otherwise noted.

Rocky Nook Inc.
1010 B Street, Suite 350
San Rafael, CA 94901
USA

www.rockynook.com

Distributed in the UK and Europe by Publishers Group UK
Distributed in the U.S. and all other territories by Ingram Publisher Services

Library of Congress Control Number: 2024936715

This book is printed on acid-free paper.
Printed in China.

DEDICATION

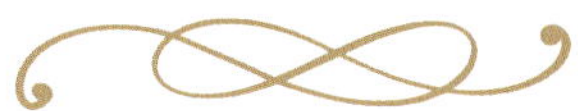

This book, which wouldn't exist without the unwavering support
and inspiration of the people I hold dearest, is dedicated to:

My parents, Sandra and Roberto, for their
endless support and encouragement;

My husband, Justin, for always believing in me
and inspiring me to chase my dreams;

My sisters, Gabi and Giulia, for being my best friends
and constant sources of love and laughter;

My aunt, Silvia, who taught me how to think
outside the box and embrace creativity;

And my grandparents, Neide and Antonio, whose love
and wisdom continue to guide me every day.

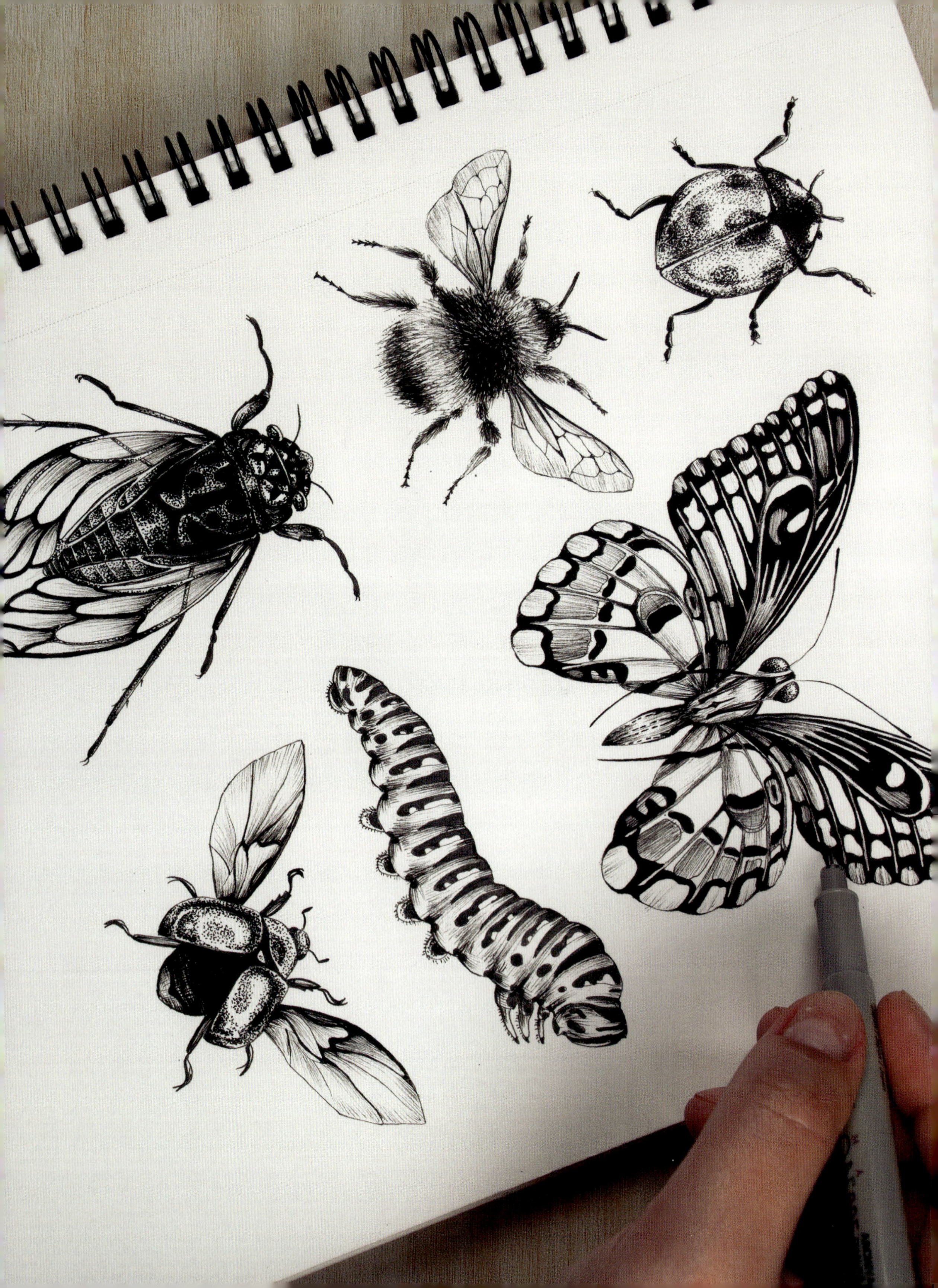

TABLE OF CONTENTS

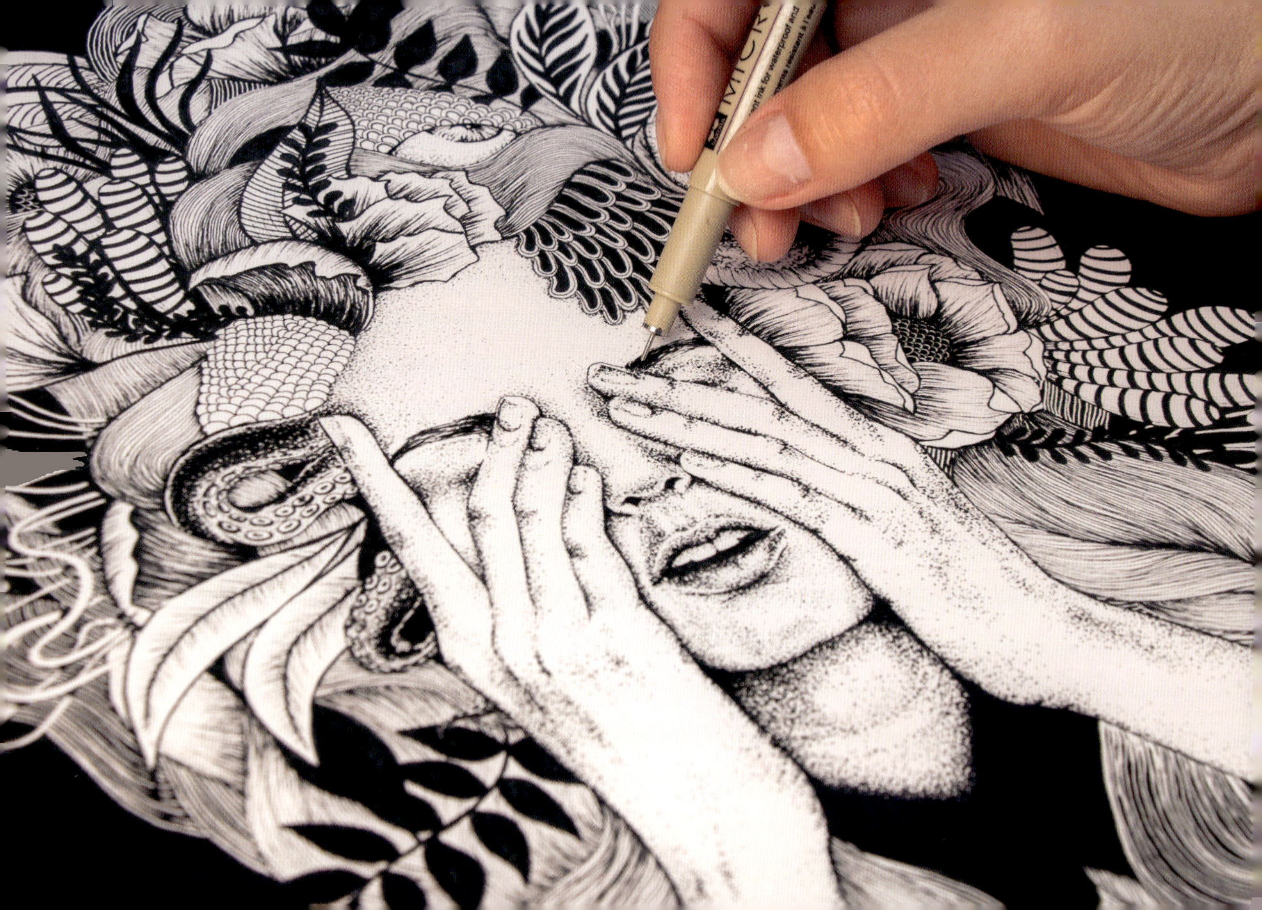

INTRODUCTION TO PEN AND INK DRAWING

The act of drawing and creating art has been a great teacher throughout my life. It taught me to self-reflect and express myself, to be patient and persistent. It gave me confidence and an incredible sense of accomplishment. From my early childhood until now, I have experimented with multiple mediums individually and mixed together, always trying to find the method that would best translate my artistic voice onto paper or canvas.

From digital to traditional art, everything felt right and not right at the same time, until I saw myself in a boring university class and the only way I could pay attention to the teacher was if I doodled on my notebook with a pen at the same time. Something about having my hands occupied and using the creative side of my brain just helped me to filter out distractions and absorb information from the class.

That year, I used my lined notebook and ballpoint pen to come up with the most creative drawings I had ever drawn. The process was so simple and practical. I could do it from anywhere and simply close the notebook and put it back in my backpack anytime—there was no mess and no expectation for me to create a masterpiece.

This was the beginning of my journey with pen and ink drawing. The pen has taught me so much about life, creativity, and expression, and I will share a little bit of those discoveries with you in this book.

WHY PEN AND INK?

Pen and ink has been a favorite choice of artists at many stages of their art journey, from beginners trying to express themselves through simple sketches and doodles, to professional artists looking to create intricate masterpieces by combining hundreds and thousands of lines to create all sorts of illusions.

It started more than 4,000 years ago in Egypt and China, where it was used for calligraphy and drawing, and then expanded to the West with artists like Da Vinci, Michelangelo, and Picasso. Today, inking remains relevant due to its simple and practical nature as an art form, as well as the possibilities it gives artists anywhere to create beautiful, bold designs in any style.

Ink drawing can be, in its simplest form, dipping a stick into a jar of ink and making a line on paper. It can also be as complex as using a variety of pens with different thicknesses, shapes, and inks, to create different effects and styles. With ink, you can express an idea for a design with a quick, rough sketch, and draw the most detailed, intricate, complex drawing you can imagine. It offers endless possibilities and a unique freedom to the artist. From fine detail work to bold, expressive strokes, the versatility of pen and ink is truly remarkable.

HOW TO USE THIS BOOK

In this book, we will explore the nuances of pen and ink drawing, through different techniques and exercises that will help you practice and improve. From understanding how to control your pen for different effects, to mastering the art of shading and texture, to developing different styles of drawing, this book offers a thorough and accessible introduction to the world of pen and ink drawing.

This book is designed to be beginner-friendly, but it also offers a lot of information for more advanced artists who wish to refine their skills. It is structured in a way that will allow you to progress at your own pace, taking the time to practice and master each technique before moving on to the next. Each chapter includes detailed instructions, tips, and sample drawings to guide and inspire you.

The knowledge you gain will help you to advance your drawing skills as well as explore yourself as a creative. I encourage you to see this book as a guide, a tool, and a friend. Use it as you see fit, skip to chapters that interest you, do the exercises at your own pace, and remember that the goal is not perfection, but progress. So, embrace the journey, not the destination. Treat every mistake as an opportunity to learn and grow. Most importantly, enjoy the process and the unique artistic expression that pen and ink drawing allows.

Whether you are a complete beginner exploring drawing as a whole for the first time, or an experienced artist in other mediums who wants to get into pen and ink art, this book was made for you. Let's begin!

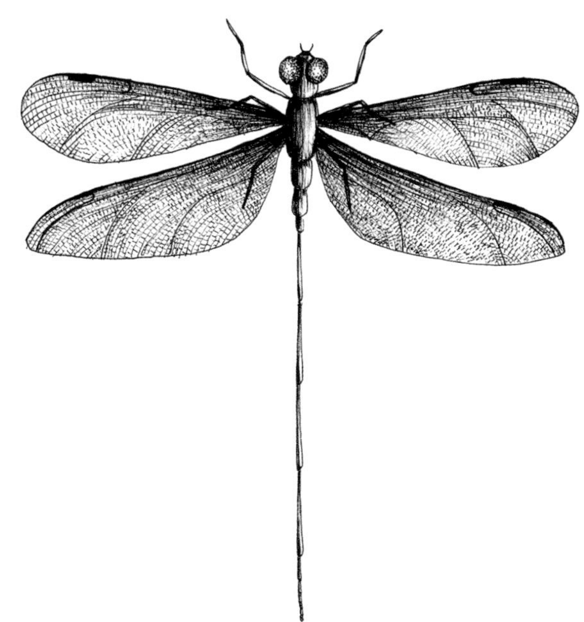

TOOLS AND MATERIALS

Before we start drawing, let's understand the materials used for pen and ink drawing. The items described in this section are not required for you to follow the instructions of this book, but simply suggestions for you to explore as you progress in your drawing journey if you wish. Everything we will draw together in this book can be done with fine-line ink pens.

Ink Choices

Ink is the most important tool for pen and ink drawing. There are many types of ink available, each with its own unique properties and advantages. Some popular choices include India ink, which is known for its deep black color and waterproof properties, and Sumi ink, which is a traditional Japanese ink used for calligraphy and brush painting.

The type of ink you use can greatly affect your final result. There are two main types of inks that artists use: pigment-based inks and dye-based inks.

Pigment-Based Inks

Pigment-based inks are made up of tiny, encapsulated particles that sit on top of the paper, rather than being absorbed by it. This makes them a lot more durable and resistant to fading. They're also water-resistant, which can be a great advantage if you're planning to use watercolors or other wet mediums with your ink work.

One of the most popular pigment-based inks is India ink. Known for its deep, dark blacks and its permanent, waterproof qualities, India ink has been a favorite of artists for centuries. However, it's worth noting that because pigment particles are larger than dye molecules, pigment-based inks can clog up finer pen nibs. Therefore, they're often better suited to broader nibs or brushes.

Dye-Based Inks

Dye-based inks, on the other hand, consist of colorant that is fully dissolved in the carrier liquid. When you put it on paper, it's absorbed and spreads out. This can result in vibrant, saturated colors and smooth, even lines. Dye-based inks tend to be less resistant to water and light, meaning they can fade over time or run if exposed to moisture. However, they can offer a wider range of colors than pigment-based inks and are less likely to clog pen nibs, making them a popular choice for detailed work.

Water-Based Inks

Water-based inks are a versatile choice for artists, especially those who work with mixed media. These inks are often less permanent than pigment- or dye-based options, but this can be an advantage in certain situations.

When first applied, water-based inks create vivid, clean lines. However, upon contact with water, they can spread and blend, creating interesting wash effects. This characteristic makes them particularly great for artists who enjoy creating gradients and soft transitions of color and tones.

Water-based inks are generally safe to use with any type of pen, including finer nibs, without the risk of clogging. They are available in a wide range of colors, allowing for great artistic flexibility.

When selecting between pigment-based, dye-based, and water-based inks, consider your artistic goals, the techniques you plan to use, and the longevity requirements of your project. If you need your work to stand the test of time and be resistant to fading or running, you might want to opt for a pigment-based ink. If you're after a wide range of colors and plan to use finer nibs, a dye-based ink could be the better choice. If you are working with mixed media, you can try water-based inks as they can create vibrant lines but also interesting wash effects when in contact with water.

As always, experimenting with these options is the best way to find what works for you.

Choosing the Right Paper

When it comes to pen and ink drawing, the paper you choose can also influence your final piece. Several factors come into play, such as texture, weight, durability, and preservation. Here are a few things to keep in mind when choosing the best paper for your pen and ink drawings:

- ✧ **Texture:** The texture of the paper can affect both the appearance and the feel of your drawing. Smooth papers can produce sharp, clean lines, making them ideal for detailed work. On the other hand, rough papers can add a textural quality to your work that can be visually interesting.
- ✧ **Weight:** The weight of the paper is also crucial. Heavier papers are usually indicated by a higher gsm (grams per square meter) number and are generally more durable. They will be able to hold more intense techniques without tearing or warping. Lighter papers are more susceptible to damage and may not hold up well to the demands of pen and ink, especially if you are working on a detailed drawing that requires several layers of ink.
- ✧ **Durability and preservation:** The longevity of your artwork depends on the durability and preservation qualities of the paper. Acid-free papers are designed to resist yellowing and deterioration over time, making them a good choice for artworks you wish to keep or display.

For pen and ink drawings, heavyweight, acid-free papers are generally a good choice. Bristol board, for example, is a type of heavy, smooth paper that's great for detailed ink work, and a personal favorite of mine. It's sturdy, holds ink well, and allows for sharp, precise lines.

If you prefer a bit of texture, try hot-pressed watercolor paper. Despite the name, this type of paper is not just for watercolors. Hot-pressed watercolor paper is smooth compared to other watercolor papers but still offers a slight texture that can add depth to your ink drawings.

Sketch paper or simple printer paper can also be useful for practice and preliminary sketches, but it's typically too thin for finished ink drawings.

Types of Pens for Pen and Ink Drawing

While the range of pens available for pen and ink drawing is vast, this book will primarily focus on drawing with fineline ink pens, also known as liners, and technical pens. These pens are affordable, user-friendly, and perfect for beginners and experienced artists alike. However, you will be able to apply the knowledge from this book to any other type of pen used in ink drawing, so here's a brief overview of them.

Fineliners

Fineline ink pens or liners are the main focus of this book. They are versatile, affordable, and very user-friendly. They are excellent for creating precise, clean lines and are available in a variety of sizes, making them ideal for both detailed work and broader strokes. These pens usually have a plastic barrel and a fine, felt-tipped nib that absorbs ink from a reservoir in the barrel. The nibs are slightly flexible, which allows for a bit of line variation and speed. Fineliners are great for quick, rough sketches as well as detailed finished

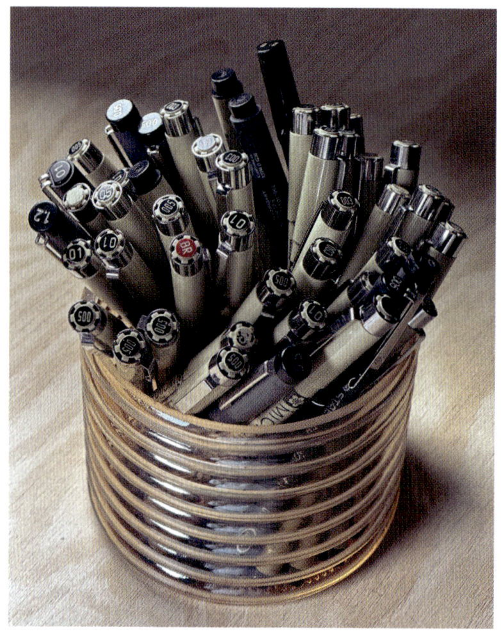

Dip Pens

Dip pens have a metal nib that you dip into a small container of ink. They were widely used before the invention of the fountain pen and are still popular among artists and calligraphers for their flexibility and the distinct character they bring to the lines.

Brush Pens

Brush pens offer the versatility of traditional paintbrushes but with the convenience of a pen. They are great for creating a variety of strokes, from fine lines to broad strokes, making them a great option when looking to work with expressive styles and calligraphy.

Quill Pens

Quill pens are traditional writing tools made from a molted flight feather of a large bird. They offer a unique, old-world charm and are often used in calligraphy.

Bamboo Pens

Like quill pens, bamboo pens are traditional writing tools. They are carved from bamboo and offer a firm but slightly flexible drawing experience.

Fountain Pens

Fountain pens have an internal reservoir of water-based liquid ink. They are known for their smooth writing experience and are used in various artistic applications.

artworks. They come in different types of inks, so keep that in mind when choosing new pens to make sure you have the right kind of ink for your drawing's needs.

Technical Pens

Technical pens, also known as drafting pens, typically have a rigid metal nib or point and come in various sizes, allowing for consistent line width. They often use refillable ink cartridges or ink reservoirs built into the pen and are commonly used in architecture and engineering for their ability to produce consistent lines of a fixed width, making them perfect for detailed work. The ink delivery system is designed to release the ink at a certain speed, making it excellent at slow and accurate line creation.

Ballpoint Pens

Ballpoint pens are perhaps the most common type of pen. They use oil-based ink which is dispensed over a metal ball at its point. They are inexpensive and a great choice for sketching and hatching.

Rollerball Pens

Rollerball pens are similar to ballpoint pens, but they use water-based or gel ink, which flows more smoothly and provides a more vivid line.

Felt-Tip Pens and Markers

Felt-tip pens and markers have a porous tip of fibrous material. The ink is usually water-based (like in highlighters) or alcohol-based (like in permanent markers). They are available in various widths and are excellent for bold lines and filling in areas.

Each type of pen has its own unique properties, advantages, and drawbacks. Experimenting with various types of pens can help you discover the best drawing tools for you and further develop your style and technique.

In the following chapters, we will delve deeper into the world of fineline ink pens. We will explore their characteristics, learn how to use them effectively, and practice several techniques that will help you develop your skills.

White Ink

In pen and ink drawing, white ink can be used as a creative tool to add highlights, create special effects, or even to correct little mistakes. This is an optional, but fun, tool to use. It can help bring your drawings to life, especially when working with realism, as we will see in further chapters. Let's explore some options for incorporating white ink into your work.

Calligraphy Ink

White calligraphy ink is often thicker than regular ink, which allows it to sit nicely on the surface of your paper without being absorbed. It's perfect for creating bold lines and intricate details, and correcting little mistakes. You can use a small round brush to apply it on your drawings.

White Gel Pens

White gel pens are a great tool for adding small highlights or intricate white details to your drawings. They have a smooth flow and provide a consistent line, making them ideal for precise work.

Fineline Acrylic White Pens

Fineline acrylic white pens offer the precision of a fineline ink pen, with the added benefit of using white acrylic ink. This type of ink is opaque and can cover dark or colored inks, making these pens perfect for adding high-lights or correcting mistakes.

There are other types of white pens available that can be used in pen and ink drawing, such as white marker pens, white ink fountain pens, and white rollerball pens. The type of pen you choose to use will depend on your specific needs and personal preferences.

Regardless of the type of white ink pen you choose, remember that it can add depth and dimension to your drawings. Use it to add highlights, enhance textures, and bring out key features in your work—and don't worry, you will learn how to do this in the following chapters. Most importantly, don't be afraid to experiment. The beauty of art lies in the freedom to try new techniques and create something uniquely yours.

Now that we're familiar with the basic tools and materials for pen and ink drawing, we'll explore techniques to effectively use your fineline ink pens to create beautiful drawings.

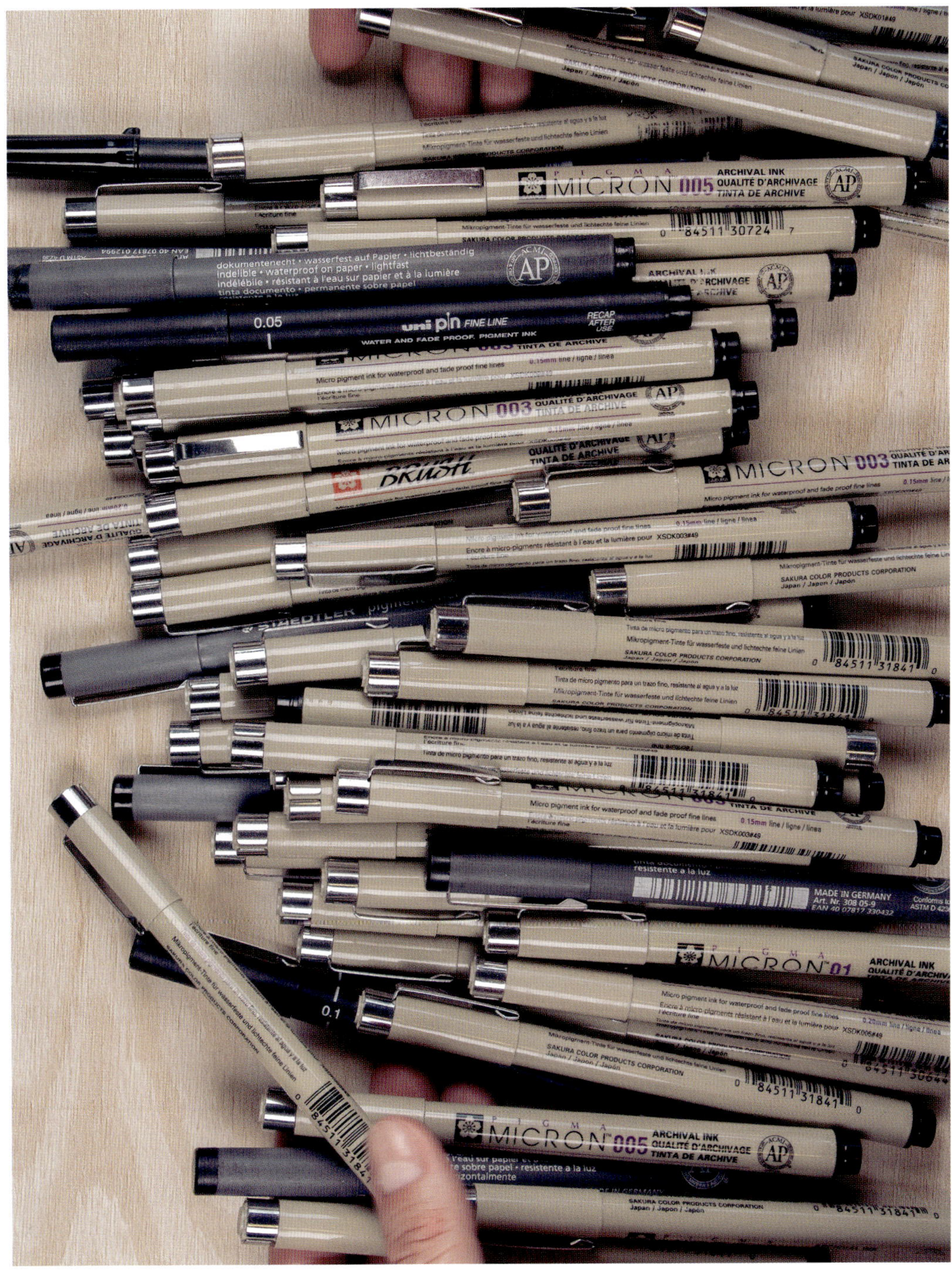

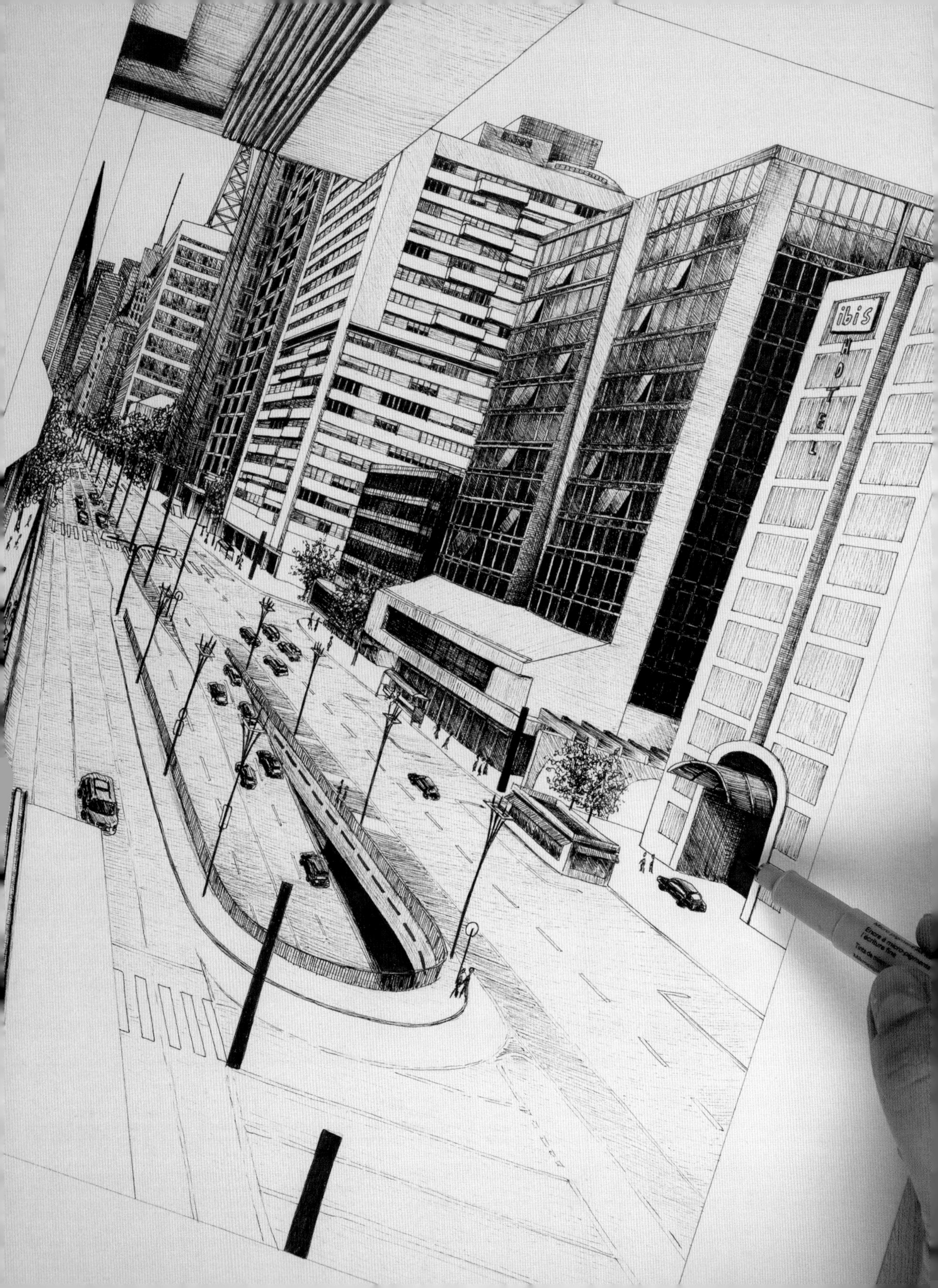

ibis
HOTEL

HOW TO DRAW ANYTHING

Drawing is often perceived as a talent that some people are simply born with, while others believe they just lack the innate ability to create art. However, this common misconception overlooks the fact that drawing is a skill that can be learned and improved through practice and dedication. In this chapter, we will explore how anyone can develop their drawing abilities, regardless of their perceived talent, and the importance of understanding drawing as a skill rather than an inherent gift.

Like any other skill, such as playing a musical instrument or learning a new language, drawing requires practice, patience, and perseverance. While some individuals may demonstrate an early aptitude for drawing, this does not mean that others cannot develop similar skills with time and effort. One of the most essential aspects of improving your drawing skills is consistent practice and experimentation. By dedicating time to draw regularly, you will gradually improve your technique, build confidence in your abilities, and potentially even develop your own drawing style.

Practice will allow you to experiment with different mediums, explore drawing different subjects, and refine your observational skills, all of which are crucial components of artistic development. Through time and dedication, you will be able to develop your own creative process.

As you embark on this journey, you will notice that drawing is more than a visual representation of ideas, but also a way of seeing the world, interpreting it, and bringing your unique perspective to life. From simple sketches to intricate illustrations, every stroke of your pencil or pen is an opportunity to explore new ideas, experiment with techniques, and push the boundaries of your creativity.

In the following sections, we will explore some of the fundamental principles of drawing and the most helpful sketching methods I encountered through my years as an artist. This chapter will offer a basic knowledge of drawing that will be useful as the starting point for any artwork.

While a self-directed practice is essential for your development as an artist, don't forget to seek guidance and feedback from other experienced artists or instructors. Attending drawing classes, workshops, or joining artistic communities can also accelerate your learning and growth as it will allow you to receive constructive criticism, learn new techniques, and benefit from the expertise of others. My expertise in drawing has grown immensely with the perspective and input of other artists. Don't take anything you read in this book—or any other source, for that matter— as the one and only right way to achieve proficiency in drawing, as I encourage you to explore beyond this book as well.

We will start by studying the techniques to draw elements with proportional accuracy and how to translate three-dimensional objects onto a two-dimensional surface, using pen or pencil. We'll build on this information to create detailed ink drawings in the following chapters, where you will learn how to use form, perspective, texture, light, and shadow to enhance your artwork and express ideas with ink pens.

SKETCHING

Sketching is the starting point of any artwork, regardless of the medium or style you choose. This is probably where you will spend a large amount of your practice time and where you will develop and improve your drawing skills over time. This stage of the creative process can help you overcome the initial fear of the blank page, offering a comfortable space to experiment, make mistakes, and refine your ideas. Unlike the final inking stage, sketching has lower expectations attached to it. It's a playground where you can let your imagination run free without the pressure of producing a polished final artwork.

Think of sketching as a warm-up routine before a workout. It's during these initial, loose strokes that your hand and mind sync up, gradually building more pen control, confidence, and precision. This stage can be inspiring and insightful. It can also be messy and frustrating. These are all natural feelings that are part of the journey, so don't let yourself be discouraged if you are not yet reaching the results you are looking for.

It's essential for aspiring artists to embrace mistakes as part of the learning process. Making mistakes is inevitable, and it's through these errors that artists can learn and grow. Perseverance and resilience are key in overcoming challenges and art blocks while helping you persist in your practice and continue progressing on your artistic path. Over time, consistent sketching will result in smoother lines, better proportions, and increased confidence in your drawing abilities.

Sketching is not just about creating preliminary drawings. It's a dynamic process that will allow you to plan, develop, and refine your ideas and set the stage for your final ink drawings. In this section, we will cover practical tips on how to improve your sketching skills and how this will help you achieve better results in your ink drawings.

Pencil Sketching

Sketching with a pencil before you start the inking process can be a highly effective way to establish the foundations of your drawing before making final artistic decisions. It is a helpful first step when looking to achieve very detailed work, like realistic effects and textures. It is especially helpful when you are not very familiar with the subject you are drawing and want to experiment with something new.

Developing a consistent sketching practice will enhance your drawing skills, allow you to create better compositions, and build confidence in your abilities. This is an optional but recommended starting point when working on any design project, and that includes drawing with ink. The following suggestions specifically relate to sketching with a pencil with the intention of using an ink pen afterwards.

Working with pencil is much different than working with pen, since the pencil is erasable and allows you to experiment more freely. It also allows you to create different values—that is, lights and darks—more easily. You will have much more freedom and confidence to start, knowing no stroke is permanent.

For the purpose of sketching with a pencil in preparation for an ink pen drawing, the process is simple. The first step is conceptualizing an idea, by brainstorming concepts for your artwork—in other words, defining what to draw. Sometimes, simply drafting those ideas on paper, with fast, rough strokes, can get you in the right creative mindset and inspire you with good ideas for a drawing. Instead of jumping straight to a detailed sketch on a high-quality drawing paper, you could also start with thumbnail sketches on simple pieces of paper instead. These are small sketches where you draw rough, simple shapes to represent the elements of your illustration to explore different compositions and arrangements. It will help you quickly visualize your ideas and determine the most effective layout for a final illustration.

Next, work on a larger preliminary sketch of the chosen composition, using light pencil strokes to loosely outline the main elements on the page. Then refine the sketch with more details and any necessary corrections or adjustments to improve the overall balance and coherence of the composition. Don't worry, you will learn more about composition later in this book.

Once the sketch is finalized, it will be used as a guide for your first inking strokes. After carefully outlining the most important lines with ink, erase the pencil marks and proceed with the drawing process using ink pen techniques. Go back to the pencil if you need new supporting guidelines. Feel free to move back and forth between pen and pencil.

Although using a pencil to sketch before a more detailed ink drawing is a common practice, it's easy to smudge it, especially if you don't have the right tools. You want to make sure the final result is a beautiful ink drawing on a clean paper, without any left-over pencil lines. To achieve this, there are some crucial steps to follow before you start a new drawing.

- ✧ **Choose the right pencil:** The choice of pencil for the sketching stage can significantly influence your results. The best pencils for sketching are not the same pencils used for detailing and shading in a pencil drawing, for example. Pencils are categorized into H and B grades based on how hard or soft their graphite core is. Pencils in the H range, from 9H to 2H, are going to be your best choice for sketching before an ink drawing. The "H" stands for hardness, and these pencils have firmer graphite leads that make lighter marks on paper, which is helpful since it allows

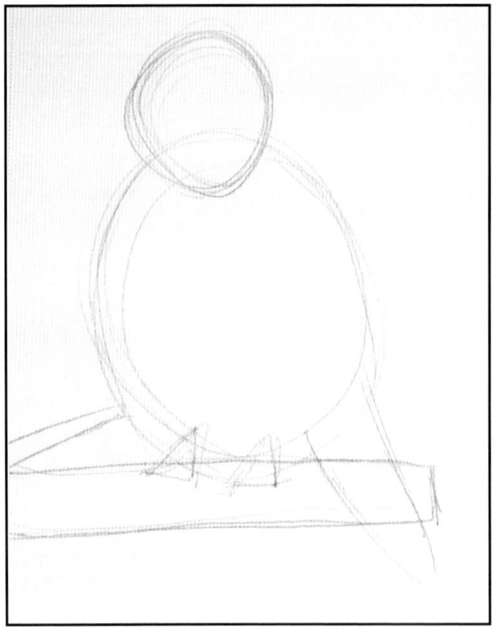
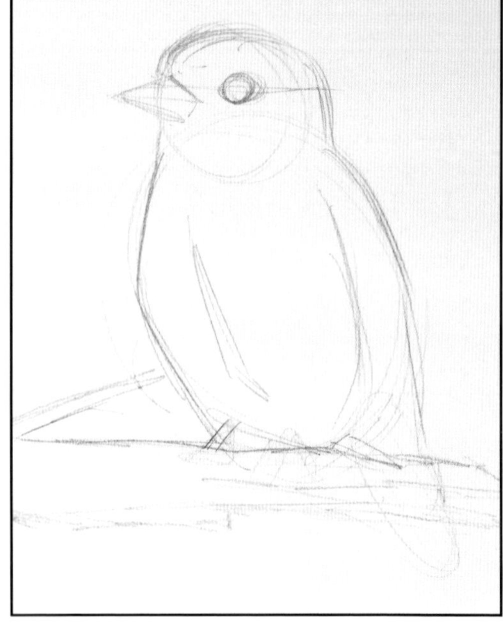

for more precise and controlled lines. The higher the number next to the H, the harder the graphite will be. Also, the harder the pencil is, the easier it will be to erase it, especially in comparison to B pencils. H pencils will definitely do a better job in keeping your page neat and clean. You will be able to experiment and refine your sketches until you're happy with the result without dealing with a messy page. Pencils in the B range (like 2B, 4B, 6B, and so on) have softer graphite leads that make darker and richer lines. These pencils are great for adding depth and contrast to your pencil drawings, but they are not ideal for sketches given that they are harder to erase and tend to smudge a lot more.

✧ **Choose the right paper:** Smooth or hot-pressed paper will be your best choice when working with ink, especially if you are starting out with a pencil sketch. They will make it easier to erase the pencil marks without damaging the paper's surface or removing too much of the dried ink, in case you are erasing over it. This is often the preferred choice when pencil sketches need to be removed entirely. Rough or textured paper, on the other hand, can make erasing slightly more challenging. The texture of the paper can trap graphite from the pencil, making it harder to erase completely without leaving behind some faint marks.

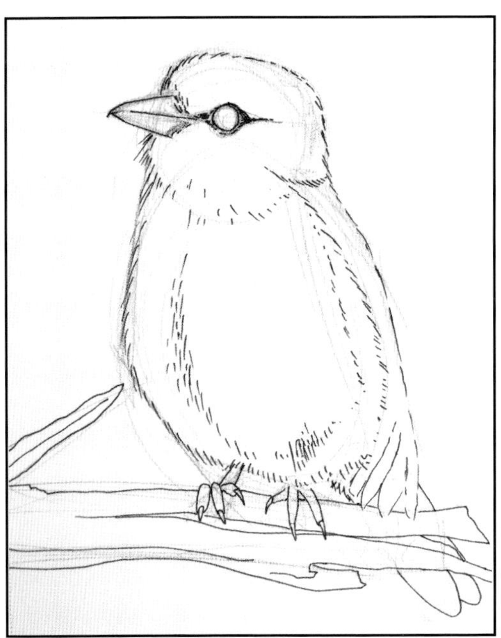

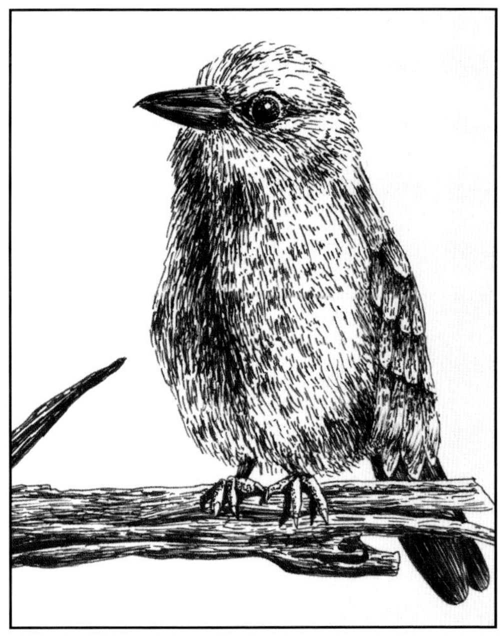

◇ **Choose the right eraser:** The type of eraser you use also plays a role. Kneaded erasers or vinyl erasers are often preferred for their ability to lift graphite cleanly without leaving much residue on paper. Applying gentle and even pressure with a clean eraser is less likely to damage the paper compared to aggressive or uneven erasing.

◇ **Wait for the ink to dry before erasing:** This seems obvious, but you would be surprised at how many times I rush to erasing and forget to wait for the ink to fully dry, ending up with an ink smudge. Depending on the area and size of the damage, this can be fixed, but most times you just have to start over. Once you start the inking process and don't need the pencil lines anymore, it is best to erase it as soon as you can to ensure a clean paper in the end. Even though the ink generally dries pretty quickly, it can vary between different brands of pens. So be patient and make sure you give a minute or two after inking to start erasing the pencil marks underneath.

These are not absolute rules by any means, but simply some helpful information to help you find a starting point. I encourage you to experiment with different tools in order to find your favorites based on your drawing style and technique.

Pen Sketching

Sketching directly with a pen, as opposed to using a pencil first, can be liberating and challenging at the same time. To try this approach, you will need to embrace your spontaneity and let go of the need for perfection. It will help you build confidence in your lines and boost your ability to make intentional, decisive strokes.

When sketching directly with pens, you are committing to every mark you make on paper. There's no erasing or redrawing as you would with a pencil. This might seem scary at first, but it can also be a great exercise in accepting imperfections and improving your observational skills. If you struggle with shaky, insecure lines, this can be an excellent exercise to help mature your technique and draw solid, confident lines. It can also help you develop a more unique sense of style to your art, since it will allow you to create more imperfect strokes and add more personality and decisiveness to your work.

Sketching with ink will also sharpen your observational skills and train your eye to see shapes, forms, and details faster. It welcomes a different kind of focus that is more relaxed and confident.

You can sketch in a similar way as you would with a pencil, by roughly defining guidelines and shapes to direct your final drawing, leaving those draft lines visible simultaneously with the final lines, or simply jump straight to drawing your subject, without any guidelines or previous planning. This allows for much simpler and stylized drawings. What makes a good drawing in this case is the quality of your lines, as exemplified in the sketch below.

Here are some tips for sketching directly with fineliners:

⬦ **Start with fast strokes:** Begin with quick pen strokes to lay down the main lines of your subject. Focus on the angles, leading lines, and main shapes as opposed to small details. You can later go over these initial lines with more decisive, darker strokes to define your drawing and add more visual information, like shadows and textures.

⬦ **Embrace mistakes:** Every line you draw is a reflection of your observation and interpretation of your subject. If a line doesn't turn out as planned, accept it as part of your artistic process and move on to the next lines. Often, what is perceived as a mistake can add character and style to a drawing.

⬦ **Vary line weight:** By varying the pressure and thickness of the lines, you can add depth and dimension to your sketches. Lighter, thinner lines can suggest distance or give a sense of lightness, while thicker, darker lines can be used to indicate closeness or give weight to certain elements of your drawing. This can be done by using fineline pens with thicker and thinner tips or experimenting with a chisel or brush pen in different positions towards the paper.

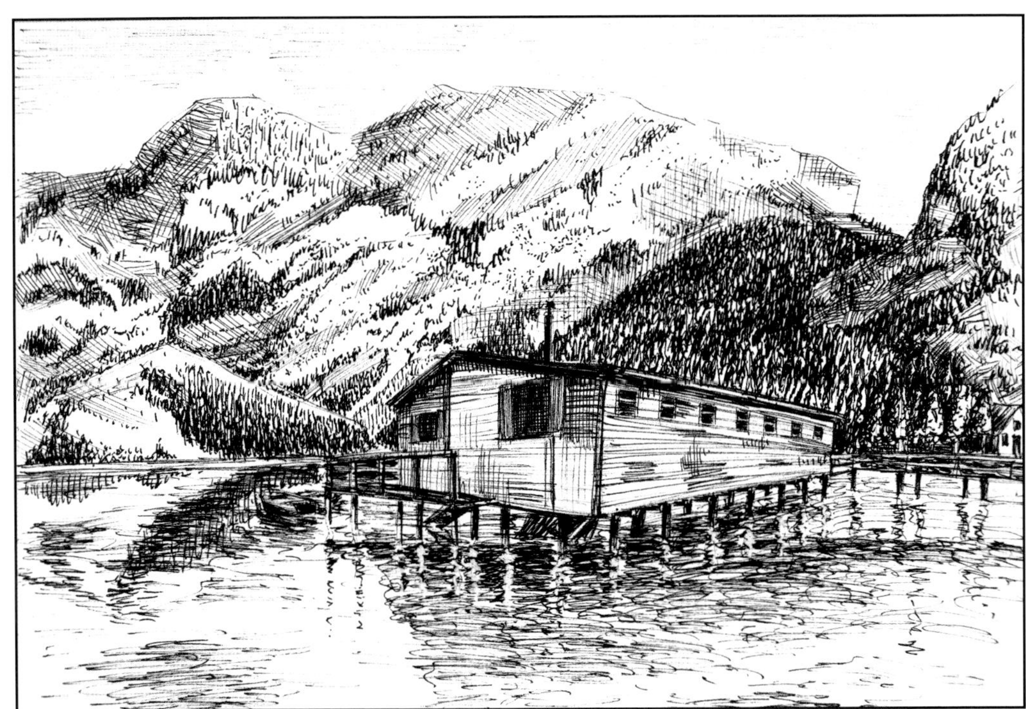

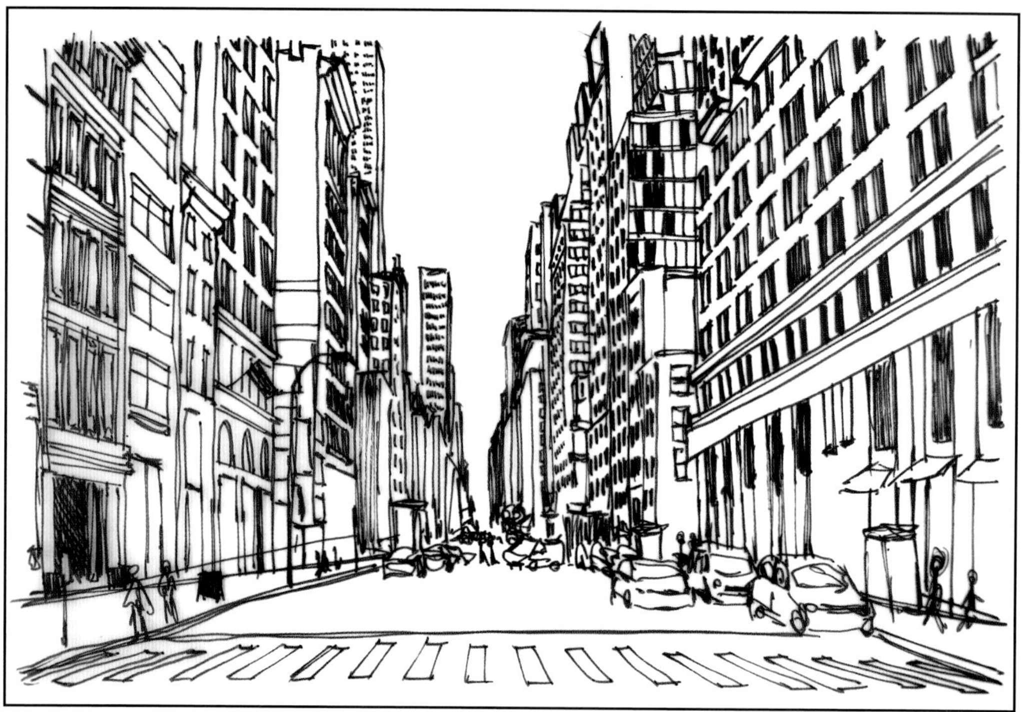

- ✧ **Experiment with techniques:** Try using different techniques like hatching, cross-hatching, stippling, and contour lines directly with your fineliner. Each technique can provide a different texture and feel to your sketches. We will discuss these and other inking techniques in Chapter 3.

Sketching directly with fineliners is not meant to replace pencil sketching. It's simply another tool in your artistic toolbox and a different approach to starting a new illustration. It encourages a different mindset and creative process that can help you grow and develop many important skills as an artist.

Line Accuracy and Pen Control

Being able to draw confident lines, exactly where you want them to be, will greatly improve the overall appearance of your drawing. A decisive stroke illustrates a clear understanding and interpretation of the subject, which is often a mark of an experienced artist. On the other hand, insecure or hesitant lines can sometimes suggest uncertainty or lack of clarity. By practicing regularly and gaining familiarity with your tools,

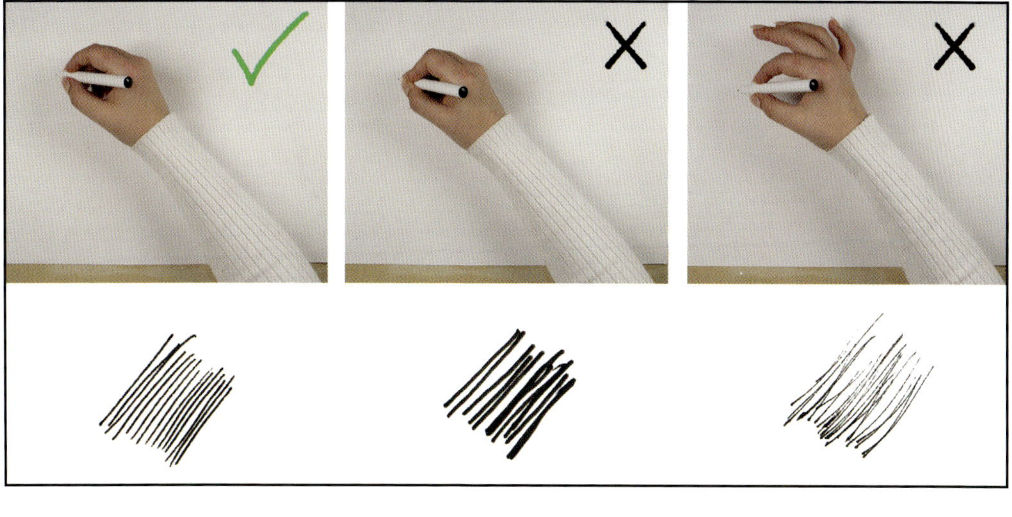

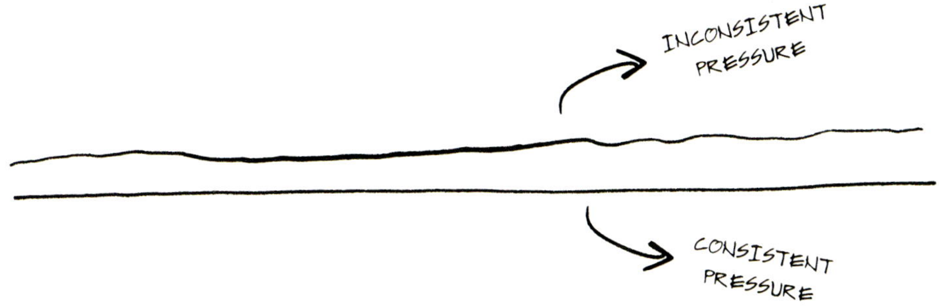

you can boost your confidence in your skills and improve the overall quality of your ink drawings. Learning and practicing different types of movements is crucial for controlling the pen based on your specific drawing needs. Here are some things to practice:

◇ **Balance and grip:** Hold the pen comfortably but firmly. If your grip is too tight and tense, if can cause fatigue. If your grip is too loose, it might be easy to lose control of your lines. Find a balance between a firm grip for good control and a relaxed hand to avoid fatigue and keep your lines fluid.

◇ **Consistent pressure:** This is key for line accuracy. Practice applying an even amount of pressure when you draw, unless the change of pressure is intentional, like when applying the hatching technique. Too much pressure can thicken lines and even damage your pen, too little can make your lines faint and inconsistent. Practice different pressure levels on scrap paper to understand how much is needed for different line weights and intensities. This will vary from pen to pen and how new or used your pen is, since ink pens release less and less ink

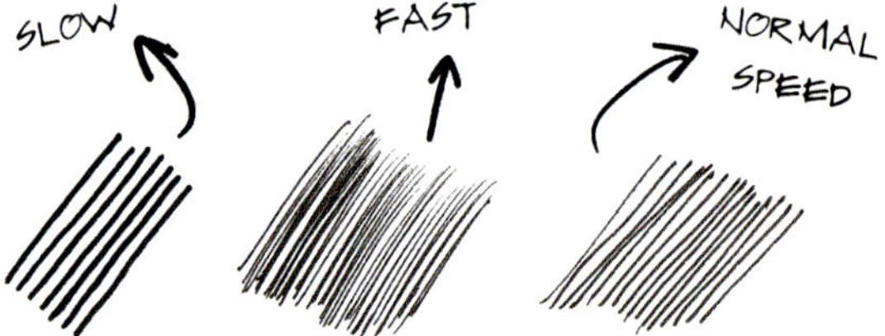

the more you use them. In summary, it is important for you to be capable of drawing solid lines from start to finish.

- ✧ **Speed control:** The speed of your pen movement affects line accuracy. Moving too fast can cause wobbly, inconsistent, or faded lines, while moving too slow can cause blotchy or uneven ink distribution, especially with brand new pens since the ink release is faster and more abundant.
- ✧ **Hand movements for detail:** When you need to work on small, intricate elements within your artwork, focus on your hand movements. This allows for a high level of precision and will help you create the smallest details. Keep your wrist relaxed but steady, using it to guide the pen across the paper. You might feel more comfortable by supporting your hand or wrist on the paper as it will give you more stability.

- ✧ **Arm movements for larger strokes:** For longer lines, shading, or covering larger areas, engage your entire arm in the movement. Lock your wrist and pivot from the elbow or shoulder, depending on the scale you are working with.
- ✧ **Wrist movements for short strokes:** If your goal is to create precise strokes or repeat line patterns, rest your wrist on the paper's surface and use it as a pivot point when drawing. Try to keep your hands stable. By grounding your wrist, you minimize unwanted wobbling and shakiness and ensure a stable point of contact between the pen and the paper. If doing this for a significant amount of time, put a small piece of paper under your wrist in order to protect your drawing from smudging with the warmth of your skin.
- ✧ **Pen angle control:** Adjusting the angle of the pen in relation to the paper while drawing can create variations in line thickness and shading. For example, a pen positioned on a 45° angle towards the paper will produce thinner strokes, while a pen in a vertical position, on a 90° angle

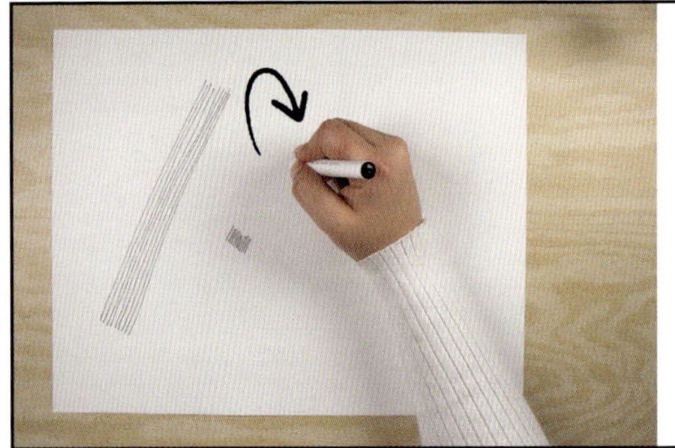

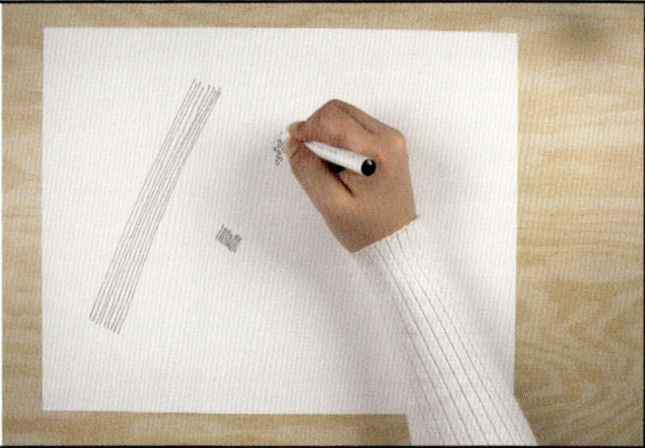

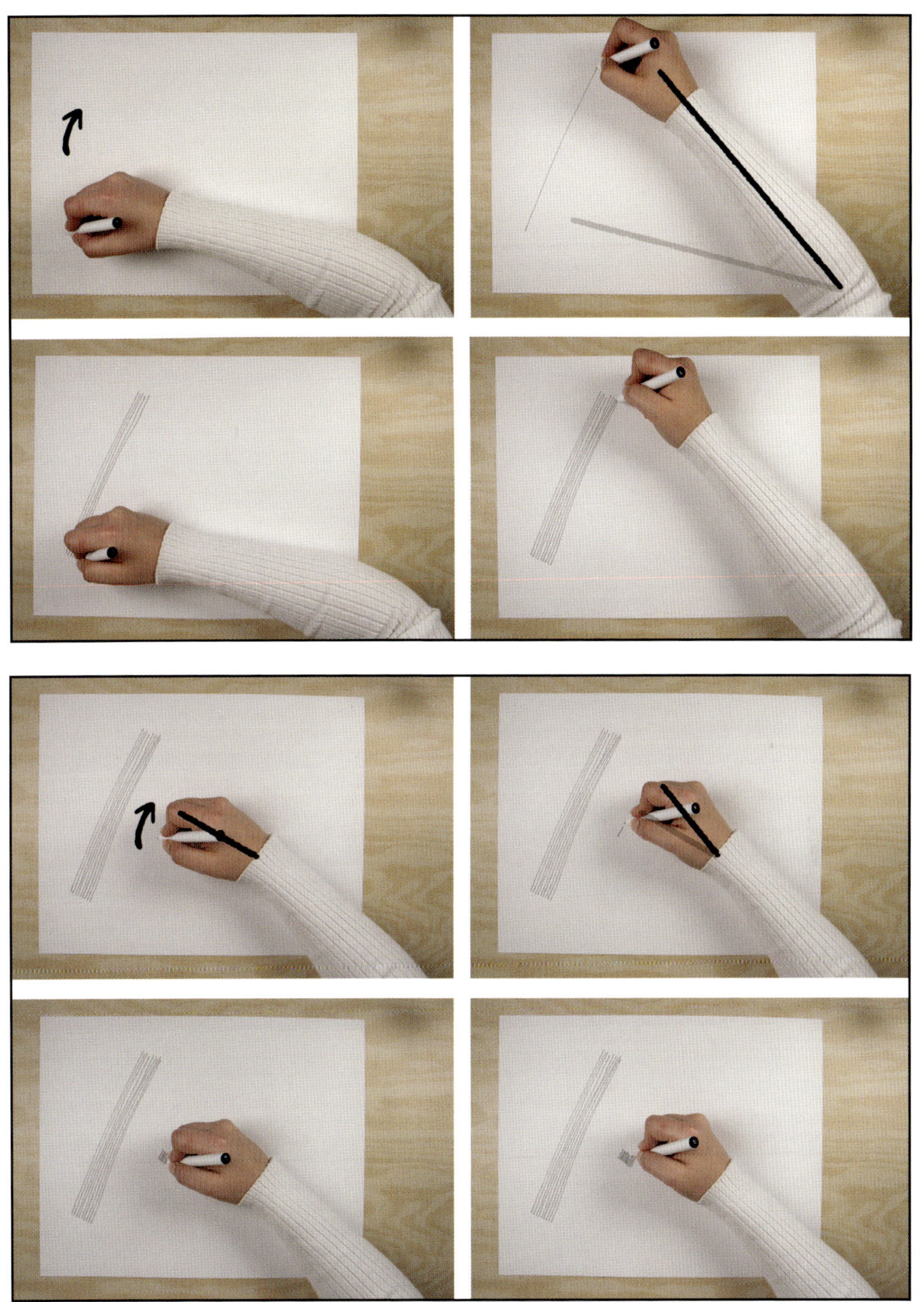

towards the paper, will release more ink and produce thicker lines. You can adjust pen angle to add depth and dimension to your drawings by manipulating the line weight and darkness.

I encourage you to practice integrating these pen control techniques into your ink drawing process. Try them on a simple piece of paper as a warm-up, and over time you will gain more control over your pens, which will help bring your artistic ideas to life. Achieving proficiency in pen control takes time, and this is a learnable skill like any other. In the next chapter, you will learn how to use these techniques to render different textures, shadows, and effects in your ink drawings.

DRAWING FROM REFERENCE

Many of us want to create art using our imagination—believe me, I get it! But if you have this as a goal or want to eventually have a unique style of drawing, understanding how real objects look and behave in different scenarios can greatly influence your ability to be creative. By studying realistic proportions, textures, movements, and lights and shadows, you will be able to adapt those aspects into different styles and shapes, creating different kinds of illusions with your drawings. In this section, you will learn methods to observe and draw anything from real life, using a real reference object, model, or picture.

Drawing from reference can immensely improve your artistic skills. The practice of observing and then drawing real-life subjects will help you build visual memory. This means you will eventually be able to draw better and in more detail by simply using your memory, without a reference. It will help you to remember how subjects look and eventually be able to draw them more easily in your own style. This means that by practicing drawing your favorite artistic subjects from real life, you will inevitably get better at drawing those subjects from your imagination.

Here are some general steps that work for any method when drawing from reference:

1. **Observe:** The first element of drawing from reference is observation. It is crucial to develop your observational skills if you want to get better at drawing. Observation is the art of seeing and understanding the world around you. We will explore specific examples on how to do this later on in this book. Start by choosing an object or picture as a reference for a drawing and take some time to observe. Start breaking down your reference into lines, angles, and shapes. Observe the distances between elements, the negative space, how the shadows behave, how the object moves, its texture and any other

details you can absorb visually. Don't worry about memorizing anything, just take a mental note of these characteristics at this stage.

2. **Sketch from large to small:** Start your sketch with the largest shapes and lines you see in your reference. For example, a face might start with an oval shape, a shoe might be a rectangle, an apple might be a circle. Choose how to position the overall shapes and lines of your subject on paper, keeping the composition in mind and making sure everything is being placed in a balanced way, instead of elements being too far on one side or the other of the page, for example. Position the largest shape on paper, and from there, start adding the most prominent angles and smaller shapes.

3. **Refine and adjust:** Gradually refine the shapes to match the contours and proportions of your reference. You can do this by drawing over it or, if you're pencil sketching, erasing and redrawing as needed. Remember, these initial shapes are just guides, so they don't have to be perfect by any means.

These general tips will be useful when applying any of the sketching methods explained in the next sections, so keep them in mind when trying them out.

Grid Method

The grid method is a classic and very effective technique to reproduce or resize drawings. It involves drawing a grid over your reference photo, and then drawing the same grid on your paper. This helps to break down the image into smaller, more manageable parts, allowing you to focus on one grid square at a time.

This is a common method of reproducing art on larger scales, such as murals, for example, since it allows artists to break the final artwork into sections and work on these smaller areas one by one. Below are the steps for using the grid method:

1. **Prepare the reference and the paper:** Start by choosing or creating a reference photo and drawing a proportional grid over it. The grid can be as dense as you want, with as many squares or rectangles as you need. The smaller each grid cell is, the easier it will be to reproduce your reference with precision. Move on to your drawing paper and mark a similar grid, with the same proportions but in the scale of your choice, maintaining the same number of squares. Note that the size of the squares on the paper will determine the size of your final drawing. For example, if you want your final drawing to be twice as big as your reference, your squares on the paper should be twice as big as the squares on the reference photo.

2. **Draw one square at a time:** On top of your grid, start drawing the contents of each square from your reference into the corresponding square on your paper. This process requires careful observation. Take your time and make sure you're accurately capturing the details in each square.

3. **Check your work regularly:** As you work through each square, take a step back

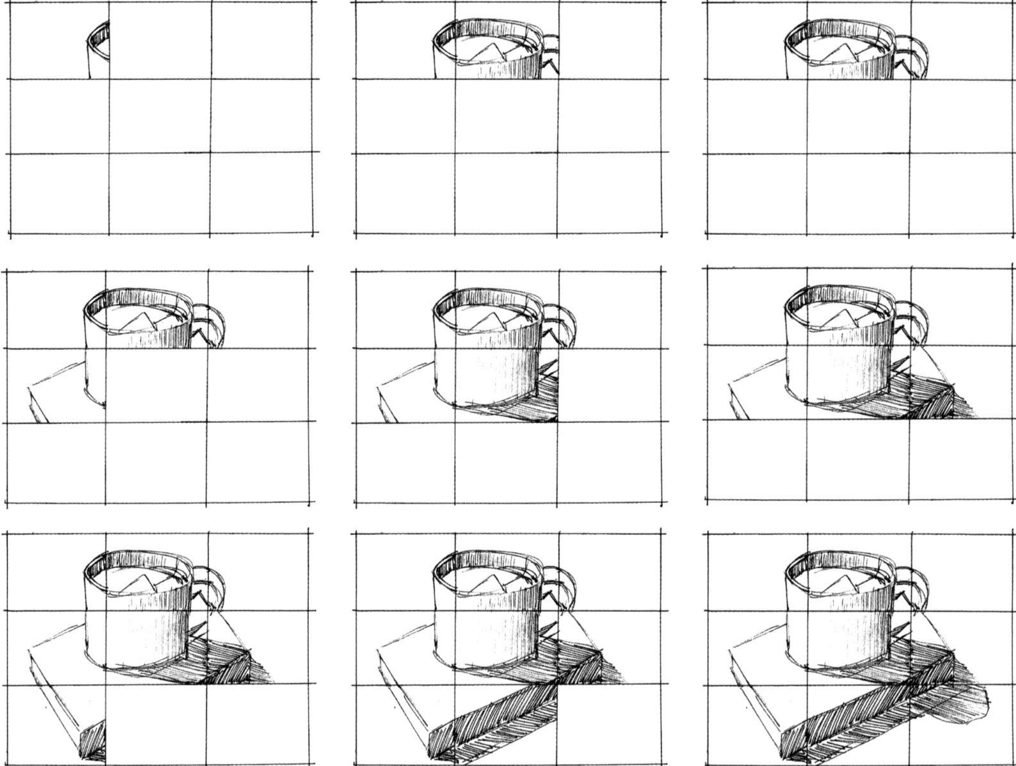

occasionally to check your progress. It's easy to get lost in the details when you're working square by square. Stepping back allows you to see the whole picture and ensure everything is coming together correctly.

4. **Refine and add details:** Once you've completed all the squares, go back and refine your lines, add more details, or erase any grid lines that are still visible.

The grid method is a great way to maintain correct proportions in your drawings and can be particularly helpful for beginners. However, it's just a guide. Don't feel constrained by it, and feel free to make adjustments as you see fit to create a drawing that you are happy with.

Geometric Shapes Method

The geometric shapes method is also a highly effective technique for drawing from reference, particularly for beginners. From my personal experience, I've found this method to be the most effective in improving my

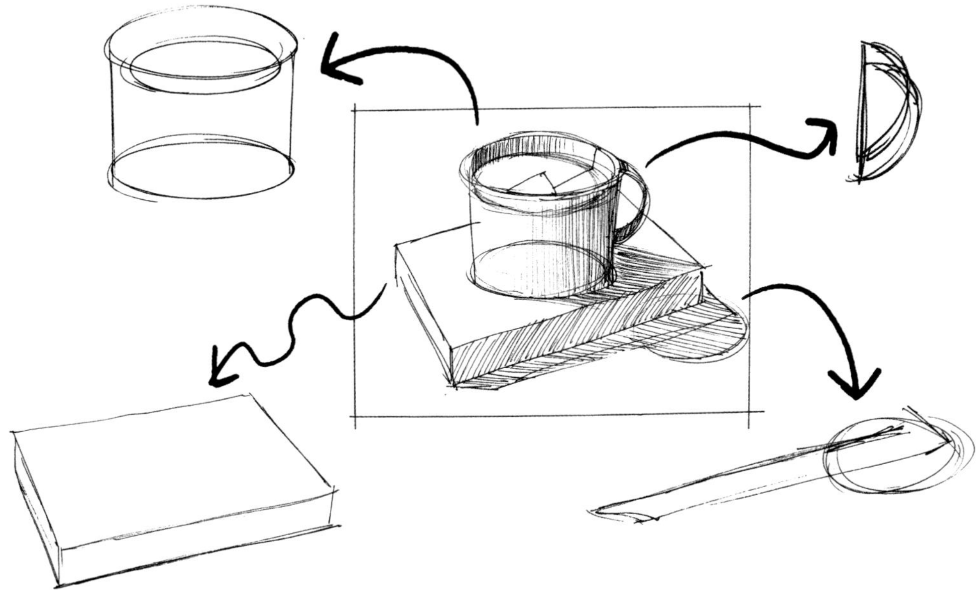

drawing skills in the least amount of time. This approach involves breaking down the subject of your drawing into simple, geometric shapes. By doing so, you create a basic framework for your drawing, respecting the reference's proportions, which you can gradually refine and add details to. At first, it might be challenging to see these shapes, but with practice you will train yourself to see them more easily. Here's how you can use the geometric shapes method in your drawing process:

1. **Observe:** Start by choosing a subject or picture as a reference for your drawing. Spend some time observing your reference, looking for the basic geometric shapes that make up the largest forms. Try to visualize these shapes and how they come together to form the overall structure of the subject.

2. **Find the negative spaces:** Sometimes it's helpful to also observe the shapes of the negative spaces, like background areas or where there are no elements to be drawn. This will allow you to position the main shapes on the space more accurately, respecting the composition of the original reference.

3. **Block in basic shapes:** Start sketching by laying down the most prominent geometric shapes you identified in the observation stage. For example, if you're drawing a face or portrait, you might start with an oval shape for the head, circles for the eyes, a triangle for the nose and a smaller oval shape for the mouth. Pay attention to the distances between each element, making sure you have the right proportions. Observing the negative space—that is, the areas around the main

subject—might help you to see these distances from a different perspective. You can also turn your reference and drawing paper upside down to help you see the shapes and distances with a clearer mind. Sketching some faint lines as guides can help you keep things aligned and proportional to the whole picture.

4. **Refine shapes and add details:** Once you have your basic shapes sketched out, start refining them to more closely resemble your subject. Adjust the shapes as needed, and begin adding smaller shapes to express the details. It's okay if your drawing doesn't look perfect at this stage—the goal is to gradually refine your sketch until it looks like your reference. If you notice that the proportion is off, go back to the previous stage and find where it went wrong, redrawing some shapes if needed.

5. **Finalize your drawing:** After you've refined your shapes and added details, you can finalize your drawing by adding shading, texture, and other elements to bring your drawing to life. When drawing with ink pens, you can choose to leave the sketch lines visible by creating them with a pen from the beginning. If you sketched with a pencil, outline the main lines with a pen and erase the sketch early, as soon as you don't need it anymore, to keep your page clean. Follow by adding the details with the ink to finish your drawing.

By breaking down complex subjects into simple shapes, the geometric shapes method makes drawing from reference more manageable. It simplifies complex subjects into simple shapes. With practice, you'll find that this approach can help you draw more accurately and confidently.

As briefly mentioned in Step 3, an interesting alternative to this method is to draw with your drawing paper and the reference picture upside down. This technique allows you to disconnect from the idea of drawing a specific object and help you focus your attention on the simplest shapes only. Since the image is flipped, it can be easier to visualize the abstract geometric forms rather than getting caught up in the details of the image. This approach can help improve your observational skills and enhance your understanding of form and structure.

Finding Expressive Lines

Another method of drawing from reference that can be especially interesting when drawing with ink pens is the expressive lines method. This is the process of identifying and replicating the most significant lines seen in your reference image. These are imaginary lines that define important angles and contours in your drawing.

The expressive lines will be the backbone of your drawing, setting the tone and structure for your piece. They capture the essence of your subject and serve as guidelines for the rest of your drawing. Here's how to apply this method to your sketches:

1. **Identify prominent lines:** Start by identifying these expressive lines, such as important angles and defining contours

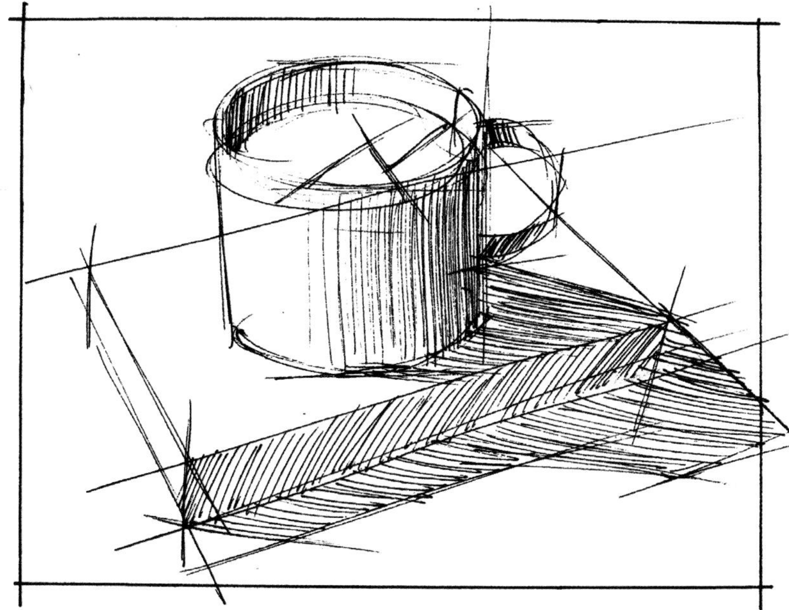

on your reference. This process requires careful observation. Try studying your reference image, paying close attention to the lines that define the form and characteristics of your subject. In real life we don't usually see lines contouring things or defining textures and depths, so the expressive lines are not necessarily obvious. Look for lines that delineate shapes, contour edges, or indicate changes in color, shade, or texture.

2. **Start with long, straight lines:** When sketching the most expressive lines, pay close attention to their angles, and start with straight, light, fast lines rather than detailed ones. This will help you create a more accurate structure for the drawing based on the reference. Don't worry too much about the precise length of the line, just make it longer than it is on your reference in order to create overlapping lines in the end, building the whole structure of your drawing.

3. **Refine lines and add details:** Once you've laid down your primary lines, you can start to refine your drawing. Adjust and elaborate on these lines as needed, adding detail and complexity to your piece. Your lines don't have to be perfectly smooth or straight—in fact, variation in line weight and direction can add interest and depth to your drawing.

As you continue to work on your sketch, refer back to your original image regularly. This will ensure that you stay true to the expressive lines of your subject, capturing its unique characteristics more accurately.

You can choose to erase these initial expressive lines by marking them with a pencil or leave them visible by doing the whole process with ink pens. These expressive lines can make your drawing look very interesting and are commonly used on urban sketches and architectural drawing, for example.

When the sketch is done, don't be afraid to let your own style shine through. While the reference image serves as your guide, your drawing should also reflect your unique interpretation of the subject. Experiment with different line techniques, such as hatching, crosshatching, or stippling, to create texture and depth. With practice, you'll develop your own repertoire of expressive lines, enhancing your ink drawings and establishing your personal style.

Ethics of Drawing from Reference

It's important to use reference pictures in an ethical way, especially when it comes to sharing or profiting from your artwork. While using reference images for learning and practicing is generally acceptable and encouraged, replicating someone else's work verbatim and claiming it as your own is not.

Profiting from or publicly showcasing a piece that is significantly similar to a reference image, especially without acknowledging the source or without the original creator's permission, may infringe on copyright laws and is generally frowned upon in the art community. This is particularly important when the reference material is another artist's work, such as a photograph, painting, or illustration.

When drawing for the purpose of practice and training, you are generally allowed to use anything as a reference, since you are not profiting from your drawings. One way to stay clear from any copyright issues is for you to create your own references or even combine multiple references for a drawing.

Here are some ideas for working with references for final artworks:

- **Respect original works:** Always be respectful of other artists' works. If you're using someone else's work as a reference, ensure your final piece isn't a direct copy but is transformed in a significant way. This transformation could be through style, interpretation, composition, color scheme, and other artistic elements.

- **Give credit and get permission:** If your artwork is heavily influenced by a specific reference, it's best to credit the original artist and, if possible, get their permission before sharing or selling your work. This is especially important if the reference you used was another artist's original work.

- **Create original artwork:** While references are helpful for learning and understanding, you can also create your own references. This can be a valuable exploration to develop your own creative process and art style. When using references, strive to create original artwork that showcases your unique interpretation and style. Use references as a tool to help you improve your skills and understanding, not as a shortcut to creating finished pieces.

- ✧ **Know fair use and copyright laws:** Familiarize yourself with the concept of "fair use" and copyright laws in your country. These laws can vary, but in general, altering a work significantly so that it doesn't infringe on the original artist's rights is usually considered fair use.
- ✧ **Use royalty-free pictures:** If creating your own pictures is not an option for you, opt for finding royalty-free photos to use as references. There are several online sources for pictures that you can download for free and not worry about copyright infringements.

As artists, we're part of a community and it's crucial to respect the hard work and creativity of our peers. Always be mindful of your sources and aim to create original works that reflect your unique artistic voice and vision.

In the following section, we will explore suggestions on how to draw from imagination, using different methods to develop your creativity and art style. With practice and persistence, you will be able to create beautiful, unique, and original artworks.

DRAWING FROM IMAGINATION

Drawing your ideas without a reference can be fun and fulfilling, but it can also be challenging without a clear path to follow. If you've ever stared at a blank page for a long time, struggling to figure out what to draw and unable to come up with anything you liked, you know what I'm talking about. Trust me, you are not alone!

Being able to have a clear art style and create unique, original drawings, is a common aspiration among artists everywhere. It's the desire to bring your unique vision to life, to create something that is entirely yours. It can help your art to be recognized and for you to be taken seriously as an artist. But with so many possibilities to experiment with, it's sometimes hard to make these artistic choices.

Although creativity is a complex topic and there are several books and studies done on this subject alone, there are some exercises that can be extremely helpful and allow you to achieve a sense of originality faster. The point of this section is not to offer a magic formula on how to draw from imagination and find your art style, but to simply give you a path to follow in this creative search.

Achieving originality as an artist requires a combination of creativity and technical drawing skills. Having a creative imagination and excellent drawing skills are two different things. You may have your mind

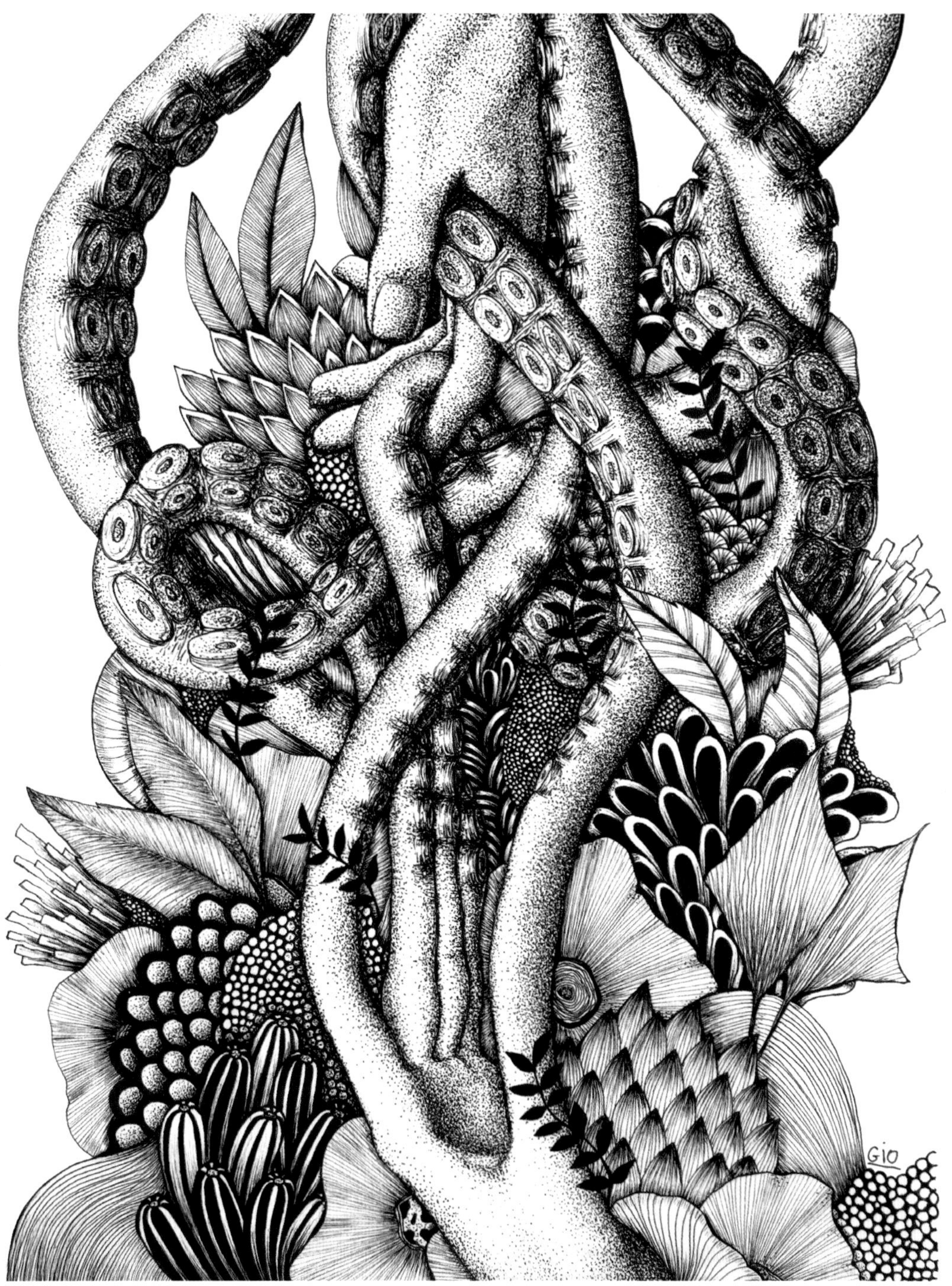

buzzing with incredible ideas, but without the necessary drawing skills, you might find it difficult to translate these ideas into art. Alternatively, you may be an extremely skilled artist, able to draw perfectly from reference, but lacking the creativity or the courage to experiment with different styles and ideas. This might make you feel like your work is missing a personal touch.

The good news is, both creativity and drawing skills can be nurtured and developed. This section will walk you through techniques that will challenge your imagination and creativity, improve your drawing skills, and ultimately, help you to create original, unique drawings in your own style.

Building Visual Memory

This might seem obvious, but you need to understand your subject before drawing it. Knowing what something looks like and having a clear visual image of it in your mind can be referred to as "visual memory." One effective way to build this skill is through the consistent practice of drawing from reference. This not only helps you study the structure and details of your subject but also understand them in detail. It will ingrain visual elements into your memory, eventually allowing you to even recreate it later without the reference. For example, if you want to draw faces and portraits from imagination, the more you practice drawing faces from reference, using different references with different positions, lighting, textures,

and styles, the easier it will be for you to draw from imagination without a reference over time. Here's a step-by-step guide on how you can practice this process:

1. **Choose a subject and draw it repeatedly:** Start with a simple subject that interests you. It could be an object, an animal, a character, anything that you enjoy drawing. Draw this subject from reference multiple times, each time changing the position, angle, or perspective. You might want to find several different references for this exercise. This will help you understand the subject in three dimensions and memorize its various shapes and forms, and with practice and patience, you will be able to draw the same subject from imagination.

2. **Test your memory:** After several rounds of drawing from reference, attempt to draw the same subject without looking at the reference or your previous sketches. This will test your visual memory and help you identify areas where you need more practice.

3. **Compare and learn:** Compare your memory-based sketches with the original reference and your reference-based sketches. Notice the details you missed, the proportions you might have gotten wrong, and the perspectives that might need improvement. Learn from these observations and apply them in your next practices.

4. **Repeat:** Continue this process with the same subject until you can draw it accurately from memory. The repetition will help reinforce your visual memory.

As mentioned in the previous section, besides practicing with existing references, creating your own references can also be a powerful way to enhance your visual memory and produce original artwork.

When you're aiming to draw an original idea from your imagination, gathering or creating your own references can be immensely helpful. This could involve taking your own photographs, setting up a still life arrangement, or even using yourself as a reference in a mirror. Creating your own references allows you to control the subject, lighting, and composition, making it easier to bring your original ideas to life.

Combining Different References

Another effective way to prepare for drawing from imagination is to practice combining elements from multiple references into a single, cohesive image. This can stimulate your creativity and help you learn how to compose and create balanced, compelling scenes. It allows you to experiment with different elements, understand how they interact in a space, and how to effectively arrange them to convey your intended narrative or concept.

This is a great way to express yourself creatively while building visual memory and improving your drawing skills at the same time. Start by sketching a composition for an illustration without much detail. Focus on simply positioning each element and deciding how they will interact on the page in a way that you can understand. There's no need for perfection or details; in fact, fast sketches can be really fun and relaxing to create.

Next, look for references for each of the elements that you have in your illustration. Be mindful of the light scheme, and that the illustration as a whole should have a cohesive light source. When looking for references, keep that in mind and try to find pictures with similar lighting. You might have a hard time finding exactly what you are looking for, so feel free to find more than one reference for each element. This is where creativity comes in. With all of those resources, you will do your best attempt to draw the elements as you pictured them in your sketch, using the references to support your ideas.

The goal here is not to copy from the references, but to be able to draw your idea as it is, using the references to help you get to the results you are looking for. For one specific element, you might have a reference for the texture, another for the lighting, and another for the position and proportions. This is a great way to draw from reference and improve your skills while being creative and coming up with your own concepts for illustrations.

The drawing on the opposite page was created with this method. I had the concept sketched first, and then multiple references for each element.

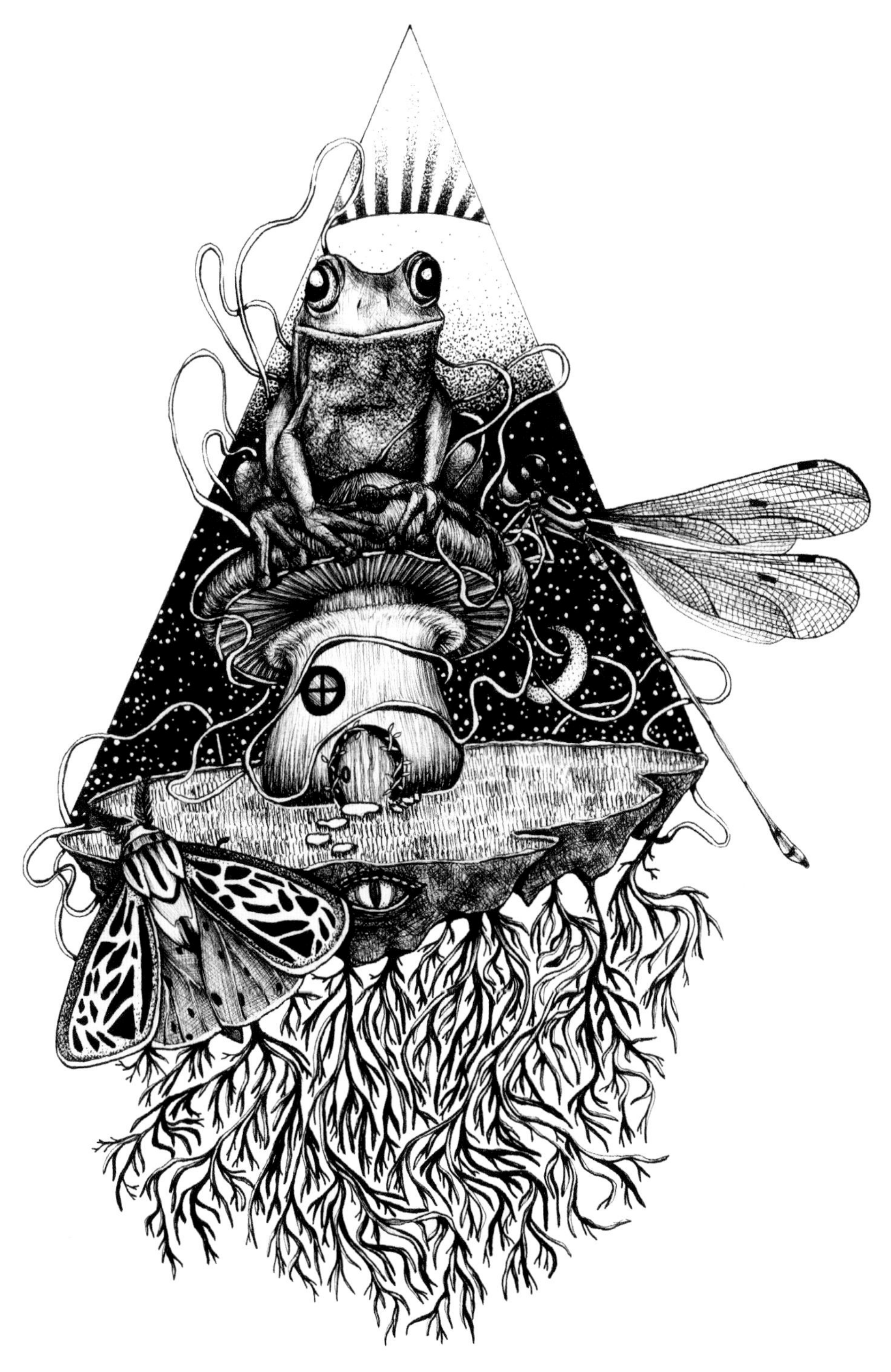

Studying Your Favorite Artists

To cultivate your ability to draw from imagination and develop a unique style, studying the works of artists you admire can be tremendously helpful. This involves a careful analysis of their techniques, the way they apply and combine lines, colors, and shapes, their approach to composition, and how they represent different subjects.

Start by selecting a few pieces from different artists that particularly resonate with you. Spend time observing and studying these pieces, taking note of the distinct elements, techniques, and styles each artist uses. Observe what makes them look unique and original and what is different from the way you create art. Look at the way they use lines. Are they sharp and precise or more fluid and organic? Pay attention to their use of colors. How do they combine different hues to create harmony or contrast? Notice how they arrange shapes and subjects within the composition. Are their works highly symmetrical or do they lean towards a more asymmetrical balance?

Once you've analyzed these elements, try to apply what you've learned in your own sketches. Practice using their techniques, experiment with creating similar strokes, play with their color palettes, and experiment with their preferred subjects. This isn't about copying their work, but rather about understanding their approach and applying it to your own creation as an experiment and study.

Over time, as you try different techniques and styles, you'll start to notice certain elements that you particularly enjoy or that express your ideas well. You'll have the freedom to try out your own ideas in your drawings and slowly add these elements to your own work. The process of exploration, experimentation, and refinement will eventually lead you to develop your own unique style.

The goal is not to copy or mimic other artists. Instead, you're learning from their approach, gaining inspiration, and building a foundation upon which you can create something that's uniquely yours. It's about understanding the principles and techniques that other artists use effectively and considering how these can be adapted to fit your own artistic approach.

In this process, always keep an open mind and be patient with yourself. Developing a unique style takes time and lots of practice. It's an ongoing journey of discovery, experimentation, and growth. Celebrate each step forward and remember that every artist, even those you admire, went through a similar journey.

Getting Out of Your Comfort Zone

Creativity thrives on novelty and change. Often, we find ourselves settling into familiar patterns, routines, and schedules that feel comfortable, but can potentially limit our creative reach. Stepping out of your comfort zone can offer new perspectives, inspire fresh ideas, and stimulate your creative mind.

Thinking creatively not only applies to artistic scenarios but is a mindset that can be applied in your daily life. By exploring your creativity outside of your drawing practice, you will inevitably feel more creative and have different ideas when making art. Here are some suggestions on how you can cultivate a creative mind, inside and outside of your artistic process:

✧ **Introduce new challenges:** One way to push your creative boundaries is by introducing new challenges in and out of your art practice. In your art practice, this could mean experimenting with new

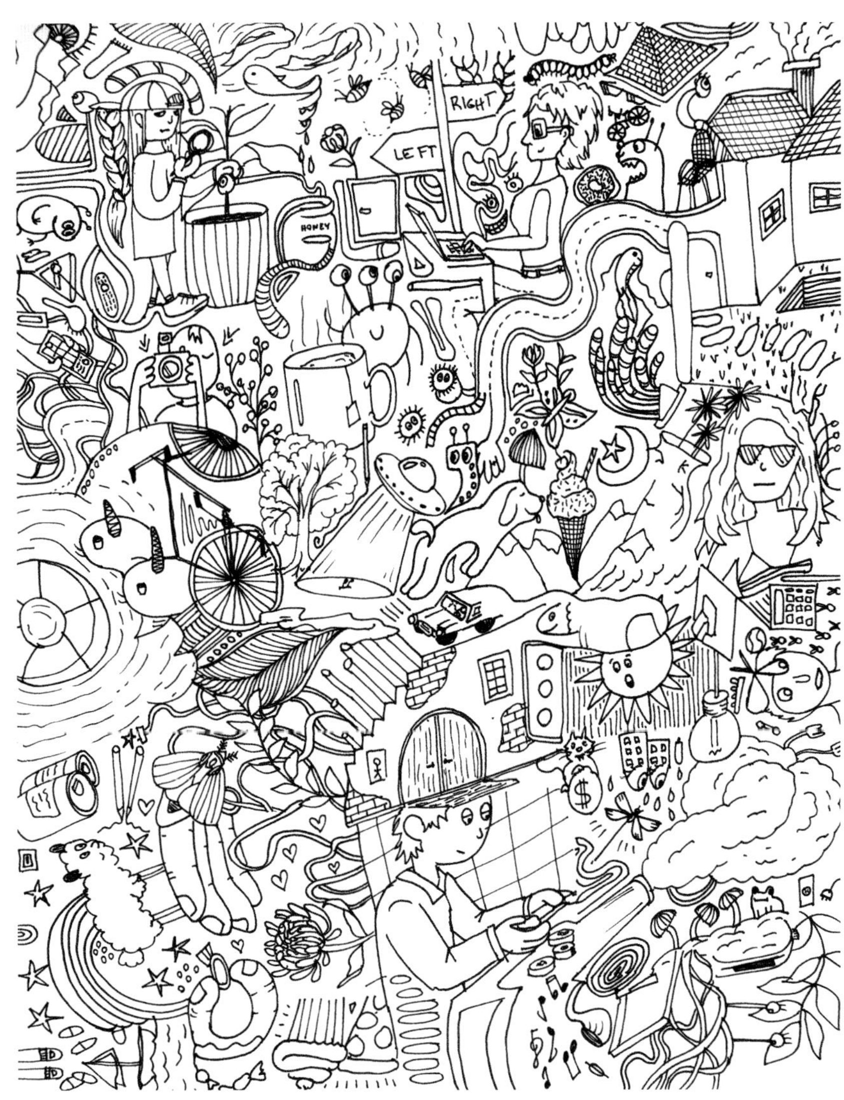

subjects, trying out different art styles, or working with unfamiliar materials. Each new challenge presents a unique problem to solve, inviting your brain to think creatively and come up with new solutions. Outside, in your daily life, this could be doing everyday activities in a different way, like brushing your teeth with the opposite hand, making an impulsive stop at the ice cream shop on the way home from work, or doing something new that you've never done before.

✧ **Change your environment:** Your environment can greatly influence your creativity. A change of scenery, whether it's rearranging your workspace, sketching outdoors, or visiting a new place, can provide new visual inspiration and spark new ideas. You feel different when you are in different places, so embrace change often.

✧ **Learn from different disciplines:** Cross-pollination of ideas from different fields can lead to unique and innovative artistic ideas. Try to explore your knowledge base beyond art. You could delve into science, history, philosophy, or any other field that interests you. The insights gained from these disciplines can provide a fresh perspective and inspiration and inspire creative thinking.

✧ **Participate in group activities:** Collaborating with other artists or participating in group activities can expose you to diverse ideas and styles. This can be a great source of inspiration and can help you view your work from different angles. It also challenges you to go beyond your known and comfortable artistic process to open your mind to new methods and styles. Receiving feedback and criticism can be scary, especially when it comes to art, since it's such a subjective topic, but you might find it to be extremely valuable and rewarding information that will help you move forward in your artistic journey.

Creativity is like a muscle—the more you challenge it, the stronger it becomes. Stepping out of your comfort zone might be intimidating at first, but with time and practice, you'll find that it's an exciting journey of continuous learning and growth. So, embrace change, welcome new experiences, and let your creativity take over.

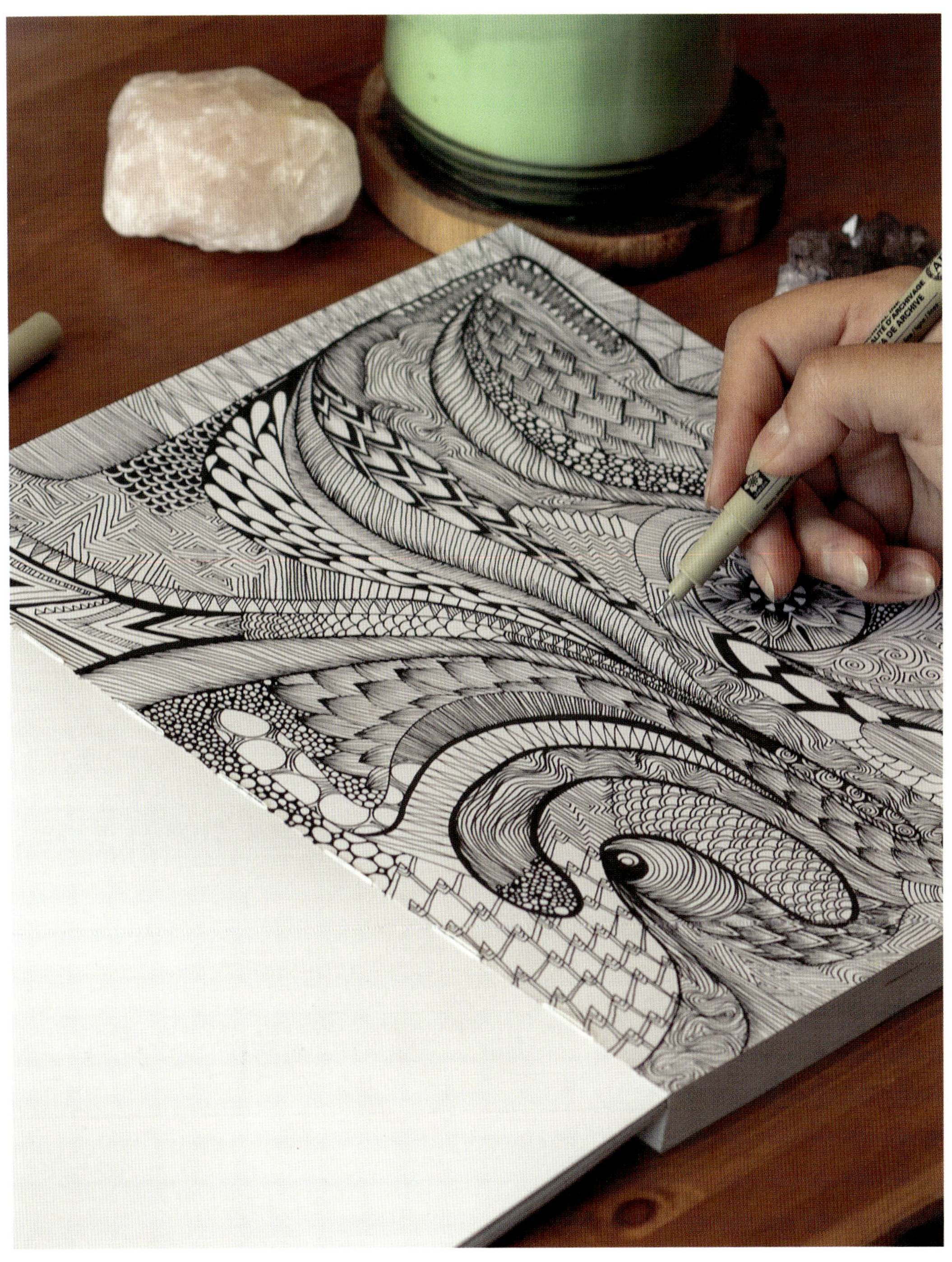

INKING TECHNIQUES

When drawing with ink or pencil, you are working on a black and white scale. Since color isn't available to separate and identify each element, it's important to learn how to create precise tones in grayscale. Luckily, there are plenty of techniques that can help you achieve a wide range of tonal values.

By adjusting these tonal values, you can create the illusion of different textures, depth, and distance between elements. You can also effectively represent lights and shadows and create incredibly three-dimensional effects in your drawings. Don't worry, we'll explore how to do that later in this book.

Understanding the nuances of grayscale and learning techniques for precise tonal control will help you to convey mood, emotion, and atmosphere in your art, making them more captivating and evocative depending on the style you are pursuing.

In this chapter, you will learn several techniques and styles of line art that you can explore with your pens, and the many variations and possibilities that come with them. As we progress through this book, we will go over these techniques and explore how to effectively use them to represent different subjects. With practice, you will see that mastering grayscale is not just about achieving realistic illusions but also about developing your unique artistic style and expressing yourself creatively.

STROKE STYLES

There are many stroke styles used in pen and ink art to create different effects, and many of the ones presented in the chapter will be referred to in the following chapters. These styles can improve the artistic expression and visual impact of your artwork, and the exploration of different combinations of these styles might help you develop your own unique drawing style or achieve specific textures and effects. By using these different stroke styles, you will be able to explore a wide variety of textures and tones, adding depth, dimension, and complexity to your drawings.

Each stroke style has its own unique characteristics, and I encourage you to play with them to control the level of detail, shading, and contrast in your artworks. The styles presented here are not the only ones available in ink pen art by any means, but simply popular and useful styles that can serve as inspiration for you to create certain effects.

By experimenting with these styles, you will be able to adapt them, blend them into one another, play with line weight and stroke size, and vary the patterns to create unique styles. Here are some of the most popular styles that will be used often throughout this book:

Hatching

Hatching is a technique that uses parallel lines to create shading and value. The length and density of these lines determine how light or dark an area appears. Darker shading is achieved by using longer lines placed closer together, while lighter areas are created by using shorter lines with more spacing. By adjusting the angle and weight of your hatching lines, you can give your subjects a three-dimensional look and make them appear more solid.

 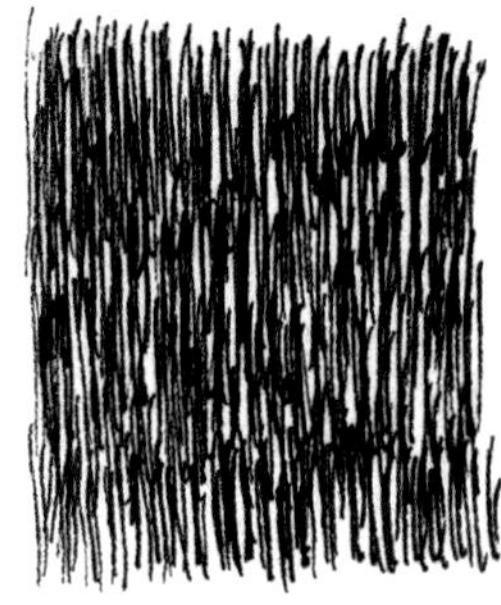 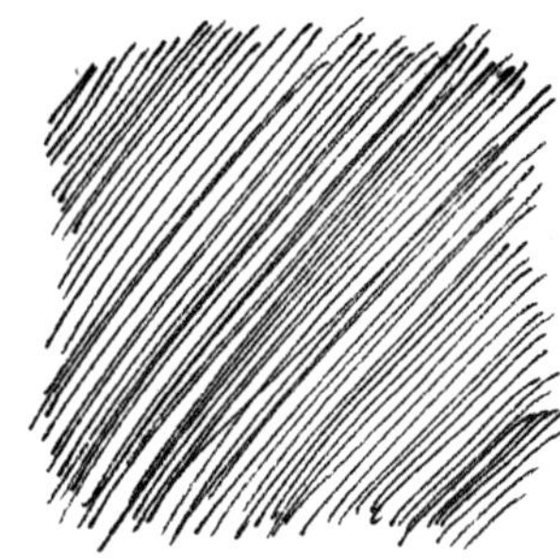

Crosshatching

Crosshatching involves layering sets of lines at different angles to create shading. Adding more layers makes the shading darker. This style is great for creating depth and texture in your drawings. Try using different angles and degrees of overlap to achieve smooth transitions in value or highlight intricate textures.

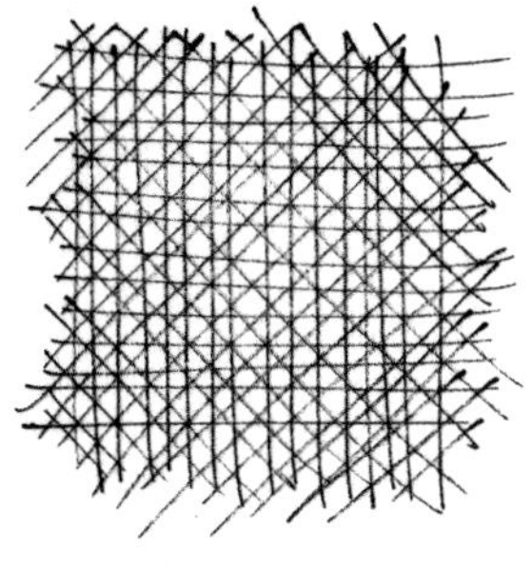

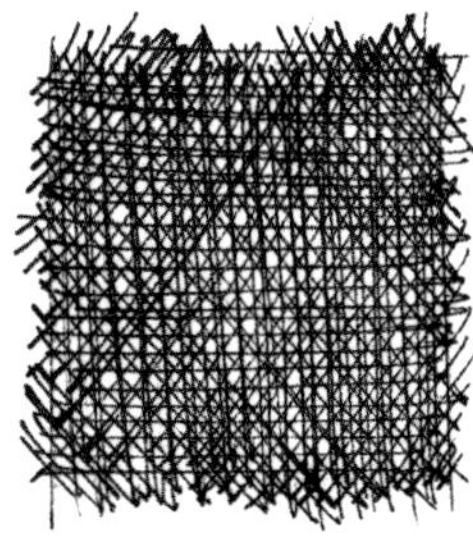

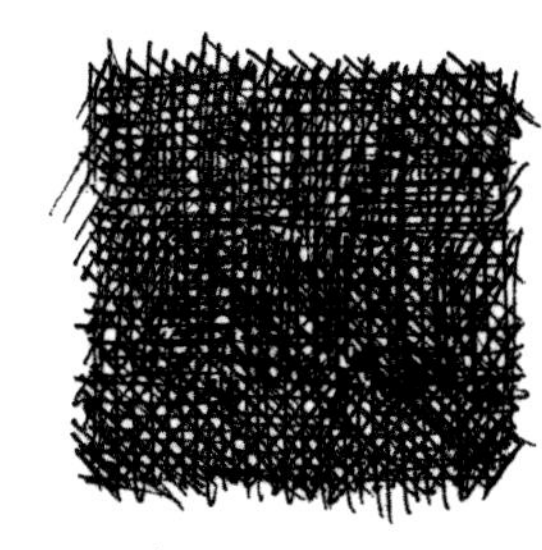

Weaving

Weaving is a technique where you crisscross lines to create patterns that suggest different textures and values. By controlling how tight or thick the lines are, you can make detailed patterns and shading effects. Weaving is a flexible technique that can be used for many things, like fabrics and foliage.

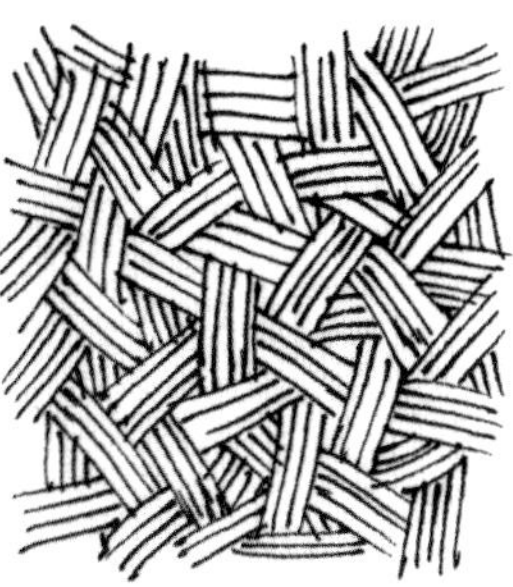

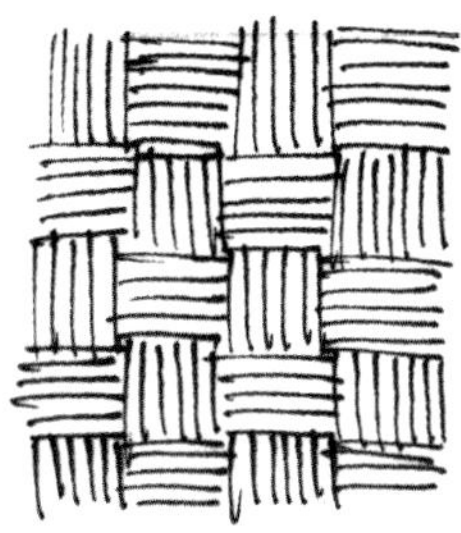

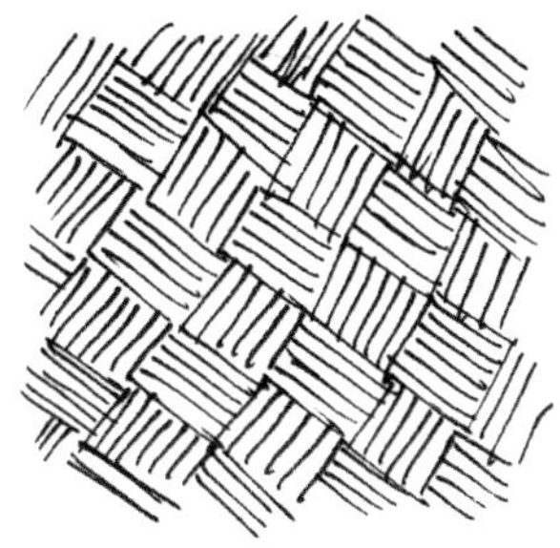

Scribbling

Scribbling is a spontaneous and chaotic arrangement of lines. It consists of quick, irregular lines to create different values. By changing the thickness and density of your scribbles, you can create a wide range of values and tones, making this a great technique for capturing the energy of quick sketches or conveying the texture of complex surfaces.

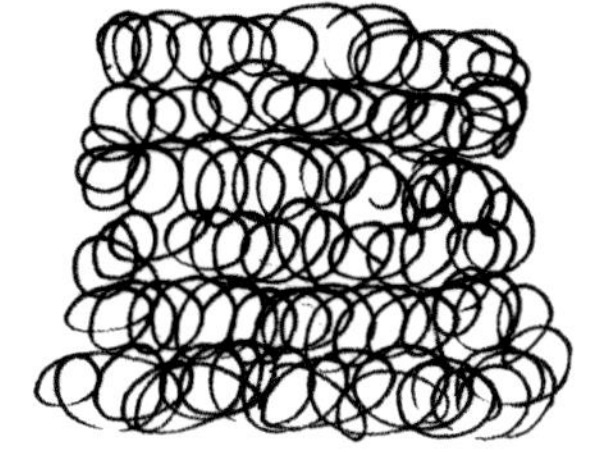

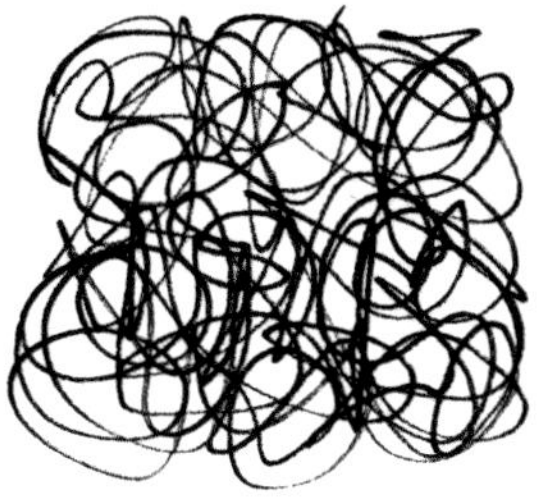

Stippling

Stippling is the process of using dots to create values. The closer the dots, the darker the area looks. Although stippling can be time-consuming, it offers a special and detailed way to add shading and texture. For beginners, it's an easier method of creating smooth transitions between different values. It's commonly used for highly detailed drawings and can create stunning visual effects.

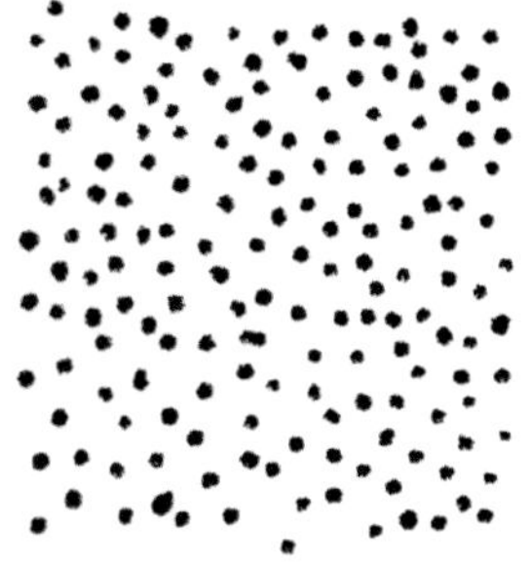

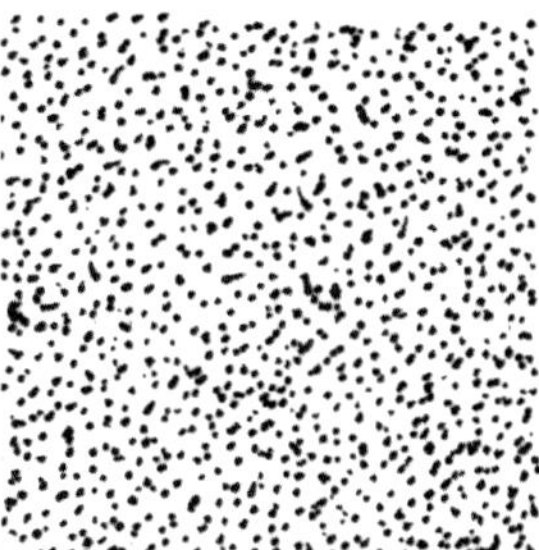

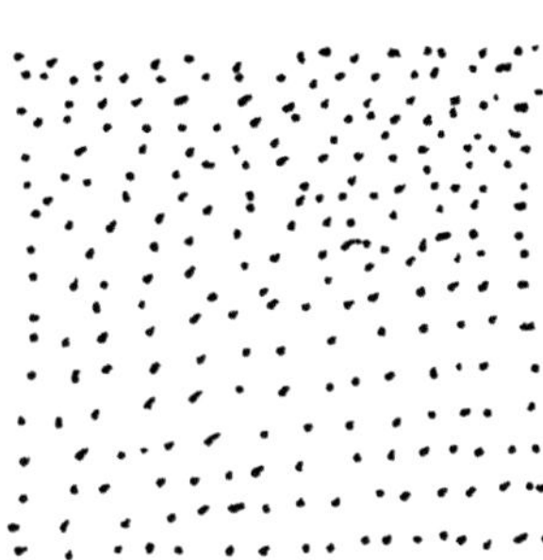

Parallel Lines

Parallel lines are drawn side by side to create different tones and textures in your drawings. You can experiment with the angle, thickness, and density of the lines to control the tone and texture. This method is versatile and can be used to achieve various tones and surfaces. The process can be very similar to hatching, but with parallel lines you can position them in rows or columns in order to create special effects.

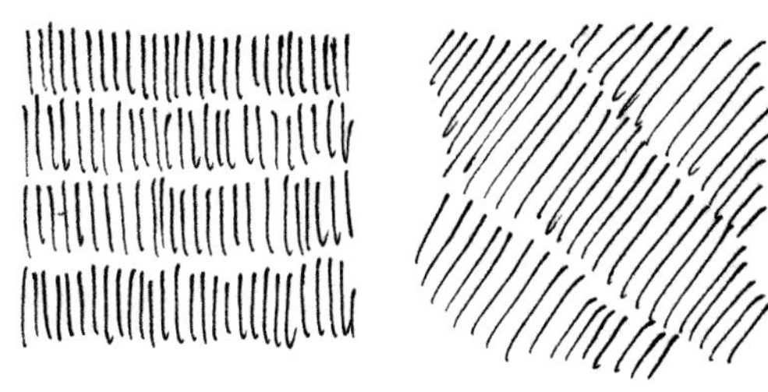

 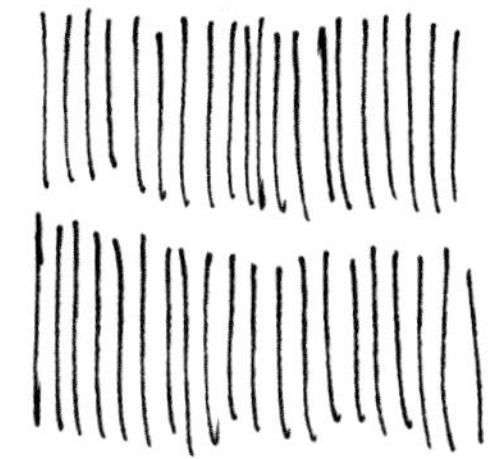 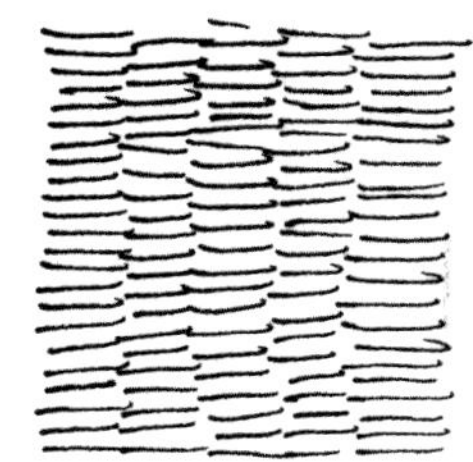

Waves

Start by sketching a wave shape. Then, keep adding more wave lines, following the first one. As you add more lines, you can vary them slightly to create different effects. Play with line thickness and pressure for depth.

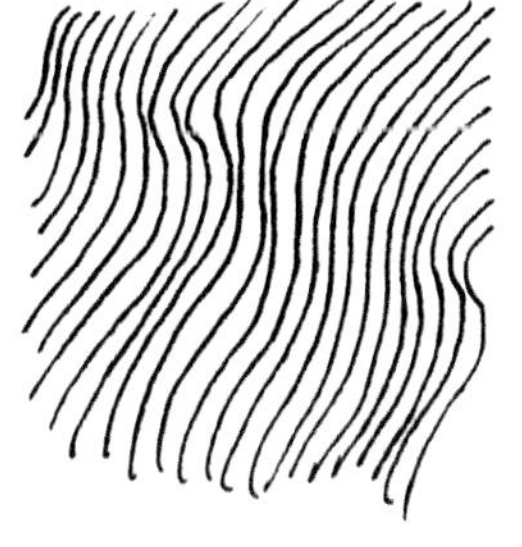 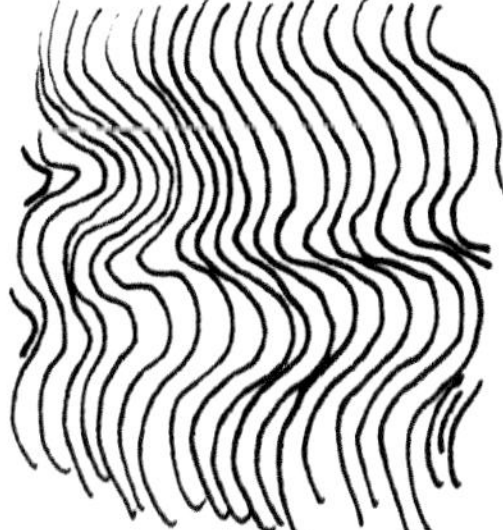

VALUE VARIATIONS

Knowing how to create a wider range of values and contrast in your drawings is a very important skill when drawing with ink pens. If you've ever felt that your drawing "looks great" but at the same time feels like it is "missing something" or looks "unfinished," you are not alone. I felt like that a lot when I first moved from drawing with pencil to drawing with ink pens. This has nothing to do with achieving a specific art style, but more about setting an intention for a drawing and being able to fulfill it. A minimalist, five-minute drawing can appear more polished and finished than a realistic, 10-hour drawing. Creating a drawing with intention and building the values the right way can help you create the effects you are looking for.

In art, values refer to the lightness or darkness of a color or tone. They play a crucial role in creating depth, dimension, and visual interest in your artworks. As artists, we are always telling stories and expressing messages through art. Whether we are aware of them or not, each illustration we create is connecting visually with whoever looks at it. An editorial illustration is visually telling the story of an article, a book illustration is depicting scenes of the story in the book, a technical illustration is visually explaining a process, system or concept, and so on.

The reason my drawings were "missing something" when I just started drawing with ink was not because they weren't good, but because I was not telling the story that I wanted to tell. There are many ways to work on your illustration's stories, and one of them is through working on the lights and shadows of your artwork. By understanding the lights and shadows in the space you create in your drawing, you will be able to direct the light to what needs to stand out and position the shadows on what needs to be in hiding, in the background, or just playing a supporting role. You will be able to create emotion, deliver subliminal messages, bring elements to the front or back to create the sensation of depth, and create three-dimensional effects. Employing light and shadow is a powerful tool that can help you to tell stories and express ideas in your art.

In this section, we will explore the foundations of creating values and contrast using ink pens, so you can have more control over the final result of your drawings, develop your own visual language as an artist, and create unique and original artworks. First, let's break down some key concepts that will be useful throughout this book.

Values

Values refer to the range of tones from light to dark in an artwork. Understanding values helps you depict form, texture, and depth.

- ✧ **Light values:** These are the areas where light directly hits an object, creating highlights. They appear brighter and have less ink coverage.

- ✧ **Mid-values:** These areas are neither in direct light nor shadow. They represent the average tones and require moderate ink coverage.
- ✧ **Dark values:** These areas are in shadow or receive little to no light. They appear darker and require more ink coverage.

Tones

An area with an even value is a tone, and you can create one by choosing a stroke style and drawing it in a consistent way throughout the whole area. Make sure the spacing, angle, size, layering, and direction of strokes is the same for each tone you create. Practice creating a tone for each stroke style presented previously.

Contrast

Contrast refers to the difference between light and dark values in a drawing. It enhances the visual impact of your artwork and adds interest. High contrast can create a dramatic effect, while low contrast can produce a more subtle or moody atmosphere.

- ✧ **High contrast:** This occurs when there is a significant difference between the lightest and darkest areas in a drawing. It creates strong visual impact and can be used to draw attention to specific areas or objects.
- ✧ **Low contrast:** This happens when the range between light and dark values is minimal. It creates a more subdued and subtle effect, often conveying a sense of calm or serenity.

Use value contrasts strategically in your ink pen drawings to add depth and three-dimensionality to your elements. Identify the light source and observe how it affects the objects in terms of light and shadow. Apply darker values to the shadowed areas and lighter values to the areas hit by light to create a convincing illusion of form and volume.

Techniques for Achieving a Wide Range of Values

There are several techniques you can employ to achieve a wide range of values, such as manipulating the ink flow, varying stroke patterns, and layering.

Position and Pressure Variation

Adjust the pressure applied to the pen tip to control the amount of ink transferred onto the paper. By applying lighter pressure, you can create lighter values, while heavier pressure produces darker values. You can also change the position in which you hold the pen to release more or less ink on the paper. If the pen is perfectly perpendicular to the paper, or if you hold if vertically against a horizontal surface, the pen will release a larger amount of ink per stroke, creating a heavier line weight. The more you tilt the pen on an angle against the paper, the less ink will be released, and you will be able to get lighter tones.

Alternatively, you can save your old pens that are already releasing very little ink to help you create smooth transitions and lighter values in your drawings.

Creating Value Scales

With your choice of stroke style, you can work your values by adding more ink when you want it to be darker and less ink where you want it to be lighter. Combine and experiment with these techniques to achieve a wide range of values in your ink pen drawings. Practice and observation will help you refine your control and understanding of these techniques, enabling you to create detailed, realistic, and visually compelling artworks.

For each stroke style, a wide range of values can be achieved by changing the size, spacing, direction, and weight of lines, and by layering the ink to create darker tones and different effects. Try creating a value scale using some or all of the stroke styles presented. This means arranging a series of shades from lightest to darkest. This exercise will help you to practice creating the different tonalities of each stroke style, giving you more control over the final results of your drawings.

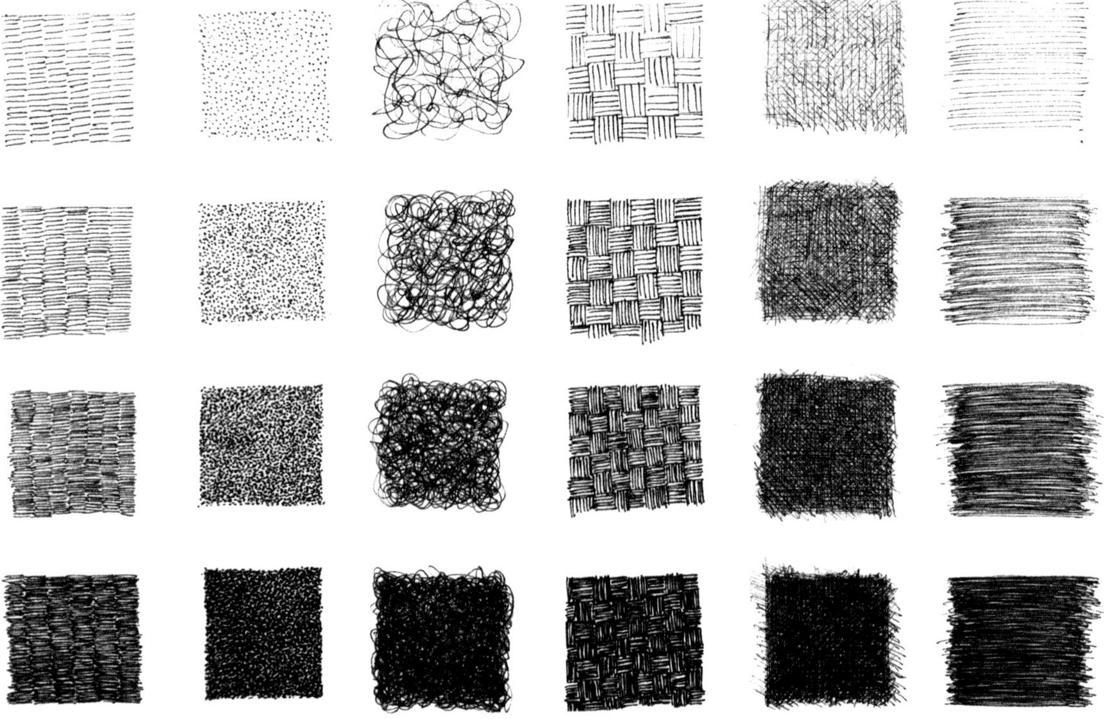

LIGHTS AND SHADOWS

Now that you have learned how to create a value scale, you will be able to create light and shadow effects in your ink drawings, which is an essential skill to have as an artist, even if you plan to create more stylized drawings with little to no contrast. Even if realism is not a style you want to pursue, understanding how the light behaves in relation to the subject you are drawing can make your work more harmonious and captivating. This chapter will explore the basics of lights and shadows and how to use lines to create the illusion of depth.

There are many ways to work on your lighting scheme using ink pens. In nature, light sources create shadows, and understanding how to draw shadows is crucial when creating the illusion of depth and dimension in your artwork. You can use a variety of techniques to create shadows, such as cross-hatching, stippling, or using thicker lines. Some techniques might create a smoother, more realistic effect, and some will create a rougher, more stylized result. There is no right or wrong—it's all about the style you choose to go with. To create the illusion of form, you need to understand how light behaves on different surfaces.

Understanding how to represent lights and shadows accurately can greatly enhance the quality of your artwork. Let's explore the concepts of lights and shadows in drawing, specifically in the context of using ink pens.

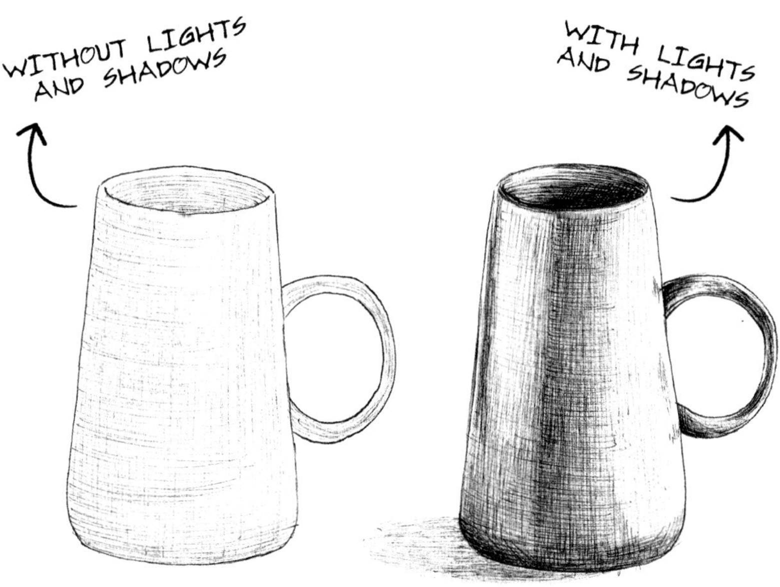

Lights

Light is the primary source of illumination in a scene. It reveals the form, texture, and details of objects. Understanding the behavior of light will help you accurately represent the areas that receive direct light or highlights in your drawing.

- **Light source:** Identify the location and direction of the light source in your drawing. This will determine where the highlights and shadows fall on your subject.
- **Highlights:** These are the brightest areas in your drawing where light directly hits an object. They are usually found on rounded or protruding surfaces and appear lighter than the surrounding areas.
- **Reflected light:** Reflected light refers to the light that bounces off surfaces and affects nearby objects. It softens shadows and can create subtle highlights in shadowed areas.

Shadows

Shadows are areas of darkness that are created when objects block the light source. They play a crucial role in defining the form, depth, and spatial relationships within a drawing.

- **Core shadow:** The core shadow is the darkest part of a shadow, usually found on the side of the object opposite the light source. It represents the area that receives the least amount of direct light.
- **Shadow shapes:** Observe the shapes and contours of shadows. They can be affected by the form of the object casting the shadow and the surface it falls upon. This is useful specially when using the geometric shapes method for sketching, since you can also break down a reference image's lights and shadows into shapes, in case they are prominent and relevant in the composition you are working with.
- **Shadow gradation:** Shadows are not uniformly dark. They can exhibit a range of tones, with the darkest areas closest to the object and lighter tones as they move away from it.
- **Cast shadows:** Cast shadows are formed when an object blocks the light and creates a shadow on another surface or object. Pay attention to the shape, size, and intensity of cast shadows, as they can add depth and realism to your drawing.
- **Drop shadows:** Drop shadows are shadows that appear below or immediately behind objects, making them look raised from the surface or background. They're used in design to add depth and make objects stand out and are very useful to create depth in your drawings.

Creating Depth

As seen in the previous section, contrast is the difference in luminance or color that makes an object distinguishable. In pen and ink drawing, contrast is achieved by placing different values next to each other. The greater the difference in value, the more the elements stand out. High contrast can make your drawings more dynamic and exciting, and you will be able to create incredibly realistic effects by using contrast to your advantage.

You can use contrast to create a sense of dimension and distance by creating highlights and shadows that give your artwork a three-dimensional quality.

The process of creating three-dimensionality to your designs will improve the more you practice your observational and technical skills:

1. **Understand light and shadow:** Study the behavior of light and how it interacts with objects. Observe elements and the life around you, and sketch what you see. Try to find (or create) scenarios with different lighting, at different times of the day, with warm or cold lights, with colorful lights, with multiple or just one light, for example. Identify the direction and intensity of the light source in your scene or reference. This exercise will help you determine where the light hits the objects and where shadows are cast, building your visual memory on the behavior of light in different contexts. Even if you are unsure initially, defining the light sources in your drawing before you start shading can help you to create a cohesive and balanced composition.

2. **Establish a range of values:** Before you start a new drawing, you can plan the range of values from light to dark to depict the different tones in your drawing. By utilizing the techniques of your choice, establish a full spectrum of values that capture the highlights, midtones, and shadows, so you can apply that to your drawing later.

3. **Place highlights:** Carefully render the areas of the subject that receive direct light, often referred to as highlights. As we know, we can't erase the black ink from the paper, which means that in order to place highlights on the elements on your drawing, you need to create shadows to make the highlights stand out. The highlights will be the lightest in value, with minimal ink coverage. Leave them as white space or use thin, delicate lines to depict the light hitting the surface.

4. **Render midtones:** For areas that are neither in direct light nor shadow, render them with midtones. Adjust the ink application and pressure to create values that are darker than the highlights but lighter than the shadows. Employ stroke styles like crosshatching or stippling to add texture and depth to these areas.

5. **Define shadows:** Observe the shadow shapes and intensities and render them using darker values. Gradually build up the shadow areas to capture the variations in shadow tones. Pay attention to the core shadows, cast shadows, and the way shadows interact with different surfaces.

6. **Enhance contrast:** To further enhance the sense of depth and three-dimensionality, increase the contrast between the lightest highlights and the darkest shadows for a more dramatic three-dimensional effect.

7. **Create gradual transitions:** Smooth transitions between values are essential to create a realistic representation of depth. Blend and transition between

different values using the techniques presented previously. Gradually layer and build up values to achieve seamless transitions and avoid harsh lines or abrupt shifts.

8. **Pay attention to edges:** The way edges are defined can contribute to the perception of depth. Softening or blurring some edges, particularly in areas that recede into the distance, can suggest a sense of depth. Define sharper and more precise edges for objects or areas that are in the foreground or receive direct light.

Textures Matter

There are many ways to create convincing shadows in your drawings. What will help you decide what stroke style to use on a specific subject is a combination of:

◇ **The kind of light:** Different types of lights create different types of shadows. For instance, a direct and intense light, like the sun at noon, will create shadows with hard edges and high contrast between light and dark areas. On the other hand, a diffused light, like on an overcast day, will create softer shadows with less contrast. Indoor lighting can also affect how shadows appear. A single light source will create strong shadows, while multiple light sources can soften shadows and reduce contrast. For example, a candle will create a warm, soft light with long, distorted shadows, while an overhead fluorescent light will create harsh, well-defined shadows.

◇ **The kind of material:** Different types of materials have different textures, and they will reflect the light differently. For example, an object made of metal will have sharp, well-defined highlights and reflections, while the same object made of stone will have much smoother light spots that blend with the shadows. A piece of clothing made of silk will have brighter, more defined light spots than one that is made of linen.

Handling light and shadow on textured surfaces can be challenging, as the texture adds an extra layer of complexity. That's why it's important to observe how light interacts with specific textures to be able to reproduce those effects using your inking techniques.

In the next chapter, we will study in-depth how light behaves in relation to many popular textures and how to choose the best stroke styles to create the right illusion. For now, let's take a step back and look into the principles of using lines to create convincing shadows in your drawings.

Flat Surfaces

Drawing shadows on flat surfaces may seem straightforward, but it's essential to consider the light source and the surrounding environment to create a believable effect.

◇ **Direct light:** When a flat surface is directly under a strong light source, the shadow it casts will be sharp and well-defined. You can portray this effect using consistent parallel lines or crosshatching on the area opposite to the light source. The lines

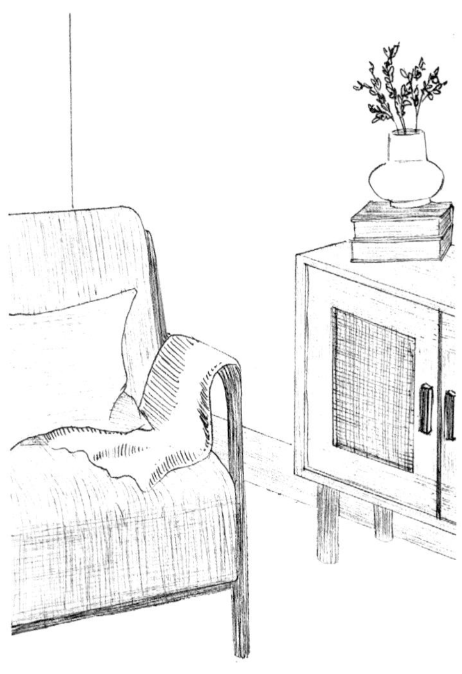 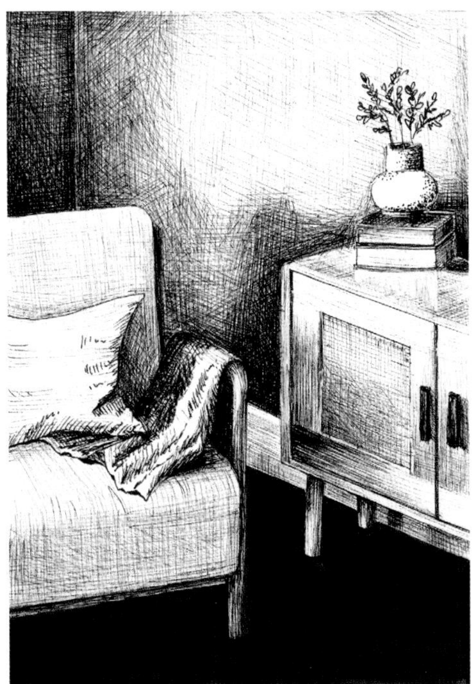

should be close together and of the same weight to create a uniform dark tone.

✧ **Diffused light:** Diffused light, such as from an overcast sky, creates softer shadows with less contrast. You can create this effect by using lighter strokes that are spaced further apart. Consider using stippling or uneven lines for these shadows, varying the density of the dots or lines to create the desired softness.

✧ **Reflected light:** Light can bounce off surrounding objects and illuminate areas that are not directly facing the light source. This is known as reflected light, which often appears on the shadow side of the object, reducing the contrast. To depict this, leave a small area within the shadow slightly lighter than the rest.

✧ **Shadows on colored surfaces:** If the flat surface is colored, it can affect the color of the shadow. For example, if sunlight (which has a warm color) is shining on a red wall, the shadow may appear cooler or more purple in comparison. With pen and ink, you can suggest this effect by changing the density or pattern of your strokes. If using a reference picture, consider removing the saturation to see the picture in black and white. This will make differentiating between values much easier and train your eye to see these differences in colored surfaces.

The key to creating convincing light and shadow effects on flat surfaces is careful observation of real-life scenarios and consistent practice with various inking techniques.

Rounded Surfaces

Creating shadows on rounded surfaces can be slightly more challenging than on flat ones, but with practice, you can master the important inking techniques to create realistic effects. The key is to understand that the curvature of the surface will affect how light hits it and subsequently, how shadows are formed.

- **Direct light:** When a rounded surface is under a direct light source, the area where the light hits the surface directly will be the brightest, while the areas moving away from this point will gradually become darker. You can depict this effect by using a hatching technique with lines that follow the curvature of the surface. Start with lighter, widely spaced lines at the brightest point and gradually increase the density and darkness of your lines as you move away from the light source.

- **Diffused light:** Diffused light creates a softer, more evenly distributed shadow on rounded surfaces. To create this effect, use a cross-hatching or stippling technique. Start with lighter and less dense lines or dots at the areas facing the light source and gradually increase the density as you move away from the light.

- **Reflected light:** Just like with flat surfaces, rounded surfaces can also have areas of reflected light. This is typically seen as a lighter band within the shadow area that is opposite to the direct light source. Portray this effect by reducing the density of your lines or dots in this area.

- **Shadows on colored surfaces:** The color of the surface can affect the shadow's appearance. The shadow may appear cooler or warmer in comparison, depending on the color of the light source and the surface. Again, you can suggest this effect by changing the density or pattern of your strokes. If using a reference picture, consider removing the saturation to see the black-and-white interpretation of the colors.

Practical Tips

- **Consider the light source:** Before you start shading, define where the light is coming from, and imagine how it hits the elements in your drawing. This will guide you on where to place the shadows and highlights. If you are using a reference, look at it and find the light source. If drawing from imagination, make this decision yourself.

- **Use a full range of values:** Don't shy away from using both deep shadows and bright highlights. This will give your drawing a full range of depth and volume. When working on white paper, you are adding the shadows and leaving enough space for the lights and highlights.

♦ **Be consistent with your light source:** Once you choose a direction for your light source, be consistent throughout all the elements of your drawing. Inconsistencies in lighting can confuse the viewer and make the artwork less convincing.

By mastering the illusion of light and shadow, your pen and ink drawings will become more visually engaging and potentially realistic, if that is one of your goals. It's through the interplay of light and shadow that we perceive form, depth, and the texture of surfaces. So, don't underestimate the power of these techniques—they can truly transform your work. In the next chapters, we will explore practical examples of how to create different textures and the most popular subjects for drawing with ink.

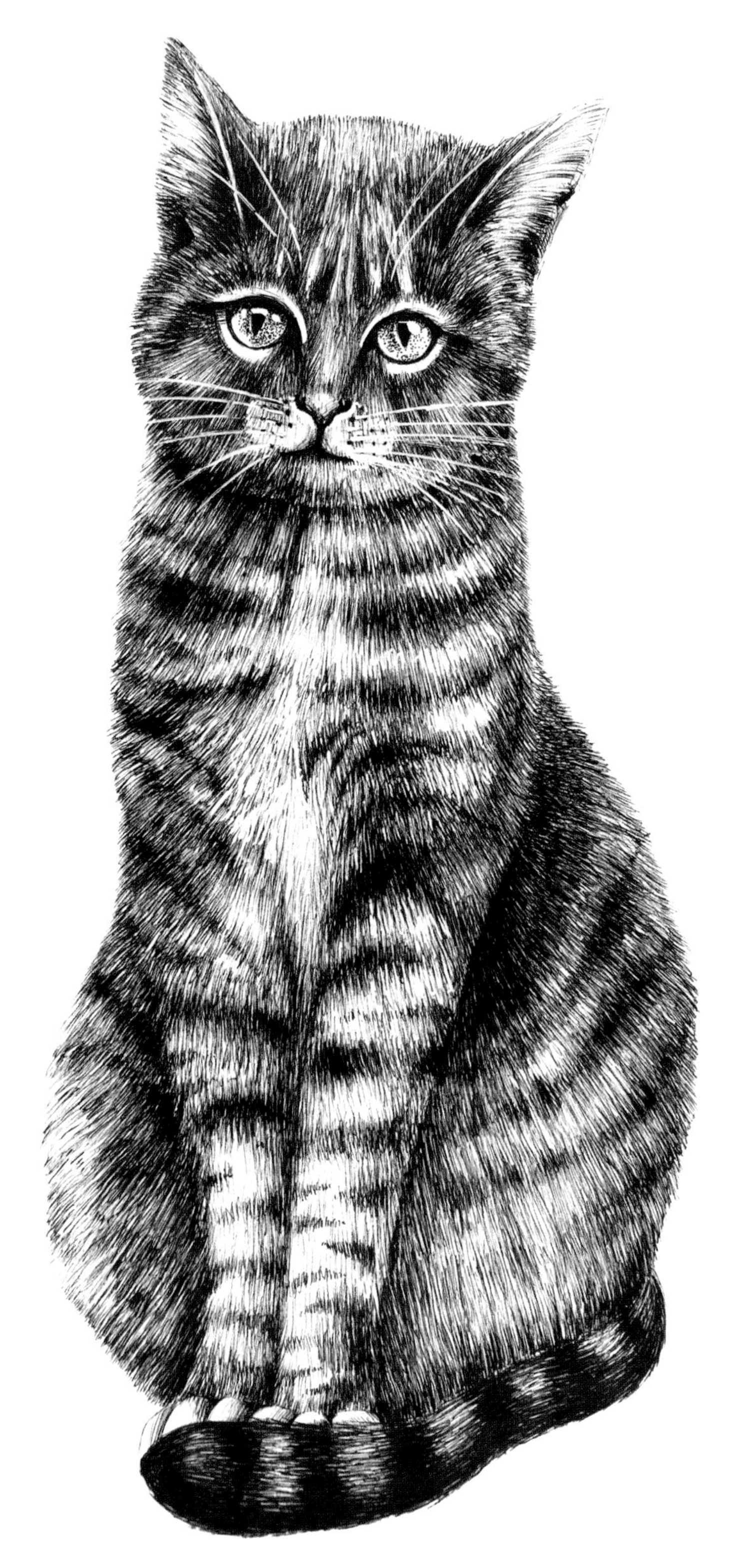

RENDERING TEXTURES: FROM REALITY TO LINES

Creating texture effects on your ink drawings requires seeing, understanding, and capturing the world around you in detail. This is not simply an observation of the physical world, but a deep perception of the textures and how to best translate them into line forms.

The goal of this chapter is to teach you how to find those lines and patterns in textures from real life and translate them into an ink drawing. This is more than a mechanical process. It's about capturing the essence of the object, its character, and its mood. The examples in the following sections will show you how to develop an eye for detail and hone your ability to see beyond the obvious.

You will also need a certain familiarity with your pens and how to use them. The tools at an artist's disposal—the pen, the ink, the paper—each have their nuances and offer different possibilities. If you understand these tools, then you know the types of lines and strokes they can produce, and how these can be used to represent different textures.

The key to mastering these techniques is to experiment. Try different methods, combine them, and observe the effects. This chapter will help you understand how a combination of lines can transform into a life-like texture on paper, and how different strokes can capture the mood of the object you're trying to portray.

In this journey of translation from reality to lines, each artist will find their own unique approach. The beauty of pen and ink drawing lies in this exploration and the infinite possibilities it offers. The following examples are not meant to limit you by providing the only possibilities to reproduce certain textures, but instead to inspire you to gain more control over your lines to create the effects of your choice.

POPULAR TEXTURES

In general, for any texture you want to draw, observe the value variations and how the light behaves. Sometimes, you will need a sharp contrast between two tones, and sometimes you will need to blend them smoothly. With patience and practice, you will be able to make better decisions about which techniques to use for each texture. The choice of stroke style or ink pattern can influence the final version of your drawing, but the most important aspects are the lights and shadows, as they are the ones that will indicate difference in texture the most accurately.

Wood

To represent wood texture, start by observing the grain of the wood closely. Notice the direction of the lines and any knots present. To replicate a wood pattern, you can use a combination of lines that follow the direction of the grain to create the pattern, combined with hatching to create texture and shadows. For uneven surfaces or to create the illusion of light and shadow, you can also use crosshatching. These techniques will help capture the defining characteristics of wood.

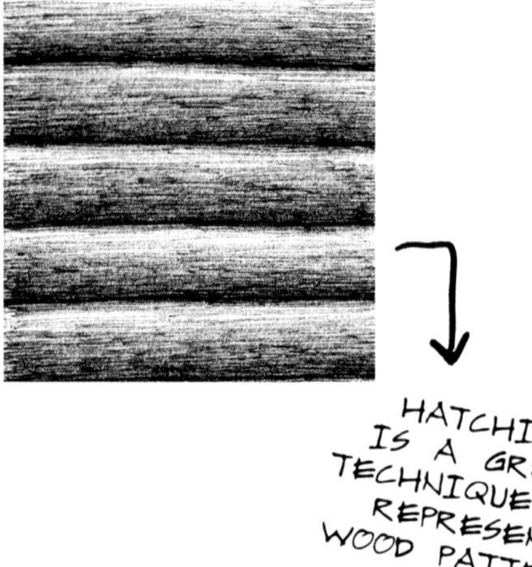

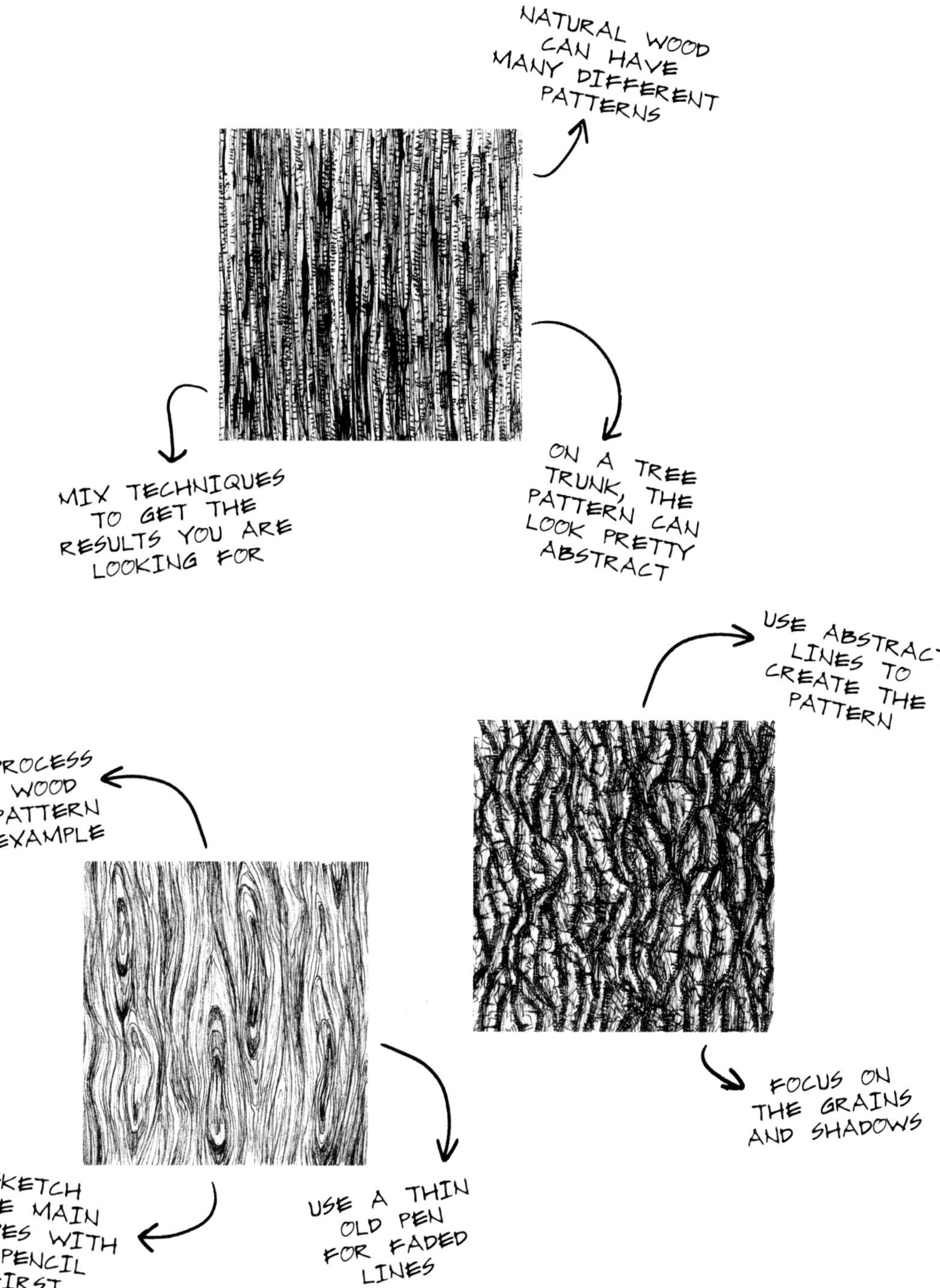

NATURAL WOOD CAN HAVE MANY DIFFERENT PATTERNS

MIX TECHNIQUES TO GET THE RESULTS YOU ARE LOOKING FOR

ON A TREE TRUNK, THE PATTERN CAN LOOK PRETTY ABSTRACT

USE ABSTRACT LINES TO CREATE THE PATTERN

PROCESS WOOD PATTERN EXAMPLE

FOCUS ON THE GRAINS AND SHADOWS

SKETCH THE MAIN SHAPES WITH A PENCIL FIRST

USE A THIN OLD PEN FOR FADED LINES

Stone, Brick, and Tile

Stone textures can be quite varied. For rough, granular surfaces like those on a boulder or an ancient wall, you could use stippling as it creates a rougher aspect. To apply this technique, use small dots to create gradients and subtle variations in light and shade, giving the coarse texture of stone. For smoother stones like river pebbles, use softer, less defined lines with minimal shading. A combination of hatching and stippling can work great to create different levels of roughness when illustrating stone. The key to capturing the authenticity of stone is observing the variability in its texture.

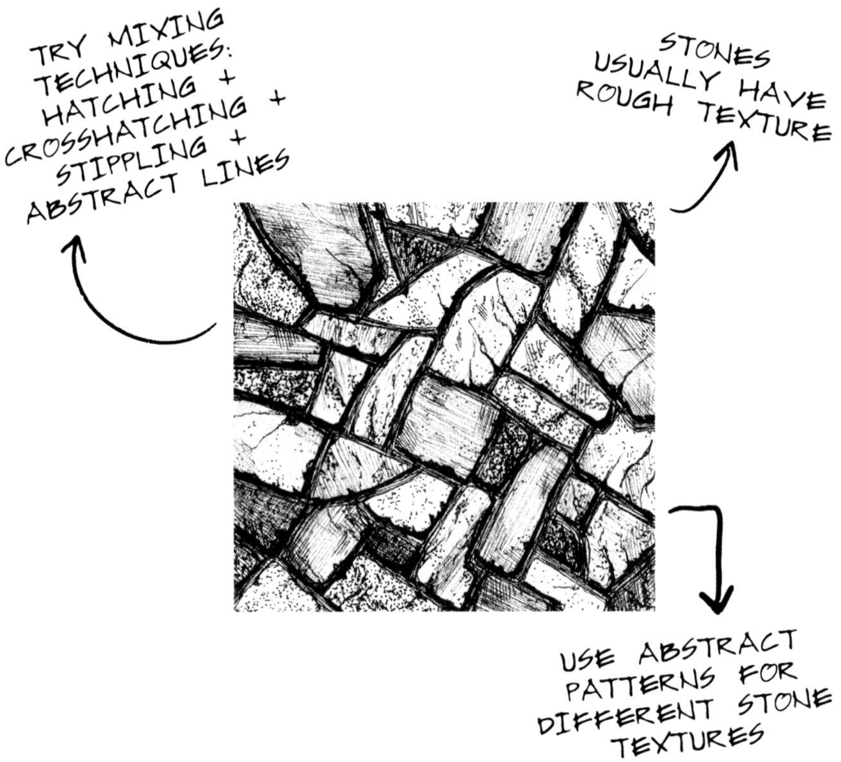

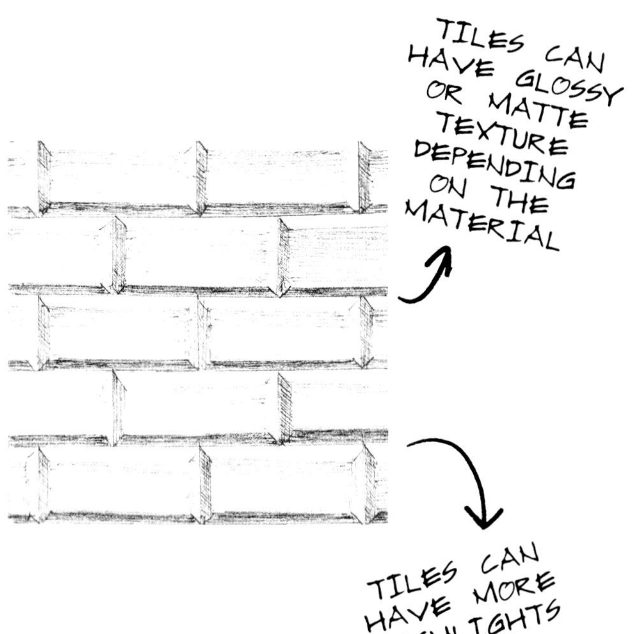

TILES CAN HAVE GLOSSY OR MATTE TEXTURE DEPENDING ON THE MATERIAL

TILES CAN HAVE MORE HIGHLIGHTS

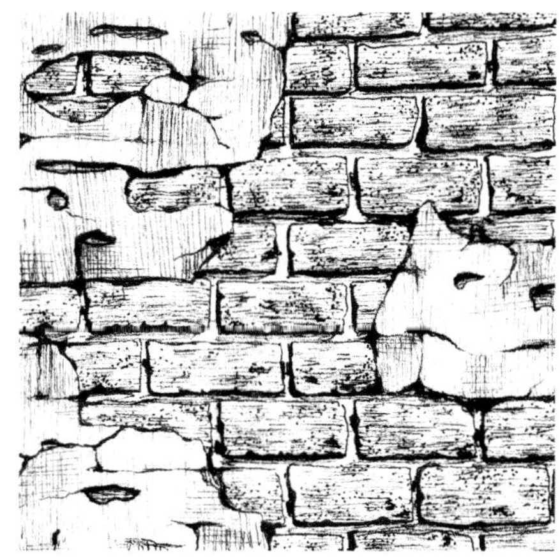

BRICKS CAN HAVE MORE UNIFORM OR ROUGHER TEXTURE

HATCHING + STIPPLING

Metal

Rendering metal textures in drawing is all about reflecting light. To create a realistic effect, focus on creating a high contrast between light and dark areas. The reflected light on metal is usually a series of lines or a shiny area. To capture this, keep your lines clean and precise, creating a quick, sharp transition between dark and light areas, as opposed to a smooth, gradual transition.

Pay particular attention to the areas of light reflection and how the shadows behave depending on the kind of light that is hitting your subject, as these nuances can make your representation of metal more realistic. You can also use stippling or any other inking technique, as long as the highlights are clear and sharp, like on metal surfaces. Things can look distorted when reflected on curved metal objects, so keep that in mind when creating your drawings.

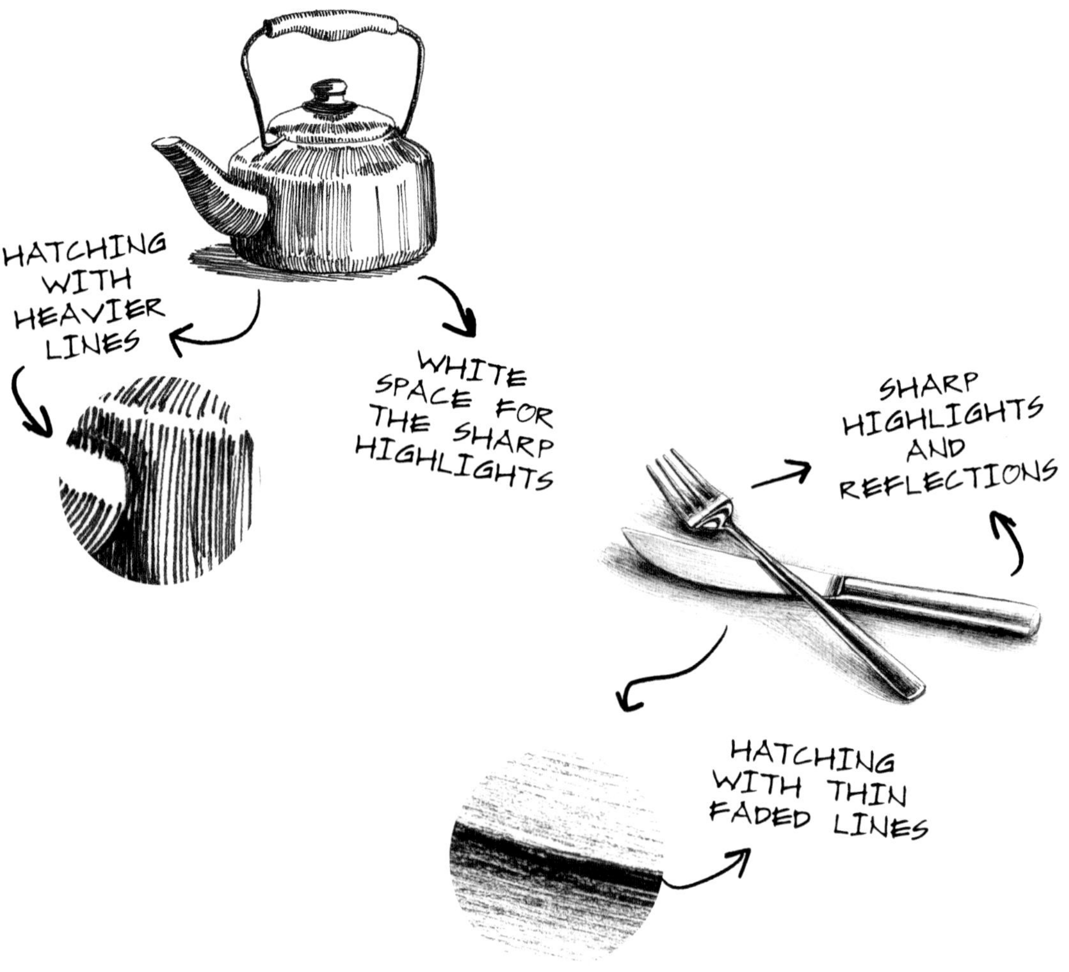

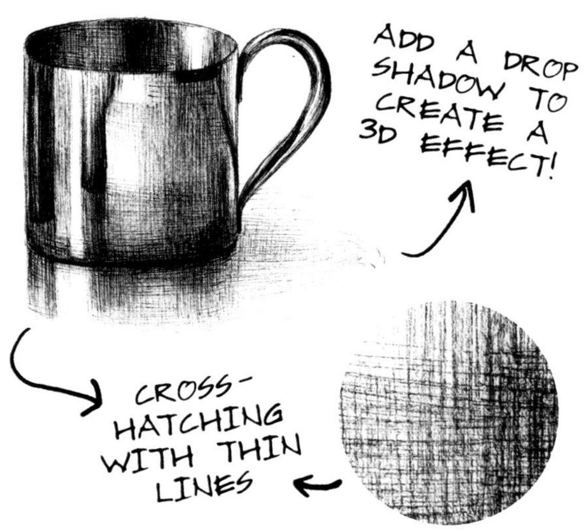

ADD A DROP SHADOW TO CREATE A 3D EFFECT!
CROSS-HATCHING WITH THIN LINES

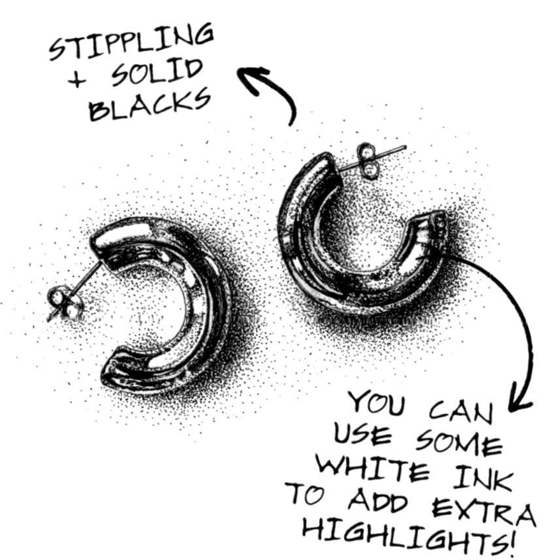

STIPPLING + SOLID BLACKS
YOU CAN USE SOME WHITE INK TO ADD EXTRA HIGHLIGHTS!

Glass

Glass, similar to metal, reflects a lot of light. On top of that effect, we usually have a certain level of transparency, which can create extra highlights and distortions. The best way to approach a complex subject like glass is to focus on the shapes of each highlight and shadow and the tonal variations between them.

Start by using smooth lines to define the shape of the glass object. To draw the reflections, the hatching technique works great, but any stroke style can help you achieve glass textures as long as the highlights are sharp and clear.

To create the transparency that is characteristic of glass, the background can play an important role. One way to depict transparency is to lightly hatch over the background area that is covered by the glass, making it slightly lighter in tone than the rest of the drawing. The goal is to make the background elements visible through the glass texture, but with the illusion of being behind it. Subtlety is key when representing glass.

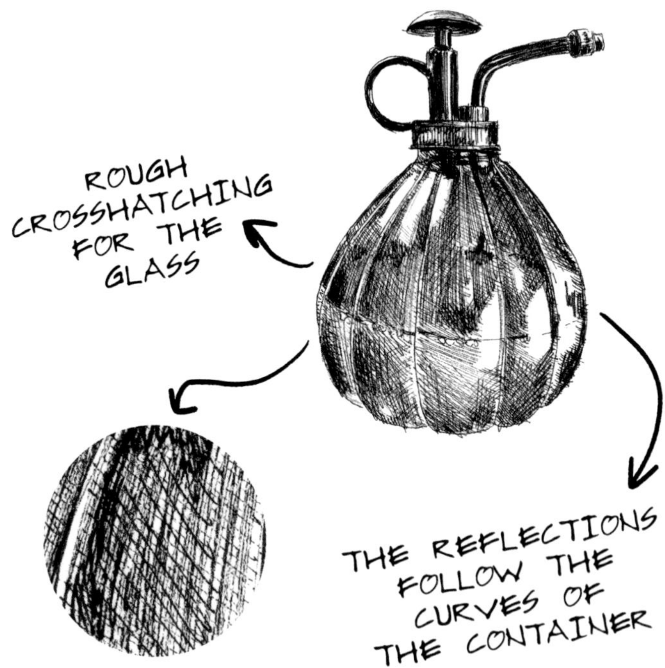

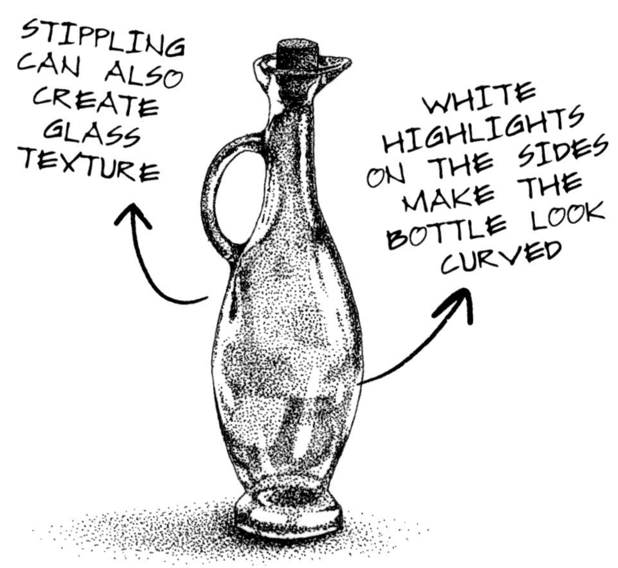
STIPPLING CAN ALSO CREATE GLASS TEXTURE
WHITE HIGHLIGHTS ON THE SIDES MAKE THE BOTTLE LOOK CURVED

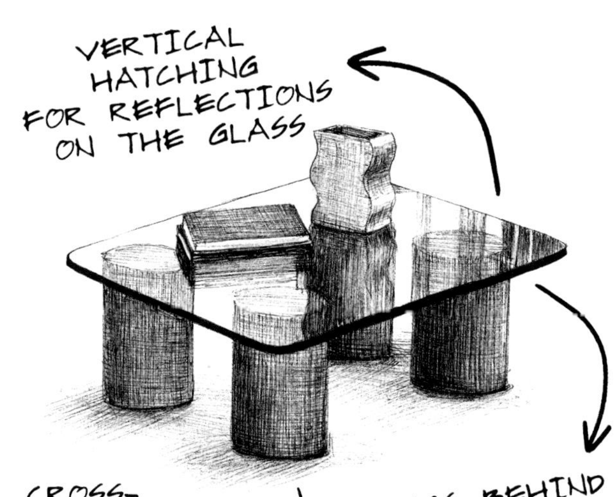
VERTICAL HATCHING FOR REFLECTIONS ON THE GLASS
CROSS-HATCHING FOR OPAQUE TEXTURES
THINGS BEHIND GLASS HAVE A LIGHTER TONE TO CREATE TRANSPARENCY

Hair, Fur, and Feathers

When drawing hair or fur, direction and flow play a big role. Start by sketching the general shape of the hair or fur. Then, add lines to divide the hair or fur into sections, following the direction from where the hair grows. To create texture and shadows, short, quick strokes work well for short hair or fur, while long, flowing lines that follow the length of the hair are more appropriate for longer hair. For curly hair, the scribbling technique can be very effective, and you can create depth by adding more scribbles on the darker spots, leaving more white space on the lighter areas of the hair. Observe the way the hair or fur lies, how it moves, and how light catches on it to make your representation more realistic.

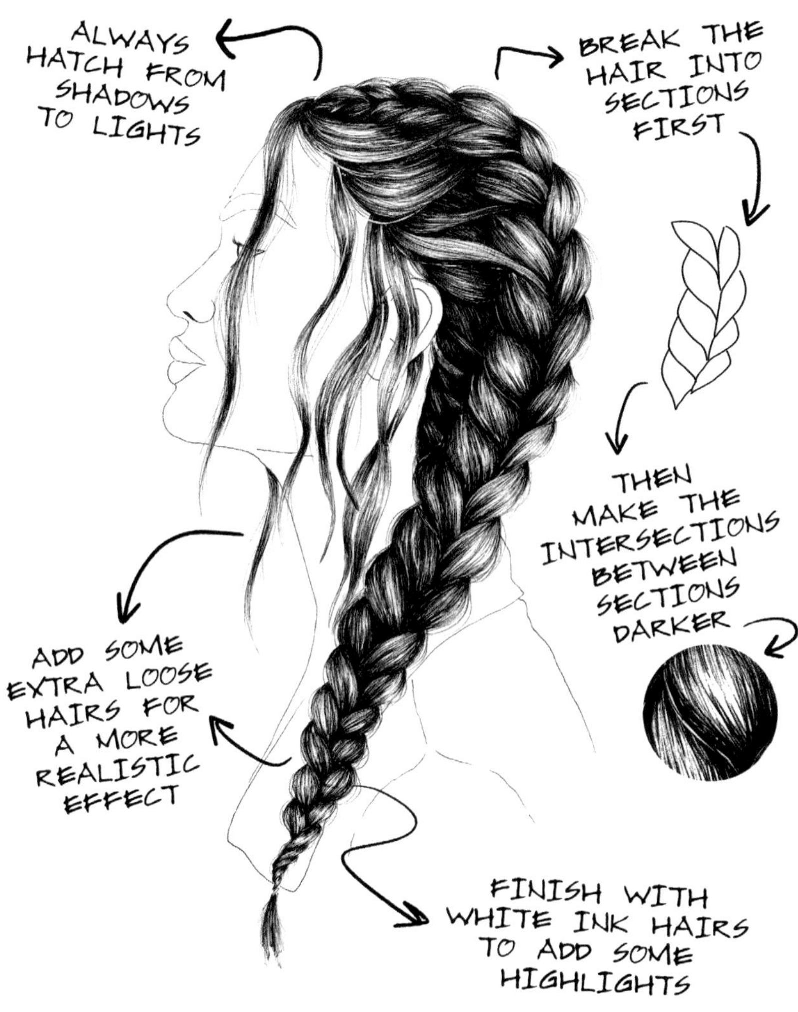

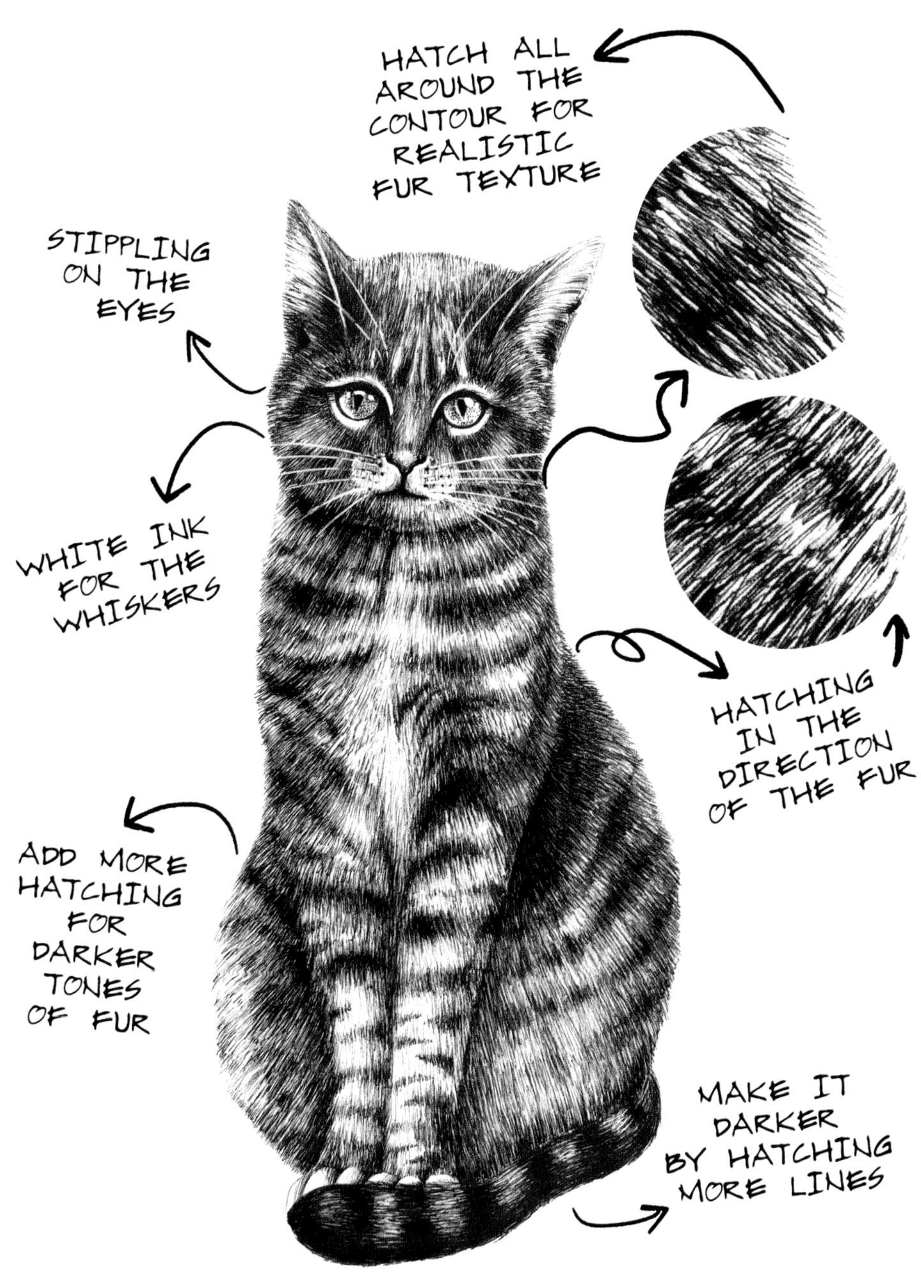

HATCH ALL AROUND THE CONTOUR FOR REALISTIC FUR TEXTURE
STIPPLING ON THE EYES
WHITE INK FOR THE WHISKERS
ADD MORE HATCHING FOR DARKER TONES OF FUR
HATCHING IN THE DIRECTION OF THE FUR
MAKE IT DARKER BY HATCHING MORE LINES

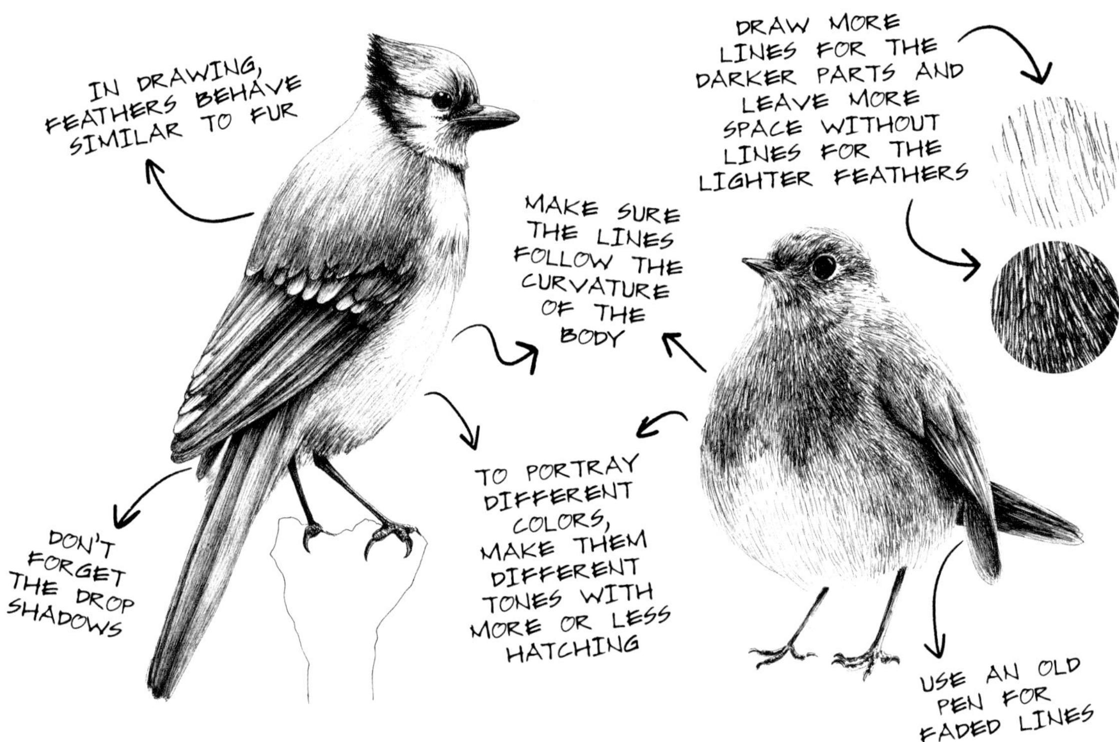

IN DRAWING, FEATHERS BEHAVE SIMILAR TO FUR
DON'T FORGET THE DROP SHADOWS
MAKE SURE THE LINES FOLLOW THE CURVATURE OF THE BODY
TO PORTRAY DIFFERENT COLORS, MAKE THEM DIFFERENT TONES WITH MORE OR LESS HATCHING
DRAW MORE LINES FOR THE DARKER PARTS AND LEAVE MORE SPACE WITHOUT LINES FOR THE LIGHTER FEATHERS
USE AN OLD PEN FOR FADED LINES

Fabric

For fabric, consider the material's weight and how it drapes. Use smooth, flowing lines for light materials like silk. For heavier materials like denim or wool, use more structured lines and add more detail to represent the fabric's texture. Studying and understanding the material's physical properties will help you depict it more accurately. Observe how the light reflects on the fabric to see how you need to place the ink on paper. Pay attention to the value variations and how smooth or sharp the transition is between them.

Other Textures

For any other textures not covered in this book, observe how light interacts with them, how the shadows behave, and any reflections that are created. In ink drawing, you are depicting the darkness and allowing the white paper to represent the light. For example, if a texture is rough and uneven, stippling can be a great way to reproduce it. If the texture is messy and highly detailed, like the foliage of trees or very curly hair, scribbling can be a quick way to draw it. When the texture has very clear, visible lines, straight or flowy, hatching can be the way to go.

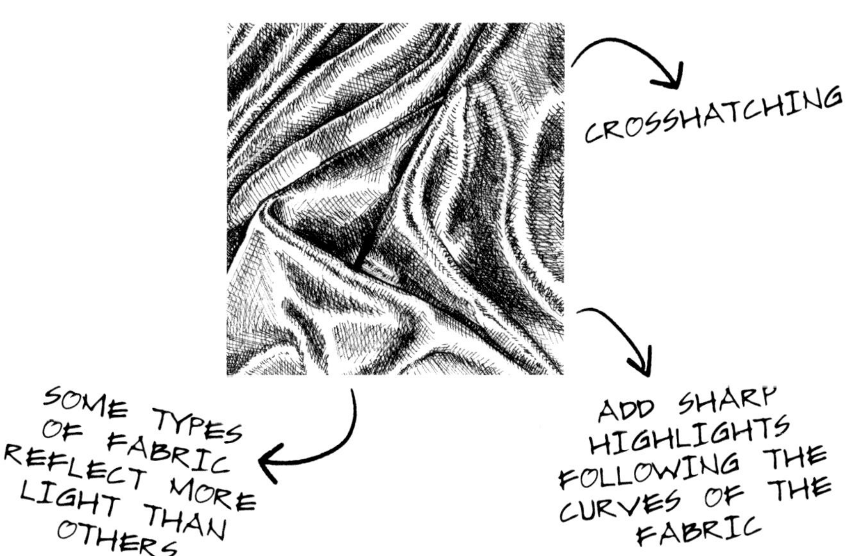

EXPLORING BEYOND REALISM

This chapter focuses primarily on realistic drawing and the realistic representation of textures. However, the world of art offers infinite possibilities and there is no right or wrong when it comes to creativity. Feel free to experiment with different inking techniques to create any texture or effect you desire. Go beyond the previous suggestions and combine techniques to explore different drawing styles. In art, anything is possible.

This section offers ideas, techniques, and exercises to expand your drawing beyond realism, encouraging you to explore your imagination and creativity.

✧ **Create fun textures and patterns:** One way to deviate from realism is to experiment with different textures and patterns. Try creating your own unique textures by combining different strokes, hatching patterns, or stippling densities. You can also play with repeating shapes or lines to create interesting patterns. Experiment with scale—a texture or pattern can change dramatically when magnified or miniaturized.

✧ **Create surreal concepts:** Surrealism defies logic, unlocking a universe of possibilities. Start by juxtaposing unexpected elements or distorting familiar objects in your drawing. Try drawing dream-like landscapes, or objects defying gravity or other laws of physics. The key to surrealism is to allow your imagination to run free.

✧ **Play with line thickness and stroke styles:** Varying line thickness can create a sense of depth and add a dramatic effect to your drawing. Thicker lines can bring elements forward while thinner lines can push elements back. Diverse stroke styles can also add a dynamic effect. Experiment with loose, quick strokes for a more spontaneous effect, or try precise, controlled lines for a more structured look.

✧ **Incorporate abstract elements:** Abstract art is another realm that allows for infinite creativity. Try incorporating abstract shapes or forms into your drawing. You can also experiment with non-representational compositions—these don't need to represent anything specific and can be a pure exploration of form, color, and line.

✧ **Play with creative compositions:** Experiment with the arrangement and placement of elements in your drawing to create a unique visual impact. Consider distorting the scale of objects, placing large elements with smaller ones, or arranging elements in an unexpected way to create a sense of surprise. Play around with symmetry and asymmetry in your compositions to create balance or tension. The rules of realism don't apply here. Feel free to let your creativity guide

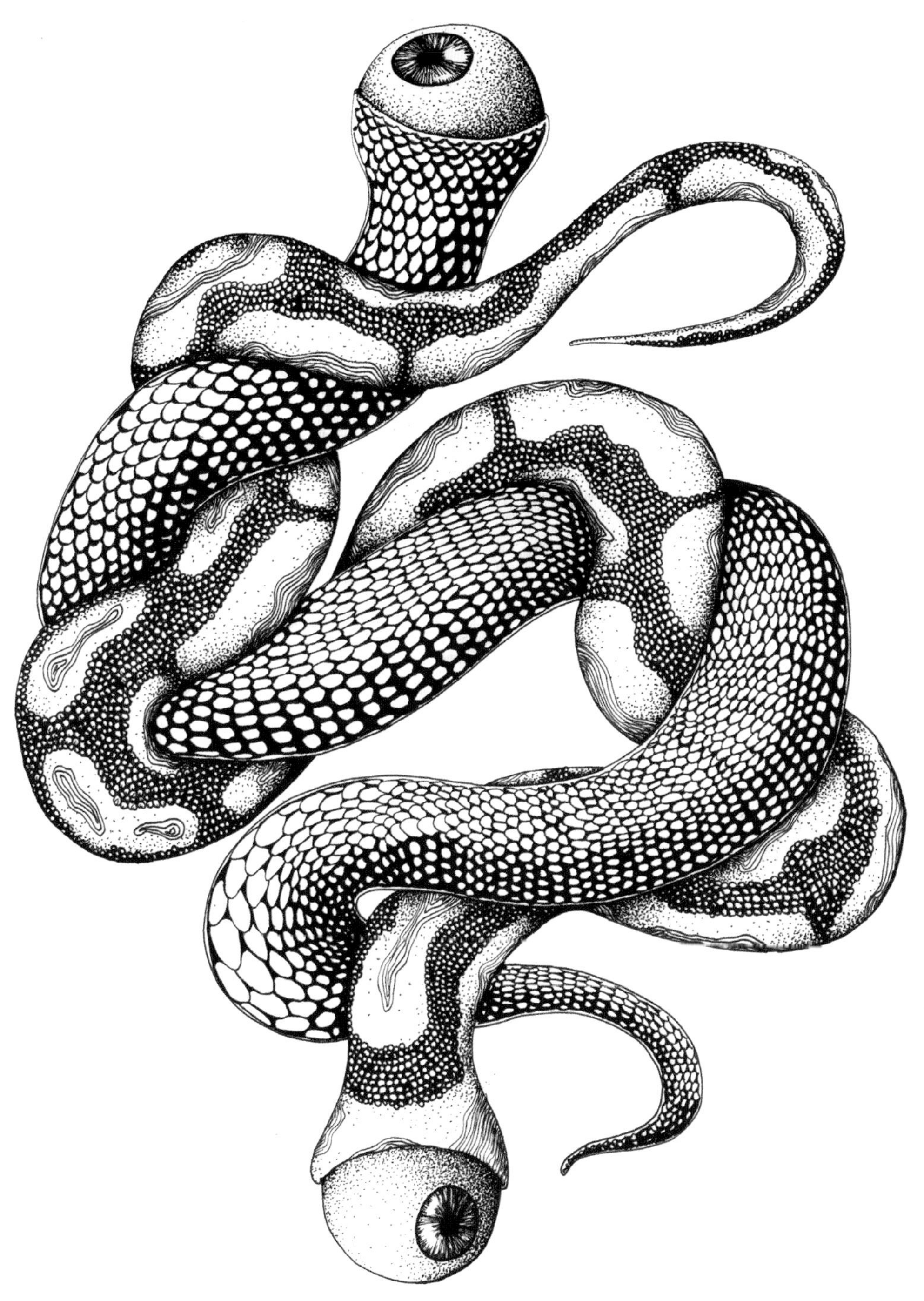

you in creating compositions that are fun, quirky, and visually engaging.

◇ **Use mixed media:** Don't feel restricted to using only pen and ink. Incorporating mixed media into your drawings can add a whole new dimension and create unique effects. Try experimenting with colored paper, which can dramatically change the mood of your drawing. You could also introduce other art tools like watercolors, colored pencils, or markers to add more depth and character to your pieces. The contrast between the precision of the ink lines and the softness or boldness of other mediums can result in visually stunning pieces.

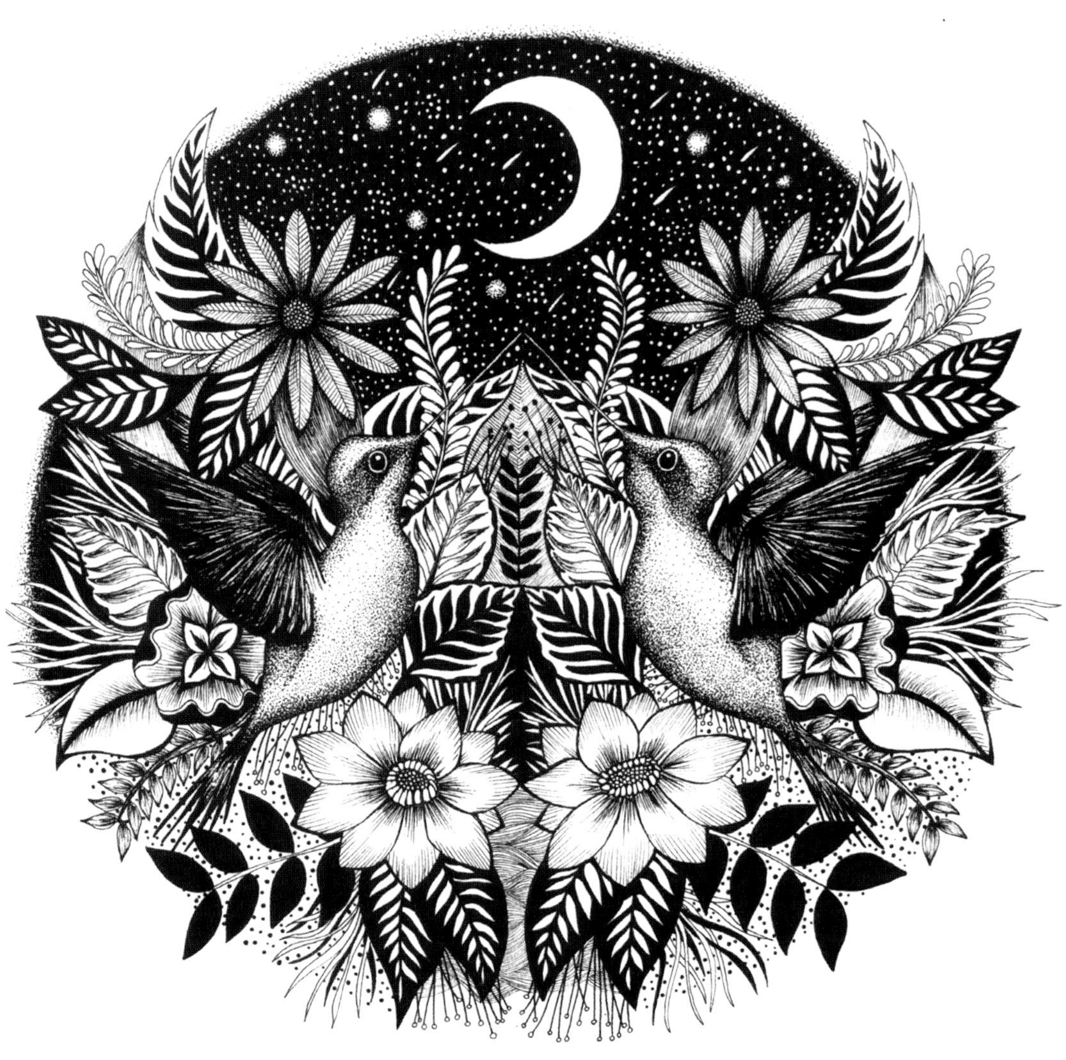

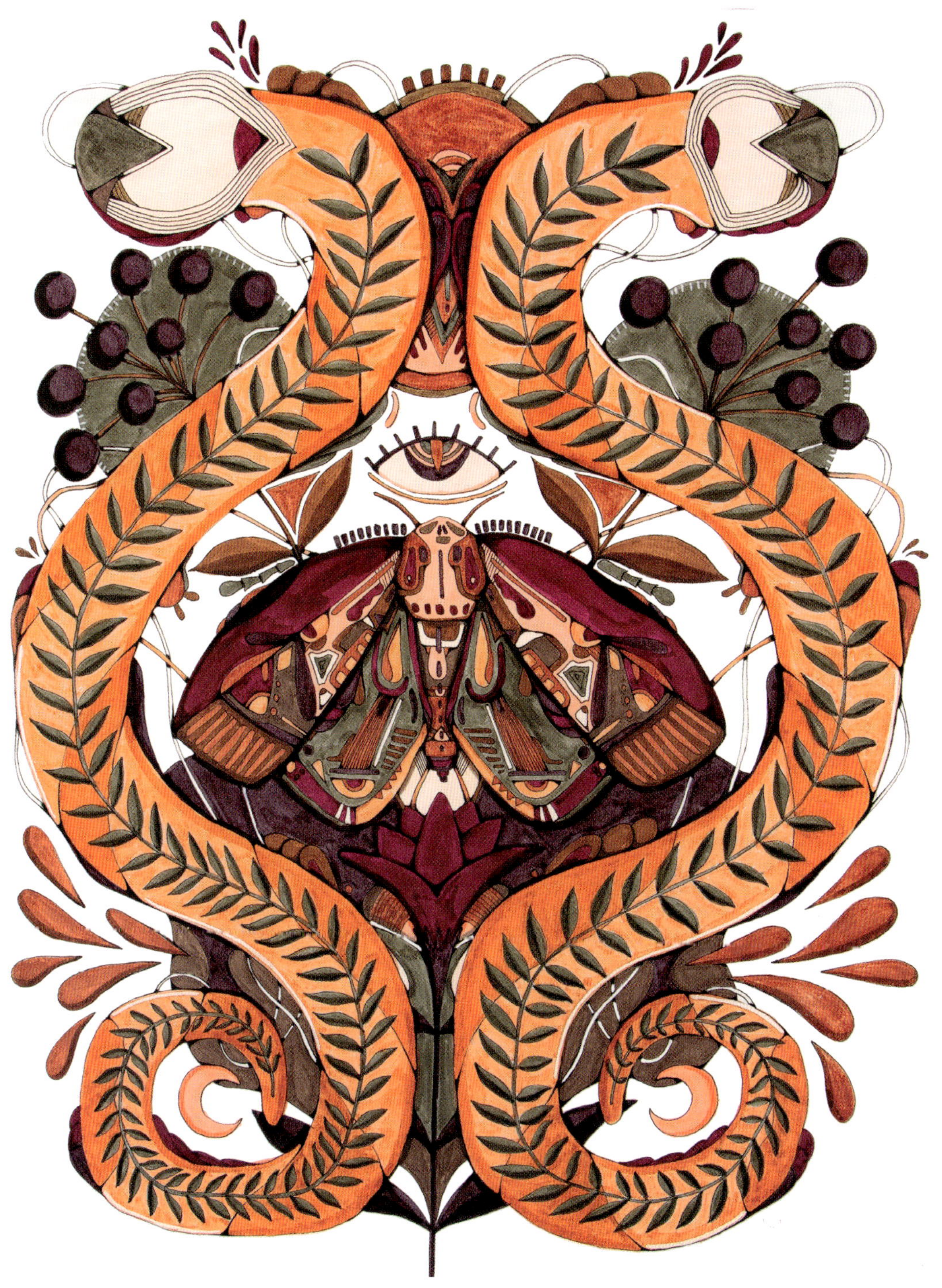

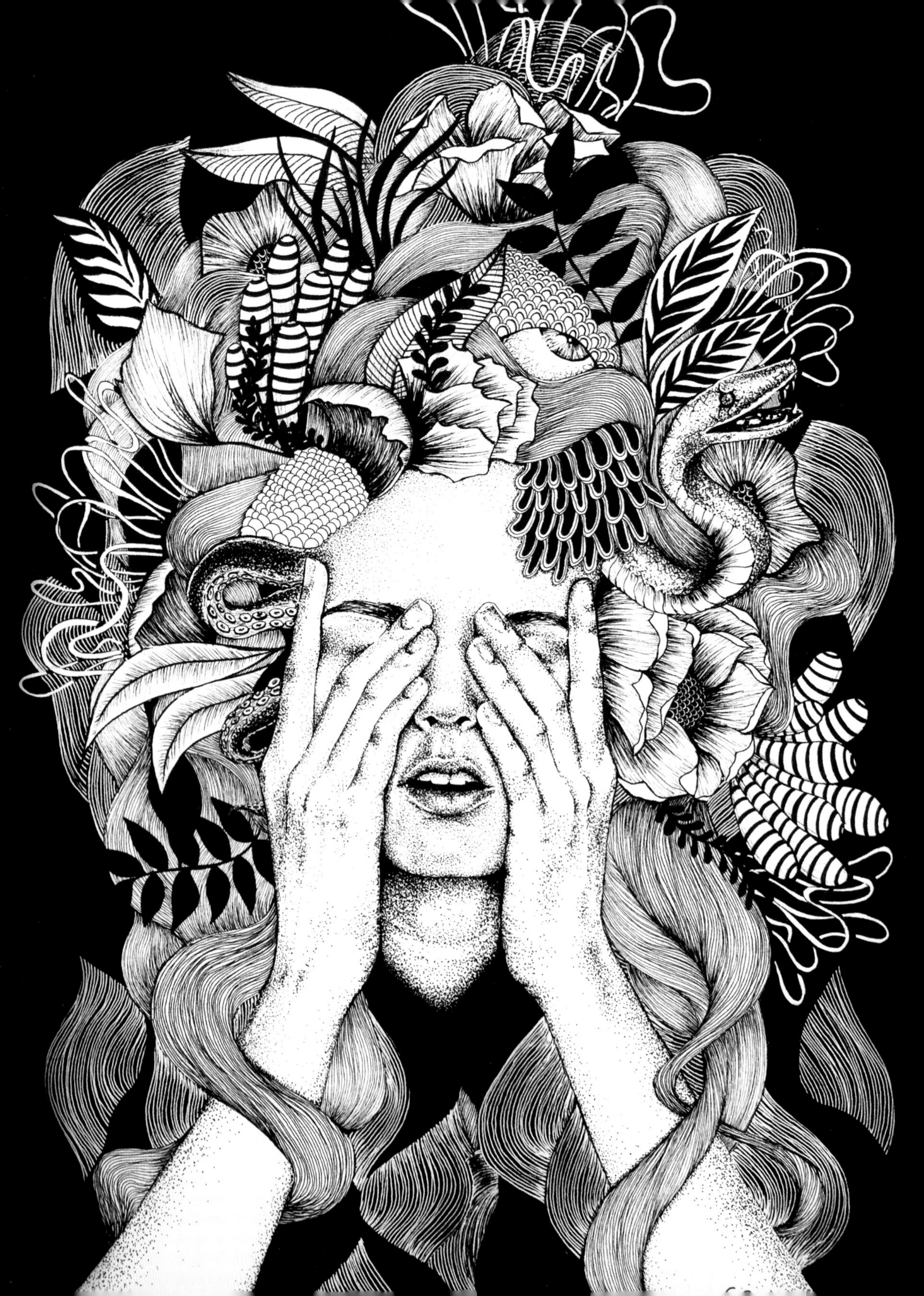

DRAWING HUMANS

Let's explore the art of drawing humans from two perspectives: faces and bodies. These drawing fields are complex and multifaceted and have been studied by artists around the world for centuries. I encourage you to experiment with what you learn here and further your study beyond this book, if the subject of drawing humans interests you.

In this chapter, you will learn a comprehensive, yet concise approach to help you begin your journey in drawing people with ink. We will cover step-by-step systems that will be useful when drawing with any medium, and then dive deeper into specific ink pen techniques that will equip you with the fundamental knowledge to create expressive, dynamic, and realistic human illustrations.

HOW TO DRAW FACES

Portrait drawing goes beyond simply drawing the physical likeness of a person. It can capture the essence of the individual, their personality and mood. Specifically in pen and ink portrait drawing, you will be able to interpret the subject through a choice in technique, style, and lighting to create the desired result. In this chapter, we will discuss everything from understanding facial proportions to mastering ink shading techniques to portray faces creatively. This guide will provide you with the essential knowledge and techniques to capture not just the appearance, but the character of your subjects, making your portraits come to life.

Facial Proportions and Guidelines

Drawing portraits with ink pens is an in-depth process that requires a good understanding of human facial anatomy and people's unique facial features.

Building a solid foundation using guidelines is crucial for creating a well-proportioned and accurate portrait drawing. Similar to drawing portraits with any other medium, the starting point is understanding the proportions of a face. Usually, a face is divided into thirds:

- ✧ Hairline to eyebrows
- ✧ Eyebrows to the bottom of the nose
- ✧ Bottom of the nose to the chin

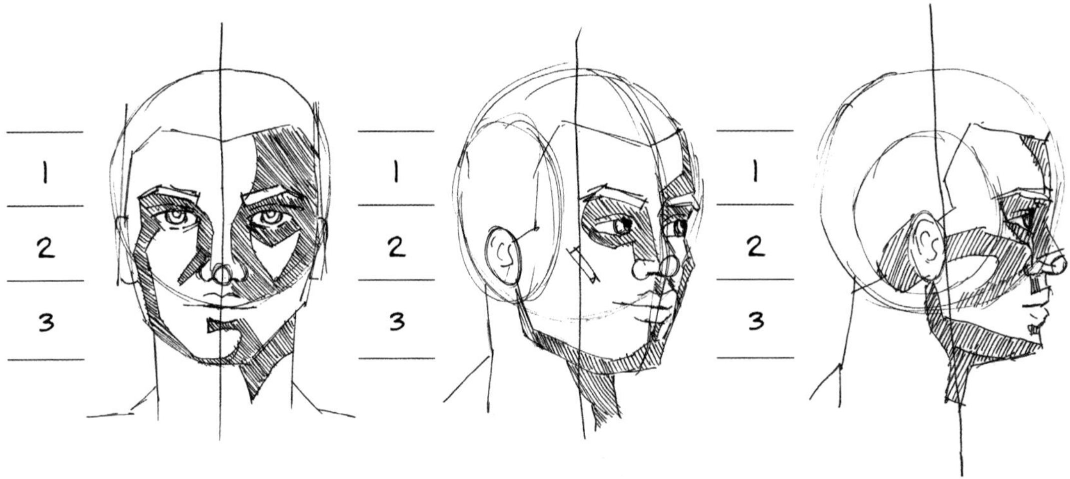

Here's a step-by-step method to get started with a front-facing portrait by sketching guidelines on your drawing. This method varies slightly among individuals, but it is a good starting point for beginners:

1. **Start with a circle:** Lightly sketch a circle to represent the overall shape of the head. This will serve as a general guide for the placement of facial features.
2. **Turn the circle into an oval:** By adding an extra section at the bottom of the circle, you will have the general shape of the head.
3. **Mark a vertical symmetry line:** Divide the oval shape in two.
4. **Draw horizontal guidelines:** Divide the circle into thirds horizontally using light, horizontal lines. The first guideline is at the hairline (so make sure you leave some space for the hair at the top), the second at the eyebrows, and the third at the bottom of the nose.
5. **Position the eyes:** Divide the middle third in half vertically to locate the eye line. Position the eyes along this line, ensuring that the space between them is approximately the width of one eye, and the spaces between the sides of the face and the outside corners of the eyes are approximately half of an eye.
6. **Position the nose:** The nostrils will be positioned on top of the third horizontal line, and they are usually as wide as the space between the eyes.
7. **Position the mouth:** Divide the space from the bottom of the nose to the chin into thirds. Position the mouth along the upper edge of the middle third, keeping in mind it is usually as wide as the space between the inner side of the iris of each eye.
8. **Mark the jawline and ears:** Sketch the jawline with sharp angles to start, noting its shape and contours. The ears should be placed roughly from the eyebrows to the bottom of the nose.
9. **Refine and adjust:** Observe the overall proportions and make any necessary adjustments. Refine the shapes of individual features, ensuring they align with the guidelines. Make sure the facial features are symmetrical by comparing the distances and angles on both sides of the face.
10. **Build up detail:** Gradually add more details, working from general shapes to specific features. Pay attention to shading, highlights, and textures as you progress.

Drawing faces in different positions like frontal, profile, or three-quarter views requires practice and an understanding of perspective, so don't be discouraged if it initially seems difficult to draw.

The oval shape is three dimensional, so the symmetry line that marks the middle of the face follows the curvature of the head shape. When a face turns, the features change based on perspective. For example, in a profile view, the far eye is not visible, and the near eye and ear align vertically. Regular practice is crucial to mastering these details.

These are general guidelines, and individual facial features can vary. Adjustments may be necessary based on the unique characteristics of each person. As you gain more

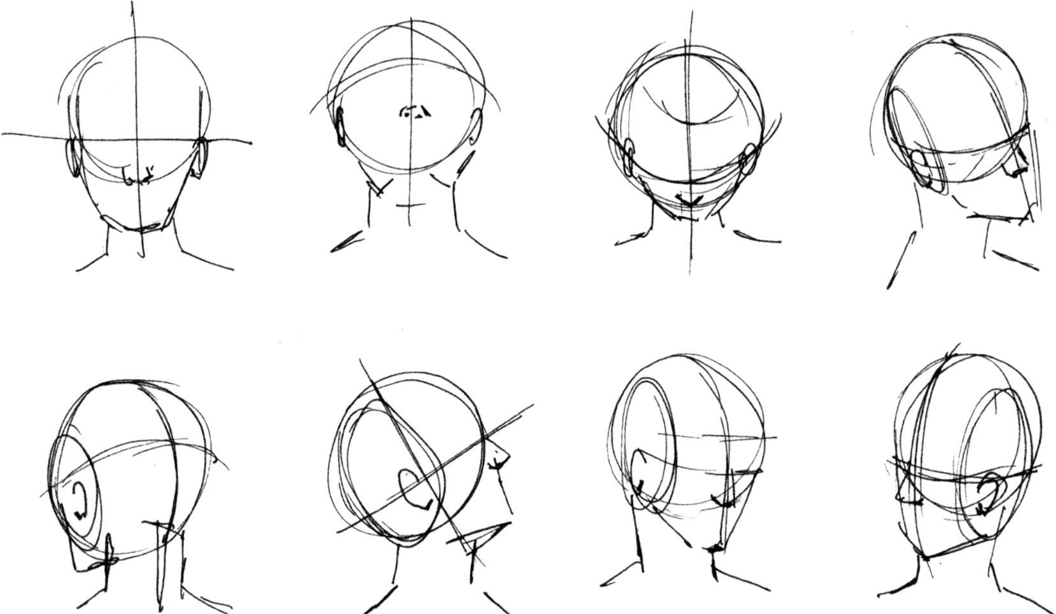

experience, you'll develop a better understanding of facial anatomy and be able to adapt these guidelines to draw any face you want.

Sketching these guidelines before starting a new portrait is not necessary, but it is extremely helpful if you want to be faithful to realistic proportions and facial expressions of your subject. Even if realism is not the style you want to pursue, I encourage you to experiment by sketching the guidelines first, so that you have a clear structure to work on when adding details and shading. With time, you will be able to create your own framework to create more stylized portraits and characters.

Individual Features: Eyes, Noses, and Lips

Here are some tips for drawing facial features:

Lips

✧ The lips can add a lot of character to you drawing. Start by breaking them down into shapes first and sketching the most prominent angles and definitions. Observe how most times the top lip tone transitions into the skin tone smoothly, without a clear, defined separation between the two. So, keep that in mind when outlining with the ink pen.

✧ If the teeth are visible, leave the lines between each tooth faded, almost invisible. Focus on the definition of the top or bottom of the teeth, if visible. If you look at your teeth in the mirror, you will see that the difference between each tooth is very delicate and light. The back teeth—the ones closer to the corners of the mouth—are shaded a bit darker, creating that rounded effect of the dental arcade.

Noses

✧ The sides and bottom of the nose should be shaded to give it a three-dimensional shape, but don't contour the whole shape. Instead, mark only the nostrils and bottom of the nose.

Eyes

✧ Start by sketching the main shapes. If using circles to render a relaxed expression, you should be able to see only the bottom half of the iris. If you let the full circle of the iris be visible, the facial expression will be closer to surprised or scared.

✧ Dedicate a good amount of time to make sure both eyes are aligned first. You can't erase the ink, so even if you portray the shadows and textures perfectly, if the eyes are slightly unaligned, the portrait will look a little off.

✧ Shade the white part of the eyes. As with anything that's white in reality, shadows will be visible. Generally, the areas closer to the corners and under the eyelashes will have a slightly darker shade.

✧ Make sure you leave a white sparkle inside the eye to give life to your drawing. Without the eye sparkle, the drawing will feel like it's missing something or have an eerie feeling. In art and cinema, the eye sparkle is sometimes removed to indicate the person is no longer alive. The eyes are often said to be the windows to the soul, and getting them right can make your portrait come to life.

Every artist was once a beginner, and every masterpiece starts with a rough sketch. Embrace the learning process, and you'll find that drawing portraits with ink can be less scary than it seems at first.

General Differences Between Faces

Each face is unique. Use models or pictures as references so you can study and experiment with different facial features and positions. Keep these general differences in mind when drawing portraits:

✧ **Male and female faces:** Typically, males have stronger, angular jawlines and thicker brows, while females have softer features and more defined eyelashes. These are general guides and can be helpful when starting.

✧ **Drawing different ages:** A person's age significantly affects their facial features. For example, babies and children have softer features and larger heads relative to their bodies. Also, the lower half of their faces are usually smaller than on adult faces. As people get older, their faces become more angular, and lines and wrinkles appear. Understanding these changes is important for creating realistic proportions and textures.

✧ **Different skin tones:** Ink shading techniques are crucial for depicting different skin tones. Darker skin tones require heavier shading, while lighter skin tones need lighter, more subtle shading. Any of the techniques you learned in this book works well for shading portraits, some being more stylized than others.

Shading and Texture

In this section, we will explore the crucial details that bring our ink pen portraits to life: shading and texture. Shading helps create the illusion of depth on a flat surface, while texture adds richness and detail, making faces appear more realistic. Before experimenting with specific shading techniques, it's important to understand how light and shadows work in a portrait. These elements are key to bringing your subject to life, giving them a three-dimensional appearance on a flat surface.

Generally, there are several main areas of shadows in a portrait:

✧ **Eyes:** The eyes are usually recessed within the face, which usually creates shadows that will help shape your portrait. This includes the upper eyelid, the area under the eyebrow, and under the lower eyelashes. Don't forget to shade inside the white of the eyes. That will make your drawing look more realistic.

✧ **Nose:** The side of the nose opposite the light source will be in shadow, as will the underside of the nose. To make the drawing more realistic, leave a lighter area at the tip of the nose.

✧ **Lips:** The upper lip is usually shaded darker as it is angled away from the light, causing it to be less illuminated, while the lower lip has a tendency to catch more light due to its position and contours.

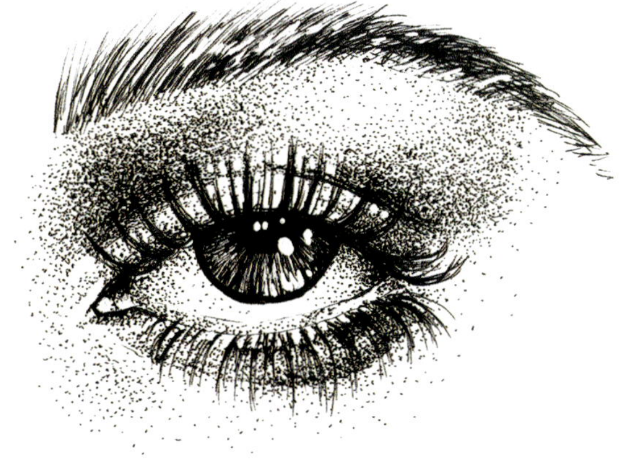

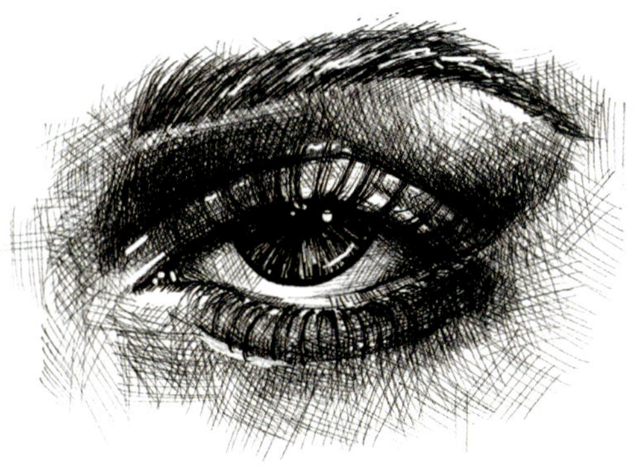

◇ **Chin:** There's often a shadow under the chin, where it overhangs the neck, and also a shadow right under the bottom lip, leaving a highlight spot at the center.

◇ **Cheekbones and forehead:** Depending on the light source and the subject's facial features, these areas may also have shadows.

Of course, this is a very general guide. The specific lighting and shading in a portrait will depend on your light source and the unique features of the subject. For example, a light source directly in front of the subject will result in a different shading scheme than a light source hitting the subject from the side.

When it comes to popular positions and lighting for portrait drawing, frontal view allows for symmetrical shading, while three-quarter view provides an opportunity to play with more dramatic shadows and highlights. As for lighting, many artists prefer to use a single, strong light source coming from one side to create dramatic, interesting shadows.

Crosshatching Portraits

Crosshatching is a popular technique used in ink portrait drawings because it allows for detailed and even realistic shading. By varying the density and angle of these lines, you can create different shades and textures, giving a three-dimensional appearance to your drawing. In reality we don't really see lines, so the thinner and more delicate the lines, the smoother your result will be and the closer you will be to a realistic texture. In contrast, thicker, more defined lines, can create very interesting and stylized textures for your portrait.

To start, lightly sketch the subject of your portrait. Once you have the basic outline, begin to apply the crosshatching technique. Start with a set of parallel lines on the darker areas of the face, then draw another set of lines that intersect the first set at an angle, blending with the lighter areas. The areas where the lines intersect will be darker, creating a sense of depth and volume.

When using crosshatching, remember the following tips:

◇ The closer the lines are, the darker the area will appear. Use this to your advantage when shading different parts of the face.

◇ Vary the direction of your lines to suggest different textures. For instance, curved lines can suggest soft skin, while straight lines can give the impression of harder surfaces. You can also use the lines to indicate the angle at which facial features protrude from the face, making the drawing look more natural.

◇ Be mindful of your light source. The areas that are closer or facing the light source should have fewer lines, while the areas in shadow should have more.

◇ Crosshatching is a skill that improves with time and practice. Start with simple shapes before moving on to more complex subjects like portraits.

The goal of crosshatching is to give your drawing depth and volume. With practice, this technique can add a new level of sophistication to your ink portraits.

START WITH
THE HEAD
SHAPE +
CENTER LINE

THEN ADD THE
FACIAL FEATURES

MAKE SURE
THE CENTER
LINE FOLLOWS
THE CURVE OF
THE FACE

FOCUS ON
THE SHAPES!

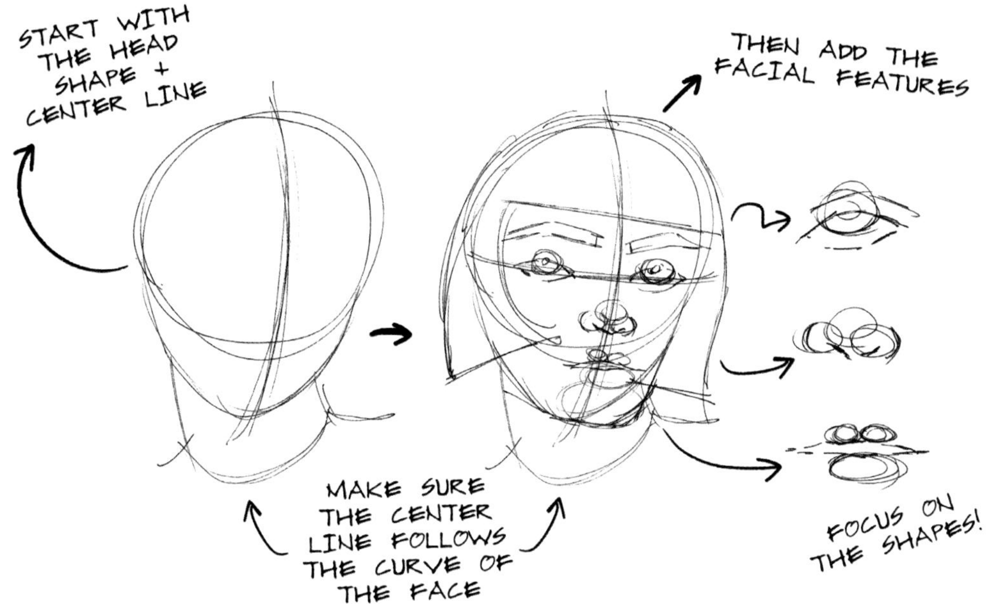

CHOOSE THINNER
FADED LINES
FOR SMOOTHER
SKIN TEXTURE

USE CROSS-
HATCHING TO
CREATE SMOOTH
TRANSITIONS
BETWEEN TONES

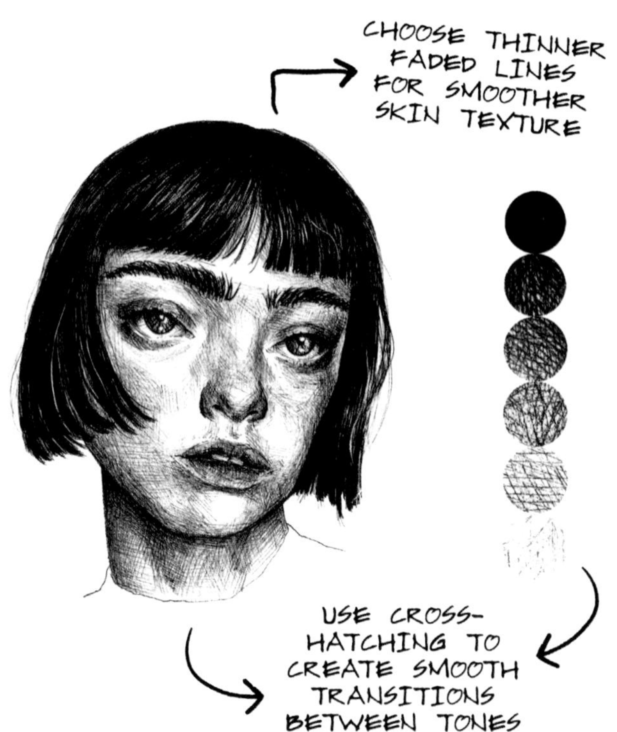

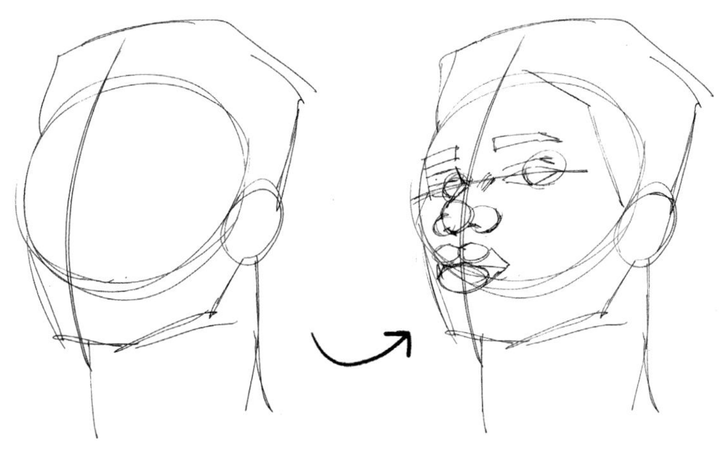

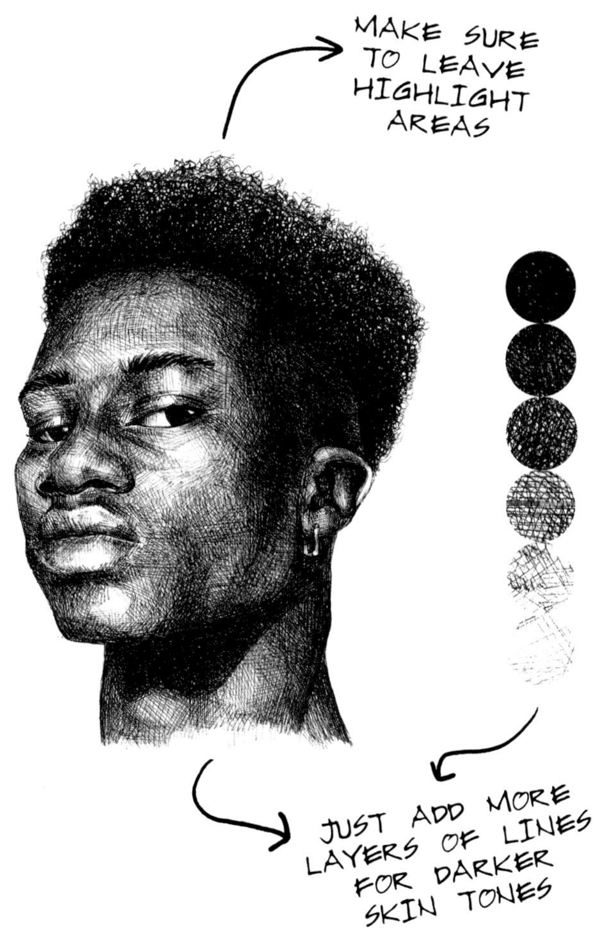
MAKE SURE TO LEAVE HIGHLIGHT AREAS
JUST ADD MORE LAYERS OF LINES FOR DARKER SKIN TONES

Stippling Portraits

With stippling, it's easier to control the amount of ink you are releasing on paper, allowing you to create beautifully smooth shadows. This is a very time-consuming shading method, but very effective.

To shade using this technique, a series of dots are created over and over, with more dots on the shadow areas and fewer dots on the highlights, giving a three-dimensional appearance. Start with a series of dots on the darker areas of the face, then gradually decrease the density of the dots as you move to the lighter areas. The smaller the dots, the smoother the shadows will be, so pick the thickness of your pen according to the results you want.

When using stippling, remember the following tips:

- ✧ The size and density of your dots matters. Larger dots and higher dot density will create darker shades, while smaller dots and lower dot density will create lighter shades.
- ✧ Be mindful of your light source. The areas that are closer or facing the light source should have fewer dots, while the areas in shadow should have more.
- ✧ Stippling is time-consuming, so be patient. The process cannot be rushed, otherwise your dots might turn into dashes and create a messy result. Practice your pen control with a steady movement when making the dots, and the final result will be worth it.

- ✧ Stippling is a skill that improves with time and practice. Start with simple shapes before moving on to more complex subjects like portraits.

The goal of stippling is not necessarily to make your drawing look realistic, but to give it depth and volume. With patience and practice, this technique can add a unique and impressive touch to your ink portraits.

Stippling is a versatile technique that can be adapted to suit your personal style and the specific requirements of your subject. Don't be afraid to experiment and find your own unique approach.

General Tips

Here are some general tips for producing convincing portraits:

- ✧ **Wrinkles:** Drawing wrinkles can be tricky. Wrinkles are just lines on the face that indicate where the skin folds. You should draw them lightly and not too harsh. The lines should be subtle and blend in with the rest of the face. After you mark the main wrinkle lines, you can shade a little from the line outward to blend it with the rest of the skin.
- ✧ **Hair:** Refer back to Chapter 4 to see in detail how to draw hair. Specifically with human hair, it's always effective to make it imperfect and add some loose hairs in black ink and white ink to make it look more realistic. For the white hairs, you can use a white gel pen or a thin round brush with white ink.

- ⬥ **Facial expressions:** The expression on a person's face can tell a story and give a lot of meaning to your artworks. Pay close attention to the eyes, eyebrows, and mouth, as these are often the parts that move more through different facial expressions. Practice drawing different facial expressions from reference first to get a feel for how the face changes with each emotion.

- ⬥ **Smiles and laughs:** When drawing a smile, pay attention to how the mouth shapes and how it affects the rest of the facial features. With laughs, it's more intense. The eyes might close, cheeks raise, more teeth show, and more wrinkles and shadows will appear. It can be challenging to define the shadows. Depending on the person, you may be able to see the gums as well, which should be drawn very delicately.

- ⬥ **White ink:** White ink can be a powerful tool in your pen and ink portraits. It can be used to add highlights, draw attention to specific areas, create contrast, or fix little mistakes. Just be careful not to overdo it, as too much white ink can make your drawing look washed out.

- ⬥ **Children and babies:** Children and babies can be challenging because they have softer, rounder features than adults. Their faces have less pronounced lines and wrinkles, so you should use a lighter touch when drawing their features.

Creative Portrait Drawing

When you've understood the basics of portrait drawing and feel comfortable with your technique, it's time to let your creativity shine. Portraits don't always have to be realistic; they can be stylized, abstract, or even surreal. Here are some ways to break out of the box and add a creative twist to your portraits:

- ⬥ **Play with different techniques:** Don't limit yourself to just one technique. Mix and match different methods like crosshatching, stippling, and line work to create interesting effects. For instance, you might use stippling for the shadows on the face and crosshatching for the hair. Experimenting with different techniques can lead to unique and unexpected results.

- ⬥ **Stylize your portraits:** Try exaggerating certain features or proportions to create a stylized portrait. For example, you could draw the eyes larger than they are in real life, or exaggerate the length of the neck. This can add a fun, whimsical touch to your portraits.

- ⬥ **Play with proportions:** While it's important to understand the basic proportions of the face, you don't have to stick to them strictly. Try playing with proportions to create fun characters. You might make the eyes larger, the nose smaller, or the mouth wider. Changing the proportions can give your portraits a unique personality.

✧ **Add surreal or abstract elements:** Combine your portrait with surreal or abstract elements to create an interesting composition. You could draw flowers growing out of the subject's hair or have birds flying out from their eyes. The only limit is your imagination.

✧ **Incorporate color:** While this guide focuses on pen and ink, you don't have to limit yourself to just black and white. Experiment with adding color to your portraits. You could use colored ink, watercolor, or even digital coloring. Adding color can bring a new dimension to your portraits.

HOW TO DRAW THE HUMAN FIGURE

Figure drawing is a fundamental skill for artists, allowing them to capture the human form with accuracy and expression. Using ink pens for figure drawing adds a unique challenge and aesthetic to the process. Drawing the human body can seem difficult due to the wide variety of body shapes and complexities, but with an understanding of basic proportions and guidelines, you will have a clear path to follow. As seen in previous chapters, we will start by breaking the subject down into shapes and lines in order to find the right proportions, and then refine and add details.

Body Proportions and Guidelines

The first step to drawing human figures is understanding the basic proportions of the body. On average, an adult figure is typically eight heads tall. Even if this varies slightly from person to person, it is used as a standard unit of measurement for drawing the figure. Use it as a starting point to get the proportions right before delving into the details of your subject.

These guidelines will look very robotic at first, but they will help you draw the human body in any position you want, as we will see in more detail further along in this chapter. Here's a simple breakdown of how to position the body's structure, starting by dividing the height of the body into eight sections, the first one being the head:

1. **Head:** The head starts as an oval shape and serves as the basic unit of measurement. The top of the head to the chin represents one unit.

2. **Torso:** From the chin to the waist usually measures two heads. This includes the neck and the torso up to the belly button. With a trapezoid, you can start shaping the chest and waist areas.

3. **Hips:** The section below will hold the waist and hips, which can be marked as a rectangle.

4. **Legs and feet:** Legs normally take up about half of the body height, which is around three heads and a half. This is divided into thighs and shins, so you can start by sketching two central lines for the two legs and two little circles in the middle of each line for the knees. From there, you can shape the legs into imperfect rectangles. The second half of the last section will hold the two feet.

5. **Arms and hands:** When the arm is extended downward, it reaches from the top of the torso, where the shoulders will be, to about the end of the hips, with the elbow falling roughly at the waistline. The hands will reach close to the middle of the thighs. It's helpful to start with the lines to mark the length of the arms, add little circles to mark the joints—shoulders, elbows, and wrists—and then the shapes to define the arms and hands a little more.

6. **Torso:** From the chin to the waist usually measures two heads. This includes the neck and the torso up to the belly button. With a trapezoid, you can start shaping the chest and waist areas.

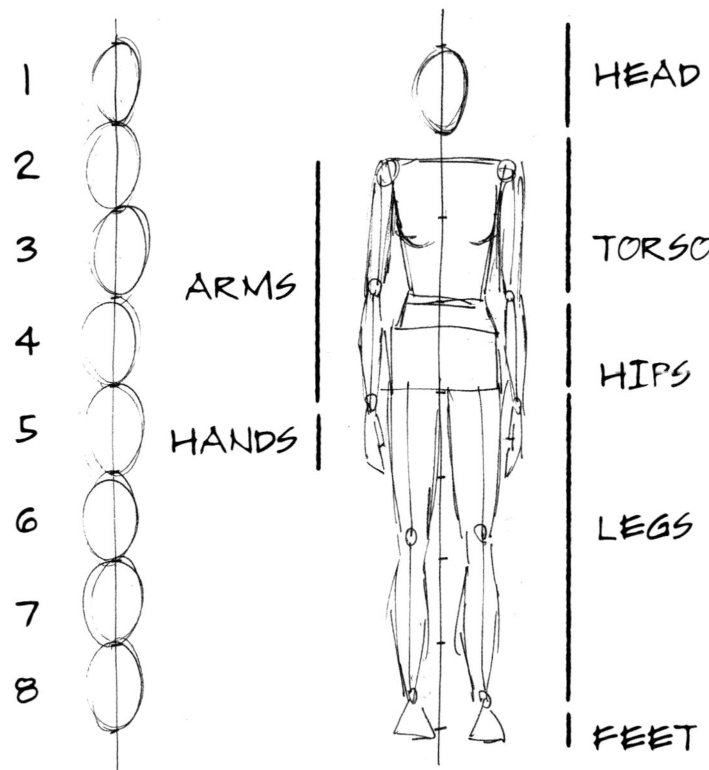

Though the general proportions are similar, there are some differences between male and female bodies. For instance, men usually have broader shoulders, while women have narrower shoulders. Female figures generally have a more defined waist and wider hips, while male figures are more rectangular. In general, men have thicker arms and legs compared to women.

With the basic shapes and joints defined with the right proportions, you will be able to play with different body positions. I encourage you to look at reference pictures for random positions and just practice reproducing the proportions properly using this method. Once you have a clear understanding of these proportions, we can move on to explore the inking techniques.

These guidelines will be the base for any drawing of the human body. From there, you can start refining your figure, adding more details like muscles, clothes, facial features, and shading. These are average proportions, and individual bodies can vary a lot. Observation will be your best tool to help measure these details.

Detailing and Shading the Body

Now that we have covered the basic human body proportions for drawing, we can explore the detailing and shading of our subjects. In this section, you will learn how to create a sense of depth and volume in your figure drawings.

Using your first sketch of the body proportions, start refining the drawing using sharp lines to shape the body. Pay attention to the angles of these lines instead of going straight to the details. It's always easier to go from big to small. Even though the body is actually made up of curves rather than straight lines, by drawing big, fast lines at the right angles, you will have a better base to then work on the details. Look closely at your subject and pay attention to the contours of the body, the muscles, and the clothes.

Once you've added the details, it's time to start shading. As we've seen before, shading with ink pens can be a little tricky because unlike with pencil, you can't simply press harder to get a darker shade. Hatching, cross-hatching, and stippling are some of the most popular ways to create convincing shadows in ink drawings. Observe the light source, noting which parts of the body are facing the light and which ones are facing away from it. In general, the areas that are closer to the light source will be lighter while the areas in shadow will be darker, and you should know the light and shadow sides before you start.

General Tips

- ✧ **Be patient:** Shading with ink pens can be time-consuming, especially if you're using techniques like stippling. Be patient and take your time. Rushing can lead to mistakes that are hard to erase with ink.
- ✧ **Practice with different pens:** Different pens can produce different lines and shades. Practice with different types of pens to see which one you prefer.

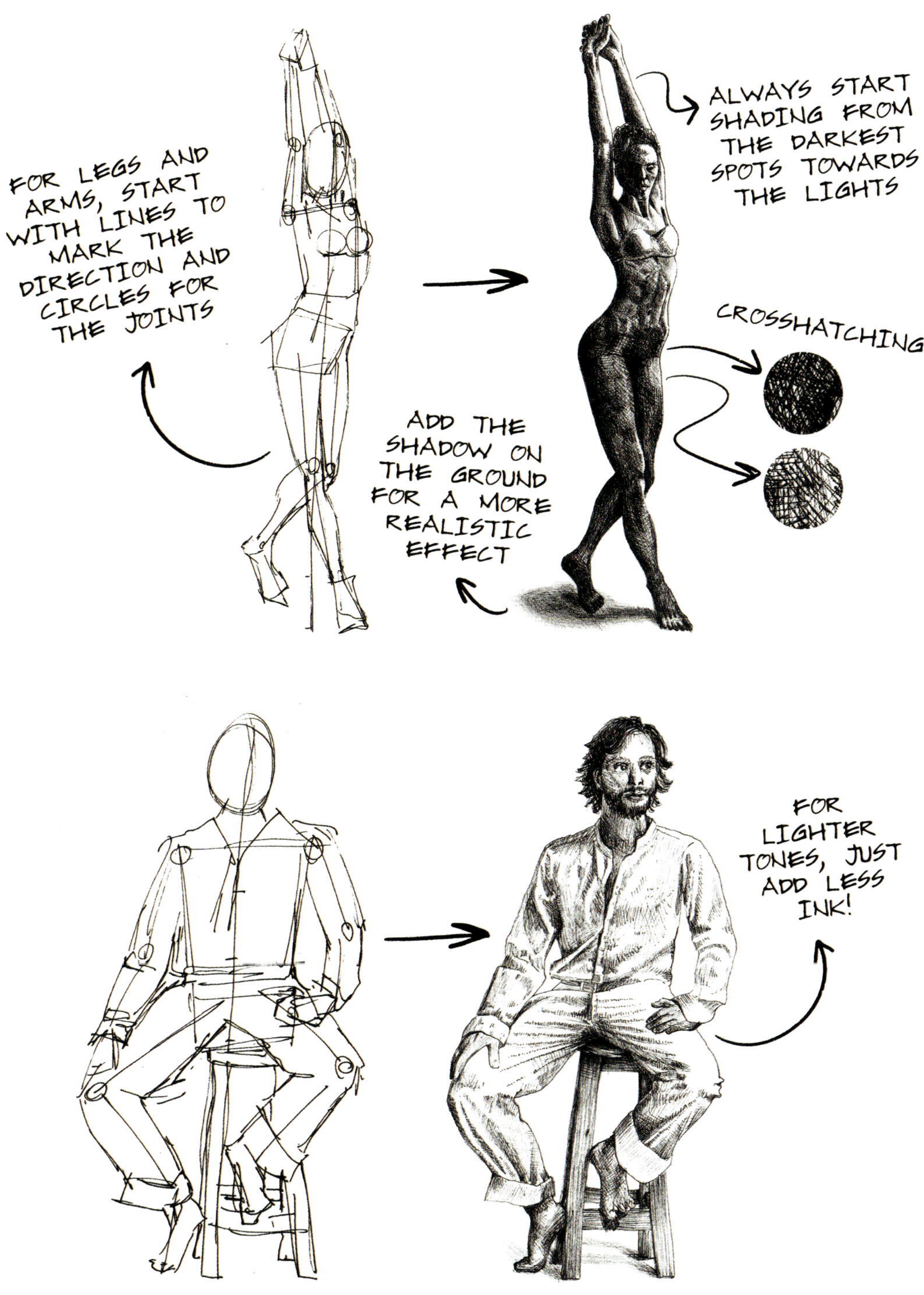

FOR LEGS AND ARMS, START WITH LINES TO MARK THE DIRECTION AND CIRCLES FOR THE JOINTS
ALWAYS START SHADING FROM THE DARKEST SPOTS TOWARDS THE LIGHTS
CROSSHATCHING
ADD THE SHADOW ON THE GROUND FOR A MORE REALISTIC EFFECT
FOR LIGHTER TONES, JUST ADD LESS INK!

- ⬥ **Use a light hand:** It's important to use a light hand if you want to create smoother shadows. The more clear the lines are, the more stylized your shading will be, while the more delicate and thin they are, the more realistic you can get. The first option will be faster to draw, while realism will require more time and patience to achieve.

Clothing and Accessories

Clothing and accessories can add a lot of character to your figure drawings. Different types of fabric behave differently. Look at reference images or even your reflection in the mirror and observe how different fabrics fall and fold on the body, paying close attention to the lighting. Because clothing is, in general, very uneven, with folds, pockets, curves, and other details, the shading can be tricky to figure out from imagination. Keep in mind your light source and sketch the folds and intricacies of the fabric with a pencil, if needed.

Consider how clothes fit on the body. Clothing can be tight, loose, or somewhere in between. Tight clothing will follow the body's form more closely, while loose clothing will have more folds and drapes. Folds can add a sense of realism to your clothing. They typically occur where the body bends (like at the elbow or knee) or where clothing is loose.

When adding accessories like jewelry, glasses, or hats, consider how they interact with the body. For example, a necklace would drape and rest on the collarbones. Pay attention to details like buttons, zippers, and seams. These small details can make your clothing look more realistic.

Stylizing the Human Figure

While realism plays an important role when understanding how to draw humans, stylizing your figure drawings allows for creative freedom and personal expression. Experiment with different techniques to transform human figures into unique artistic interpretations. Here are some ideas to spark your creativity:

- ⬥ **Exaggerate proportions:** Play with the size and shape of the figure's features or body parts. For instance, you might enlarge the eyes for a cartoonish look or elongate the limbs for a more abstract feel. This is a fun way to add interest to your drawings.
- ⬥ **Study different styles:** Don't limit yourself to one particular style. When experimenting with other art styles, such as manga or cartooning, you will be working with different proportions for the human body. It's even possible for you to create your own rules for drawing humans in your own way. A fun way to experiment with this is to draw some of your favorite characters from different shows or movies and study their different proportions and specific details. Each style will offer a unique perspective and will give you a repertoire of possibilities for drawing people.

- ◇ **Play with line quality:** Line quality refers to the thickness or thinness of a line. Vary your line quality to dramatically impact the look of your figure. Thicker, darker lines can emphasize certain areas, while thinner, lighter lines can add delicacy. You can also experiment with broken lines or dashes for a more sketch-like feel.
- ◇ **Emphasize shadows and highlights:** Get dramatic with your lighting. Exaggerate shadows and highlights to create a stark contrast and add depth to your figure. This can result in a stylized, high-contrast look that adds visual interest.
- ◇ **Create a mixed media look:** While this guide focuses on ink pens, don't hesitate to mix in other mediums. Adding splashes of color with watercolors, pastels, markers, or digital coloring can add an unexpected twist to your ink drawings.

Stylizing is all about creativity and personal expression. Don't be afraid to experiment and make the figure your own. With practice and exploration, you'll develop your own unique style of stylized figure drawing.

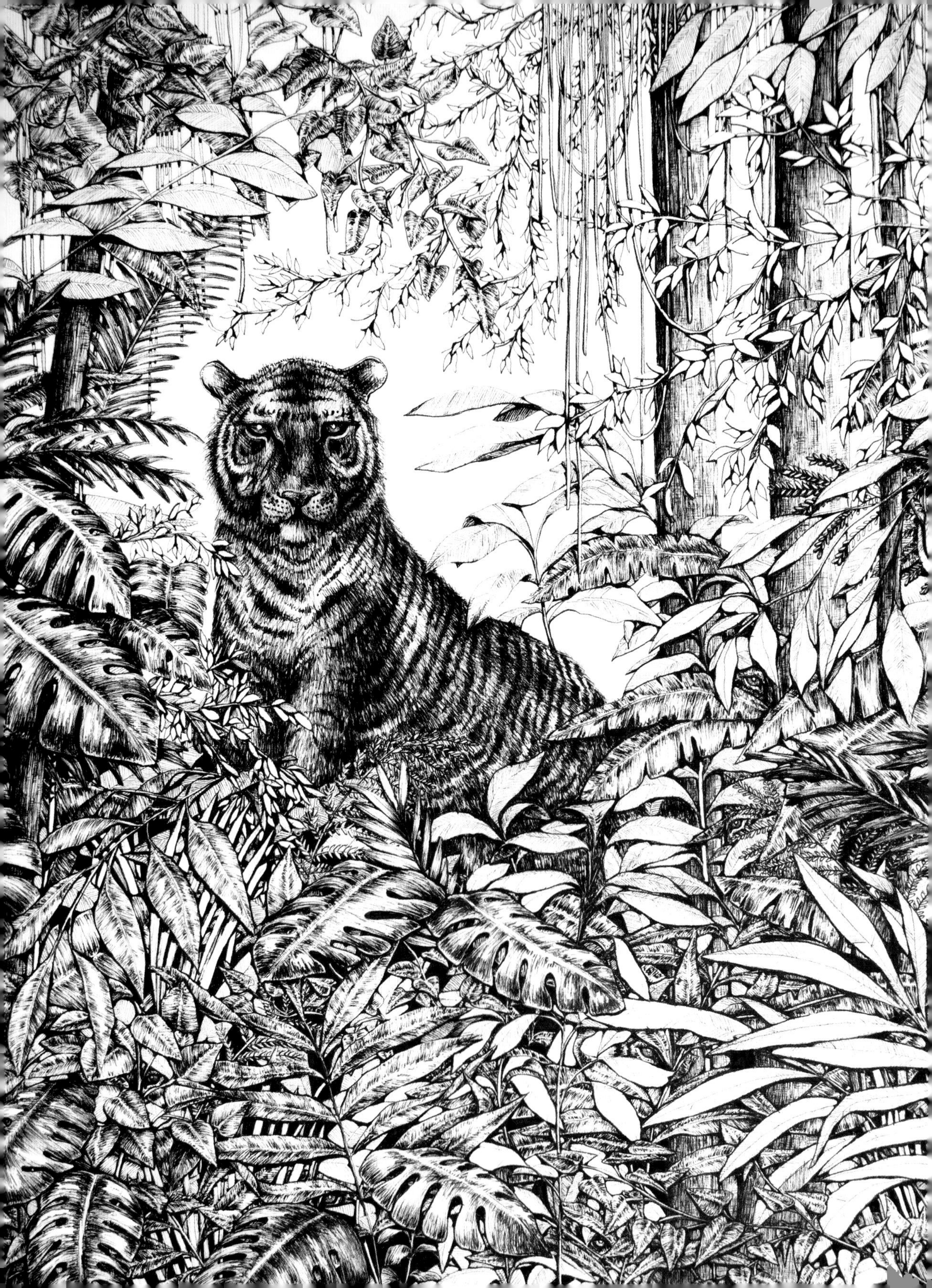

DRAWING ANIMALS

In this chapter, we will explore the process of drawing animals using ink pens. Given the vast diversity of sizes, shapes, and textures existent, it would be impossible to cover every species and break down all the steps for drawing them like we did in the previous chapter, for humans. Instead, apply one of the sketching techniques learned in Chapter 2 to build the initial lines and proportions of your drawing, then work on the textures, shading, and detailing with ink, which will be the main focus of this chapter.

There are infinite ways to use ink to represent animals, so bring your own creative approach to it. The goal of the examples in this chapters is to equip you with the most important tools to sketch any animal, from small, delicate insects to large, heavy mammals. This chapter will simply offer you suggestions on how to elaborate your animal drawings from a realistic perspective.

FIRST SKETCHING LINES

Much like human figure drawing, animal drawing also requires a basic understanding of the subject's structure. Understanding animal anatomy can be helpful when it comes to drawing animals accurately, but it is not necessary by any means. If you draw specific animals frequently, or you want to include these animals in your work more often, study their anatomy and draw them from reference in several different positions in order to gain a better understanding of the animal's structure and how it moves. This can definitely help you add more accurate details and movement to your drawings.

Since each species has its own distinct anatomy, each would have its own set of drawing guidelines to follow. It's possible to do this process with any type of animal you like, mostly by combining what you learned in Chapter 5—how to draw the guidelines for a human body—and in Chapter 2—how to sketch anything from reference. If you are not familiar with a certain animal, the easiest way to get started is to find a reference picture of the animal you want to draw, set some basic guidelines based on the picture you found, and break the animal down into geometrical shapes to position everything on paper. Here's a breakdown of this process, step by step:

1. **Choose a reference picture:** A good picture for this exercise will have good lighting, allowing all parts of the animal to be visible. Observe the picture closely, focusing on the proportions of the body. Don't hurry into the sketching just yet. Instead, take some time to just look and absorb all the information from the picture. Look at the negative space, the elements in the background, the position in which the animal is in, if it is supporting itself in any way, what direction its body is facing, where the light is coming from, the shapes of the shadows and where they are located, and if it has a facial expression or tension in any part of its body or face. Since you will have the reference next to your drawing the whole time, don't stress over memorizing anything. Just observe and take a mental note of all of these details. After some relaxed observation, identify the main shape of the animal as a whole and how it's positioned in the frame, and then the lines and smaller shapes that form the basis of the animal's structure.

2. **Break down the animal's body into shapes:** Start sketching with a pencil instead of a pen, to really give you space to develop the guidelines and shapes first. You can start by identifying one of the main general shapes. If it has a round figure, you can start with a circle. If it is long, maybe a rectangle or an oval shape. Sometimes it's also helpful to add a few important lines that identify symmetry, gestures, and specific angles. For example, the legs and arms can start with simple lines to mark the angle in which they are positioned, and then evolve into

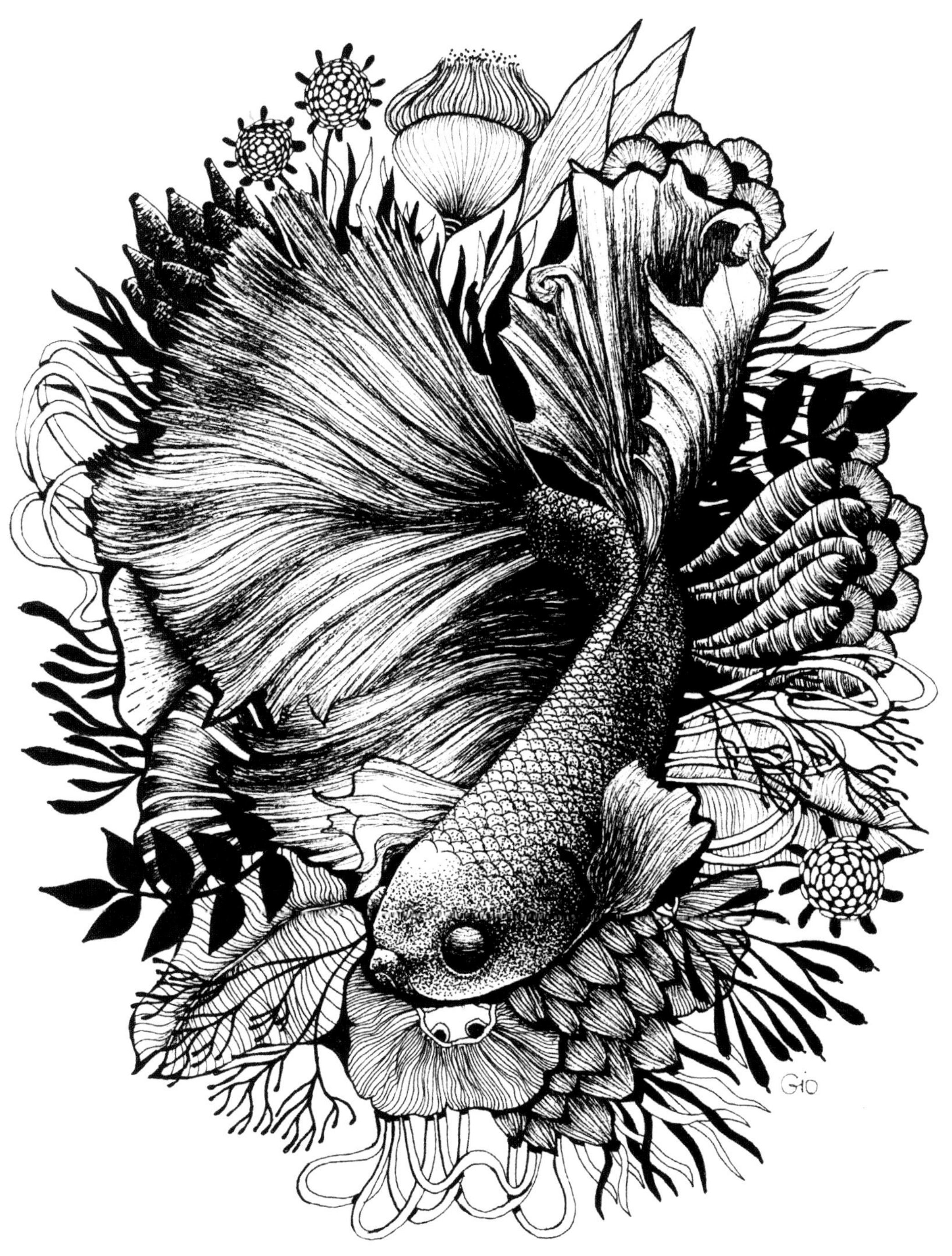

a series of rectangles or cylinders. If they have wings, pay attention to where the wings start and end in relation to the body. Observe how the body parts relate to each other in terms of size and position. Pay special attention to the angles of each line that contours the animal's body by sketching them as straight lines first, and then smooth them out and turn them into curves and other details.

3. **Render more detailed shapes:** From your initial lines and shapes, you can start detailing the drawing and adding more information to it. Look at the animal's musculature and patterns. Pay attention to the small details that make each species unique and maintain correct proportions. Always cross-check the proportions of the body parts with each other and adjust as necessary.

4. **Outline with an ink pen:** Once you have a clear pencil sketch, start outlining the drawing with your ink pen, keeping in mind the final texture you want for your drawing and remembering you can't erase the ink. For example, for textures like fur or feathers, you might want to use a light, short hatching around the body in order to create a more realistic effect. Some parts of the body might be defined only by a light shadow, instead of a line, so you can just mark that with very light dots or hatching. Add lines only where you see a clear, sharp, visible line as an outline of the animal. You can also outline and mark specific details of the animal's texture.

5. **Erase the pencil and start rendering the shadows and textures:** Once your outline is defined and you have a clear vision of what your animal should look like, erase the pencil marks to focus on the textures and shadows. Observe the textures in your reference and choose the stroke styles that will best represent them in your drawing. Feel free to use a little side paper to check and test different pens and styles before applying them to your drawing. Start with the shadow areas and move from the darker to lighter areas. Move back and forth between them in order to correctly apply the right values for each shadow area. In nature, we rarely see black lines contouring or defining animal shapes or textures. In general, lighter, thinner, and more delicate lines will help you achieve a more realistic result than thick, dark lines. The dark, black lines have their place and are essential for creating beautiful, intense, dramatic contrast in our drawings, but using them in the light spots can create simplified results rather than realistic ones. There is no right or wrong way to do this, just what feels right according to the results you want to achieve. If you want a detailed, realistic drawing, this is an important factor. If you want a more stylized and creative approach, there are no rules and you are free to experiment with any thickness and intensity of lines. With time and practice, this process will help you develop a strong foundation in animal anatomy, which will greatly enhance

your ability to draw any animal accurately. Repetition is key. Try using different references with animals in different positions and lighting to develop your animal drawing skills.

As we've explored in previous chapters, there are multiple ways and styles of representing the same element in an ink drawing.

In the next sections of this chapter, you will see examples of animal drawings of different kinds, with ideas on how to shade and detail them with ink pens. The idea of this chapter is to suggest possibilities for creating multiple textures, starting from the ink outline, and ending with the finished drawing for each animal.

HOW TO DRAW A RABBIT

1. **Outline the major shapes:** Sketch your basic shapes first. Begin with a circle for the head, and two more circles for the body—one for the torso and the other for the lower body. Draw ovals for the front legs and ears, and a small circle for the one visible back foot. When outlining the pencil sketch, suggest the fur of the rabbit by hatching short lines to contour the body. Some areas will allow for a simple line as a contour, like the nose and mouth area and ears. Pay attention to the direction in which the fur is positioned, and hatch following that direction.

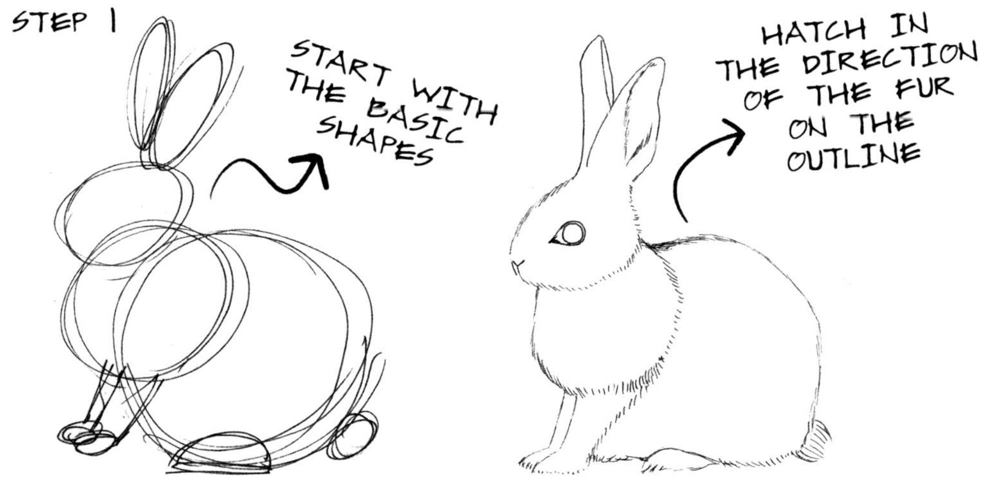

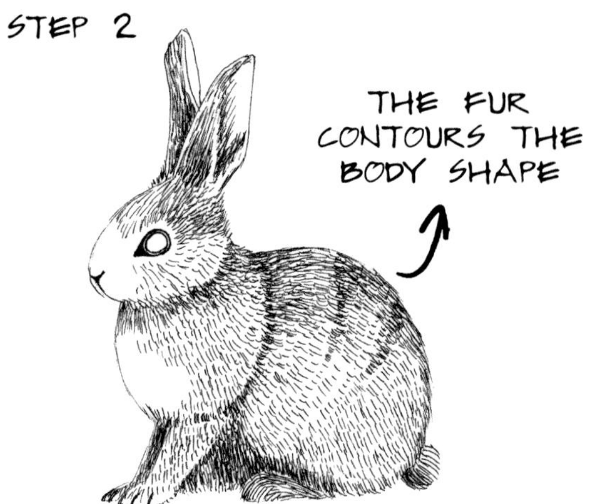

2. **Define the fur pattern:** To draw the fur, simply hatch short lines all over the fur area. Always follow the direction in which the fur grows from the body and leave enough white space for the lighter areas. In the example we are working with here, the fur on the body moves from the head downwards, contouring the round shape of the body. For the head, the fur should move from the nose and eyes outwards. Hatch some extra lines in the shadow areas to start building darker values.

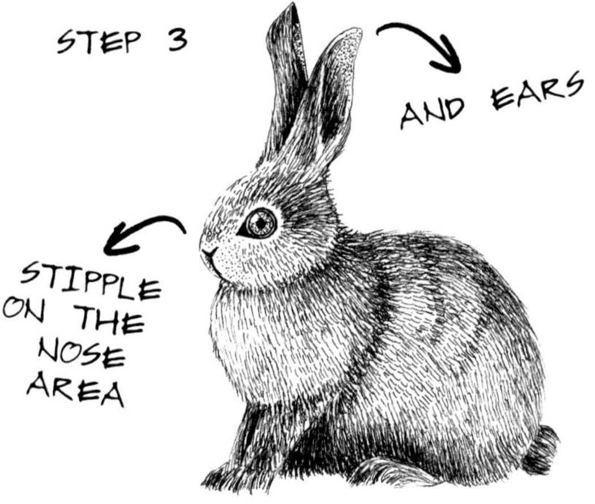

3. **Increase contrast and build texture:** Keep hatching from shadow towards light areas to create depth and dimension, always following the direction of the fur described in the previous step. Work on the transition from shadow to light, making it smoother to create a rounded effect for the body. On the nose and ears, the hatching can transform into stippling to create a skin texture without fur. Don't forget to leave a white light spot inside the eyes.

4. **Add final details:** The intersection between each section of the animal can make your drawing look unfinished or create more depth and look incredibly three-dimensional. So, pay special attention to these areas and intensify the shadows where it's needed. The stomach area that is hidden, the space between the back foot and the rest of the body, the space between the two front legs, the neck areas, right underneath the head, are all examples of these transition spaces that may require some solid blacks or more well-defined lines that help create a more dramatic contrast. The eyes will also play a huge role in making your drawing look realistic. You can use stippling to add more shadows, leaving the highlight spot untouched.

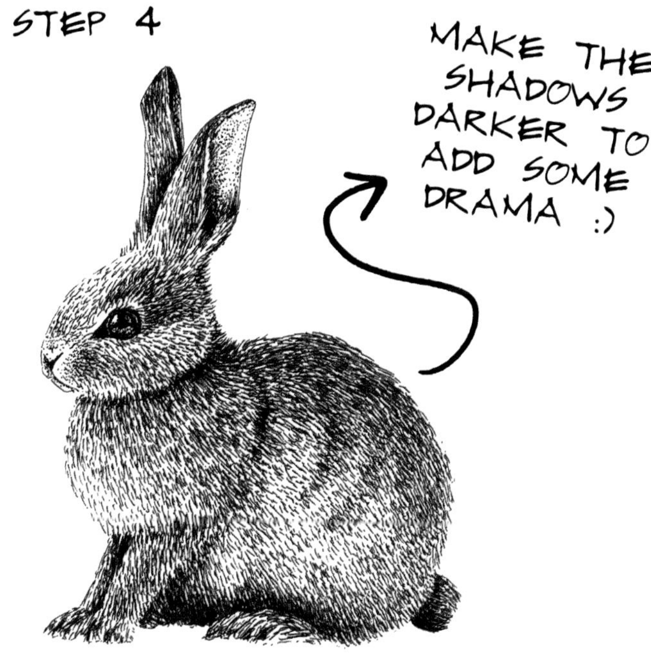

HOW TO DRAW AN ELEPHANT

1. **Outline the major shapes:** When drawing a front-facing elephant, you can start with the main shape for the body, which could be a rectangle or an oval shape, followed by a few circles for the head and ears. For the trunk, start with a line marking the curvature and angles, and then you can start adding more details and definition to your sketch, still at the pencil stage. Since we are not working with fur this time around, you will be able to simply outline the sketch with your ink pen using simple lines. Thin lines will be a little harder to control but will get you a more natural and realistic result than thicker lines.

STEP 1

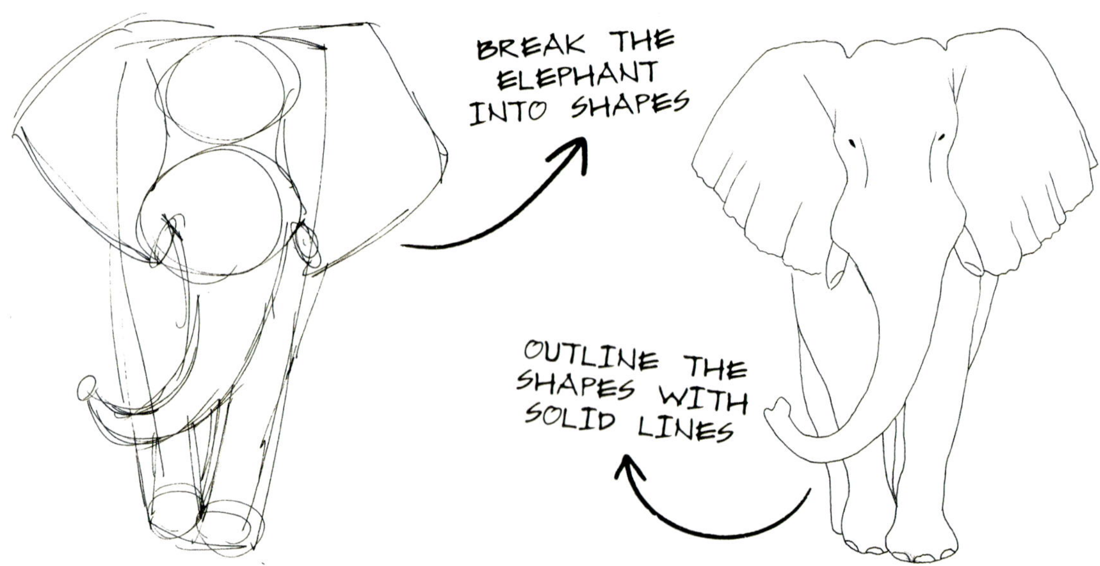

2. **Define stroke style and mark shadow areas:** Choose the stroke style to best portray the rough texture of elephant skin. Once you make your choice, start adding lines or dots to the shadow areas first, like the front leg areas under the head and trunk, the back legs, and the areas of the ears closer to the head. As I chose stippling for this drawing, the instructions will refer to this style more often. When stippling, just add more dots where you want it to be darker and smooth the shadows out by adding fewer dots where you want it to be lighter.

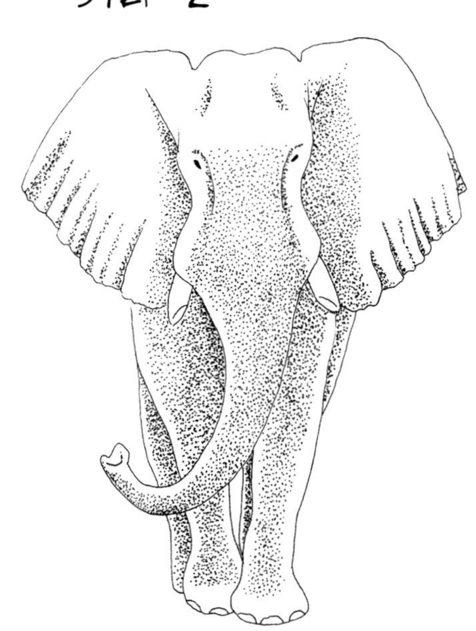

3. **Keep building your shadows:** Add more ink in the shadows, making them darker to differentiate them from the lighter areas. Keep adding dots until the whole body is covered by dots. To save time, feel free to use a thicker pen for the darker areas and a thinner pen for the light spots. This will help you cover the shadows faster and the results will be very similar to using the thinner pen for the whole drawing.

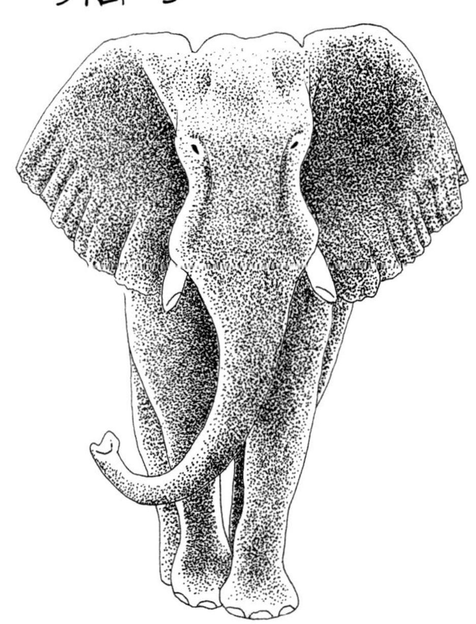

4. **Intensify depth and add details:** Cover the darkest areas with solid black to add more definition to your shadows and create more depth. Make sure that the transition from solid black to stippled areas is smooth. Any dark areas should look like they are just covered by more dots, and not painted with black using any other technique. Once the texture is done, draw the wrinkles and texture of the elephant's skin, starting with slightly curved horizontal lines, following the curvature of the face and trunk, and then add several imperfect vertical lines. The space between the curved horizontal lines should decrease as they move down towards the trunk. Pay attention to the eyes to capture the elephant's expression, and if you want, add a little hatching or stippling on the tusks.

STEP 4

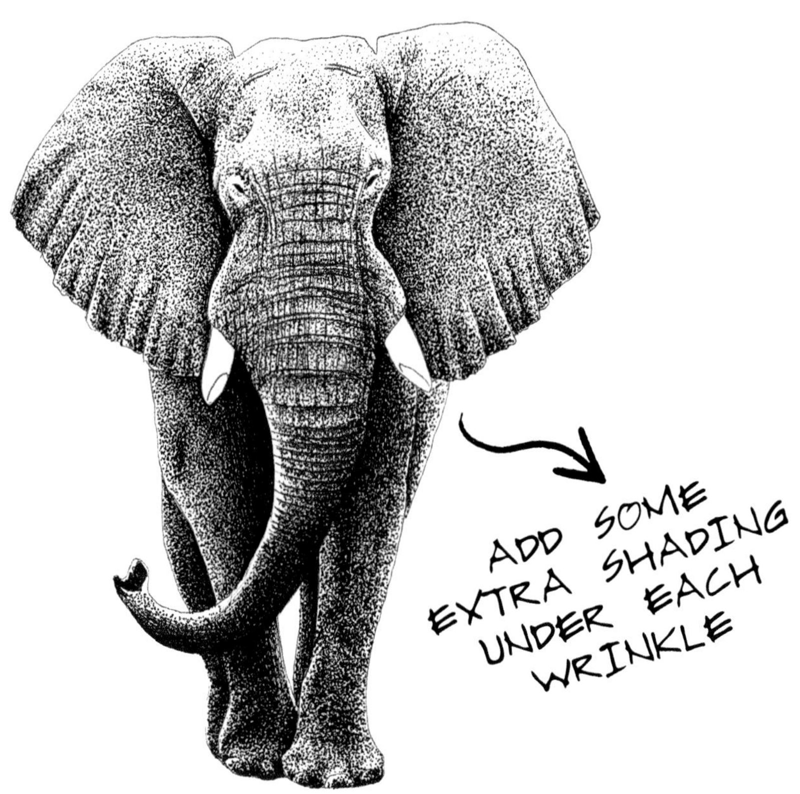

HOW TO DRAW A CAT

1. **Outline the major shapes:** With a front-facing cat, your starting shapes could be a circle for the head and a bigger oval shape for the body. Add two rectangles for the front legs and an oval shape for the tail. It's important to get the facial proportions right, so vertical and horizontal guidelines can be very helpful. Pay attention to the distances between each facial feature, and then position them accordingly. Typically, the eyes are positioned around halfway up the height of the entire head, the nose and mouth can be bundled into a circle at the bottom of the face, and the ears can be represented by two triangles that start a little bit lower than the top of the head. To outline the cat, since we are dealing with fur texture, just hatch short lines or dots all around the cat, keeping in mind the direction in which the fur grows from the body. For the face, simply outline the eyes, tip of the nose, mouth, and ears.

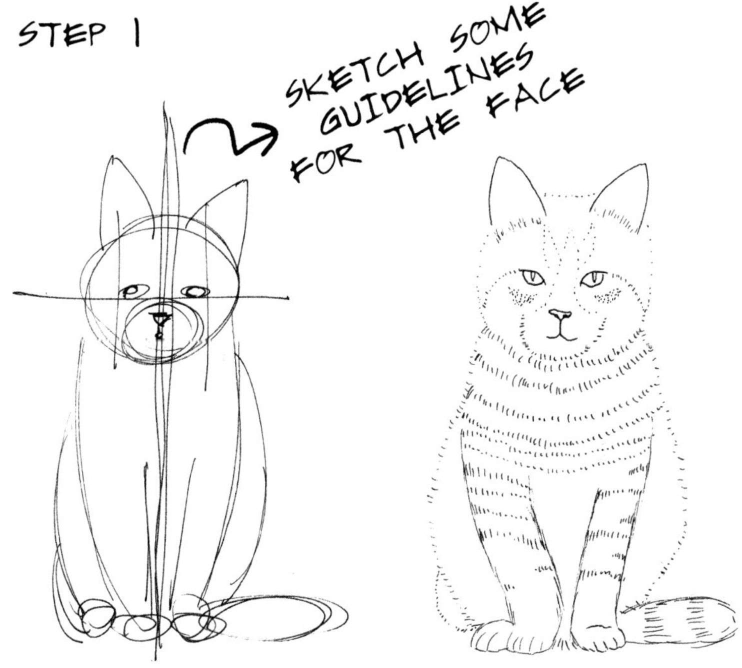

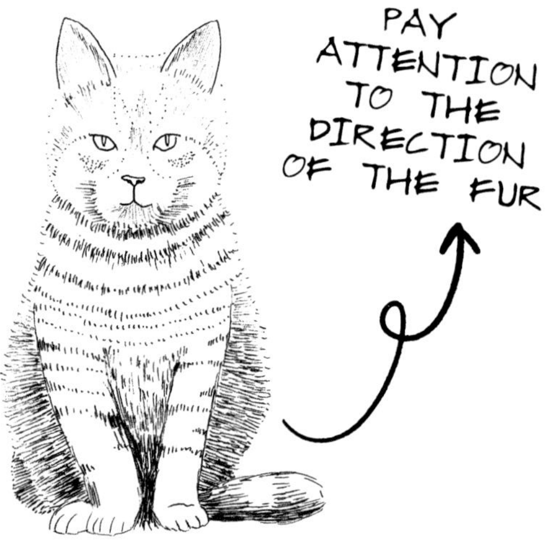

2. **Define the fur pattern:** To represent different colors in a black-and-white drawing, you can play with different values just like we do for shadows. In this cat drawing, we can create a striped pattern by hatching more short lines where the stripes will be. Keep the curvature of the body in mind, so instead of making the stripes completely horizontal, add a slight curve to them to create a more realistic effect. The fur direction is important, and some cats will have more fur than others. In this case, the body fur moves from the head downwards and out to the sides, and on the face, it moves from the center of the face outwards. Feel free to start adding extra lines for the stripes and shadow areas.

STEP 3

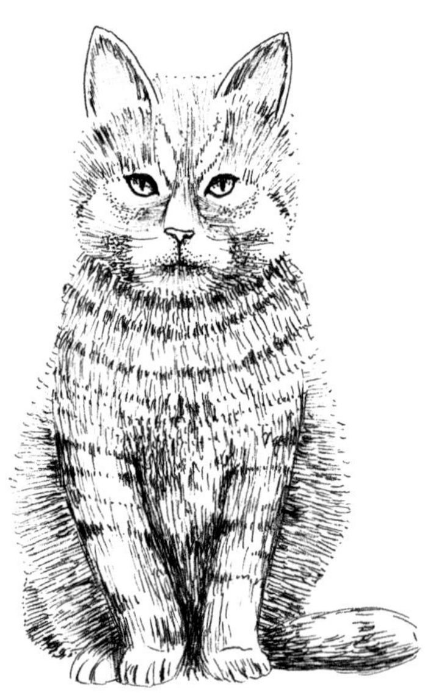

3. **Increase contrast and build texture:** Keep drawing the fur, paying attention to its direction and density. For lighter fur, use an older pen to create faded lines, as this will help you create the effect of a light color fur with a more realistic, softer texture. The scale in which you draw can also influence the appearance of the fur. The larger you draw, the more detailed and realistic your drawing can be.

4. **Add final details:** Intensify the darkest shadows, using solid black where it's needed, like the lower area between the front legs and the base of the tail. The stripes that curve back, on the sides of the body, can also be darker and more intense. The darker shadows and increased contrast will add dimension to your drawing. For the face, the process will be the same when it comes to the fur. The eyes usually have a dark, well-defined contour, and for the more delicate shadows on the mouth area, sides of the nose, and eyes, you can use stippling with a very thin pen to create textured shadows. Stippling is easier to control when working on a smaller scale, since a line in the wrong place can change the whole drawing. If you are working on a larger scale, hatching can be a great choice for the facial details as well.

STEP 4

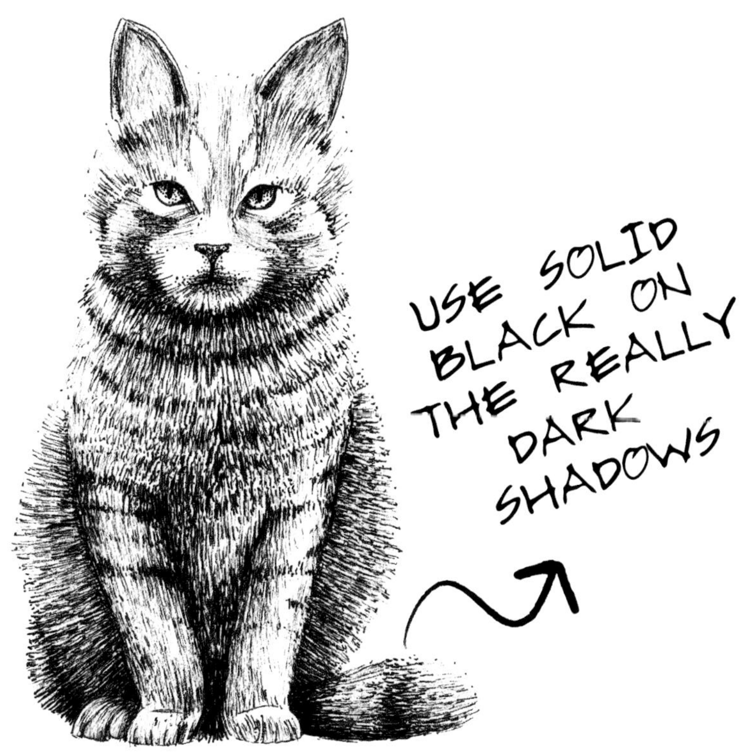

HOW TO DRAW A FOX

1. **Outline the major shapes:** Start with an oval shape for the body, then add a smaller circle for the head and add lines and oval shapes for the legs. After defining the sketch in more detail, you can start outlining it. Since foxes are covered in fur, contour the sketch lines with short hatching lines. You can also mark specific areas of the fur as a reference for shading later.

2. **Define the fur pattern:** Hatch short lines to create the fur effect, starting with the darker areas. Respect the movement of the fur by paying attention to its direction on the body. For example, the leg fur is mostly downwards, the chest fur moves from the head down and out to the sides and the fur along the rest of the body moves back towards the tail. Reference pictures can be a great resource to help improve your ability to understand and draw fur.

3. **Intensify shadows:** Finish creating the fur texture by hatching over the whole body, making the shadow areas darker and spreading the lines towards the lighter areas.

4. **Add final details:** Increase the contrast and depth by defining the darkest shadows with hatching and solid black. Add the details on the paws and use stippling to shade around the nose and mouth areas. Leave a highlight on the eyes, as this is an essential step to adding life to your drawing. To create a more natural fur effect, use a thinner, older pen to hatch short, faded lines along the body. The contrast between darker and lighter lines will help create a more accurate fur texture.

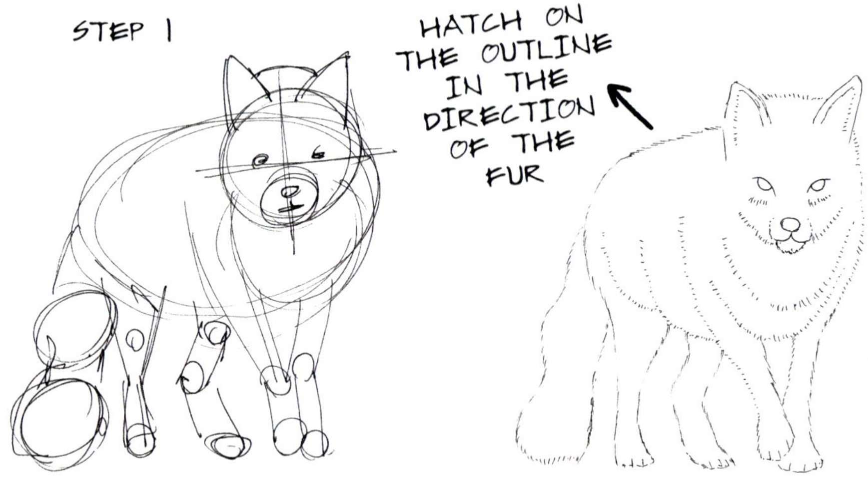

STEP 2

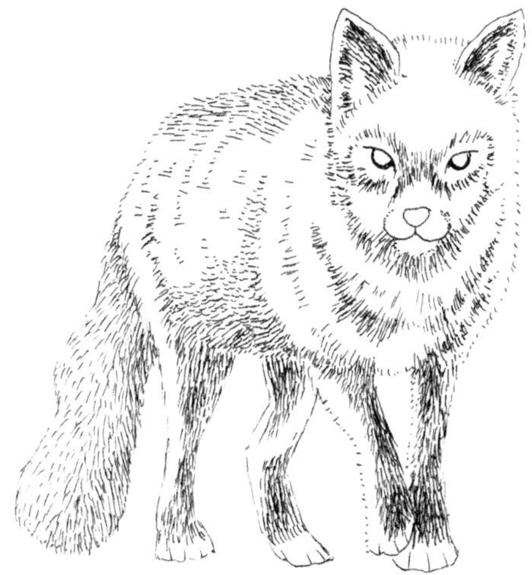

STEP 3

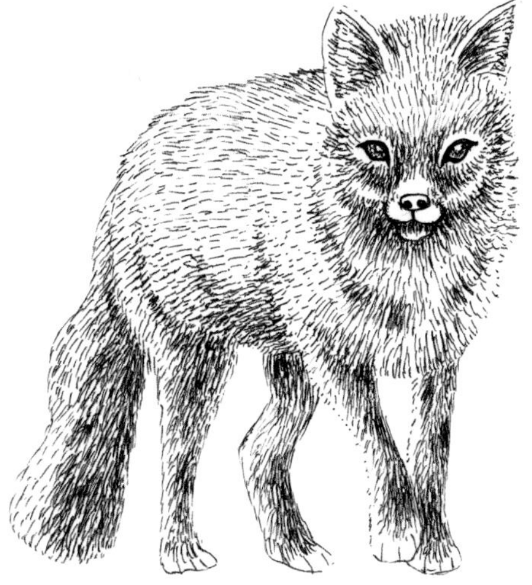

STEP 4

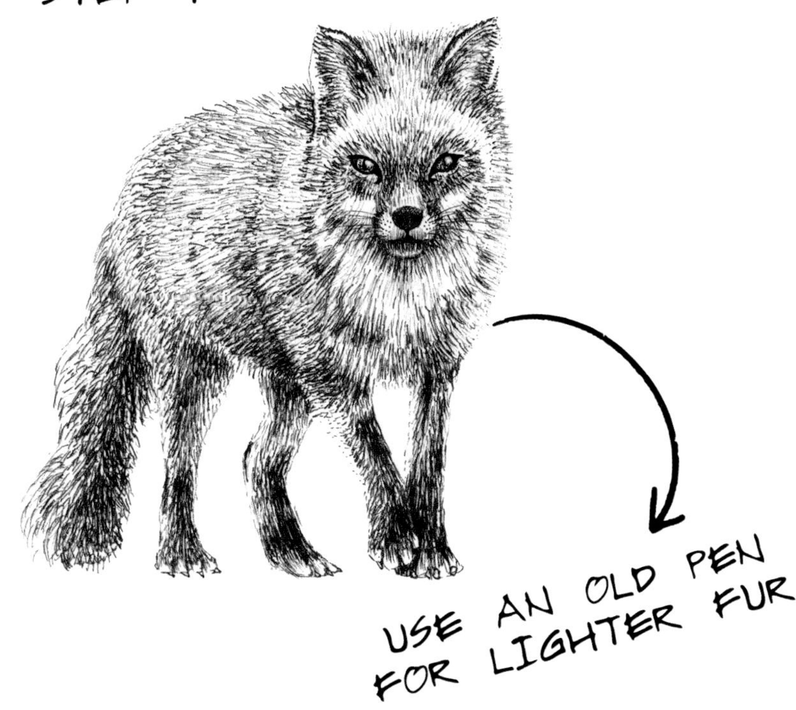
USE AN OLD PEN
FOR LIGHTER FUR

HOW TO DRAW A PENGUIN

1. **Outline the major shapes:** Let's draw an adult penguin with a baby penguin next to it. Start with oval shapes for both penguins, then add circles for the heads and oval shapes for the flippers and feet. To outline the adult penguin, simply use a solid line, as the feathers will not be very noticeable around the contour. To outline the baby penguin, use stippling and short hatching lines to outline the body as the feather texture will be more visible. Use solid lines to outline the head, beak, flippers, and feet.

2. **Define the textures:** For this drawing, you can use a few different textures to create different effects. To depict the back and flipper of the adult penguin, use stippling. For the front of the body and neck, use light, faded hatching with a thin, old pen to create a light texture. This technique maintains the appearance of light color, as this area of the penguin's body is predominantly white in real life. For the baby penguin, very short hatching lines combined with stippling are ideal to create the short feathers effect. When it comes to drawing with ink, this texture resembles fur. Don't worry about the shading just yet—simply define what stroke styles to use in each texture.

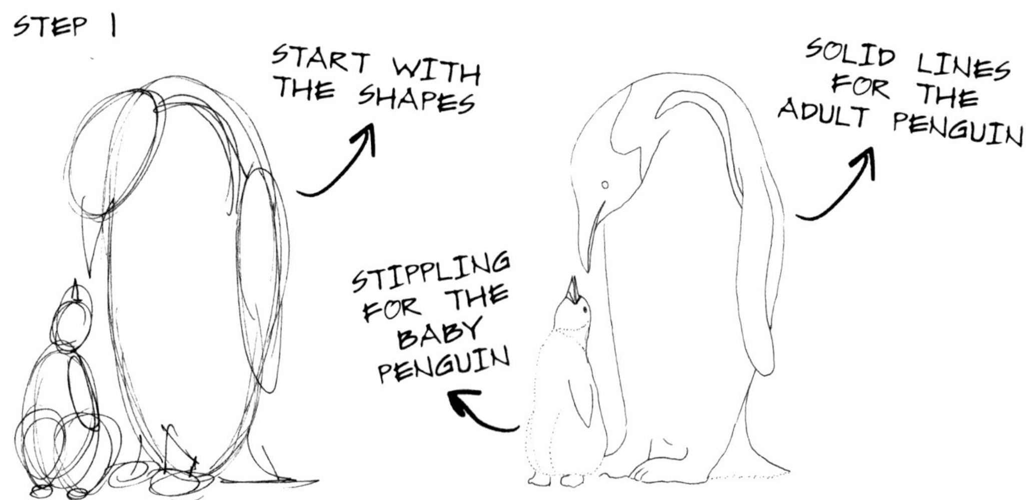

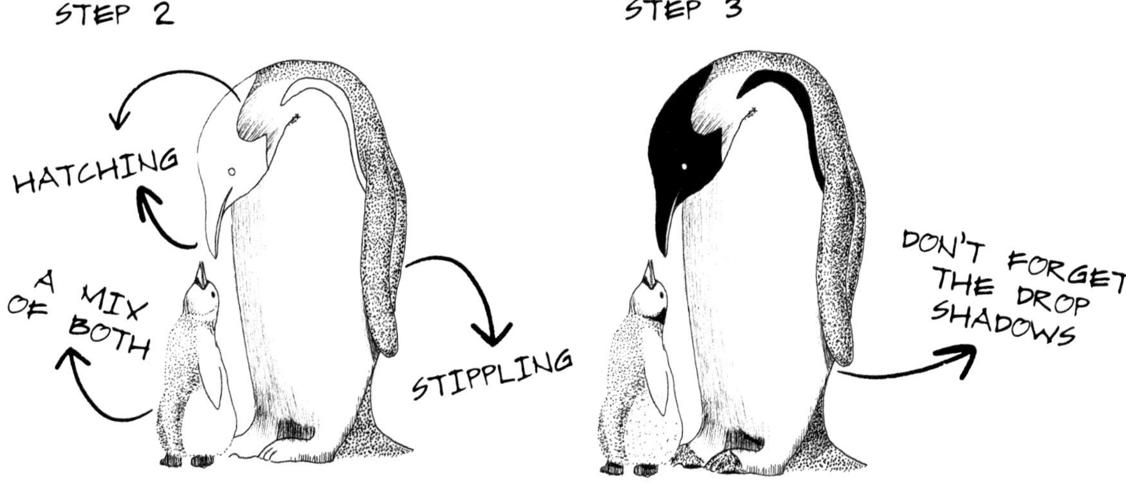

3. **Add shading and contrast:** Follow by focusing on the darker areas and intensifying the shadows using the stroke styles you chose in the previous step. Pay attention to where the light source is coming from and what areas should be darker. In this example, the back and front of the adult penguin and mostly the front of the baby penguin are darker. Add solid black on the head of the adult penguin, leaving a white line along the beak, and also at the bottom of the feet and at the back of the head of the baby penguin.

4. **Add final details:** Intensify the shadows to create more depth and make the drawings look more three-dimensional. Feel free to use some solid black lines and shapes on the darkest shadows. Also use stippling to shade the front of the body of the baby penguin, making the texture look more natural and realistic. Don't forget to roughly shade the feet and add light drop shadows underneath the flippers.

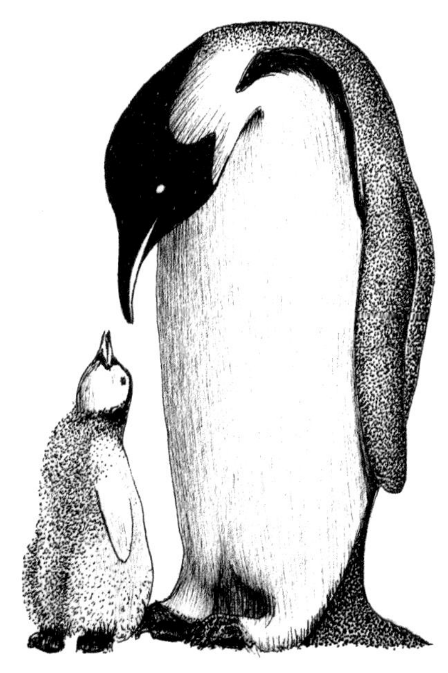

HOW TO DRAW AN EAGLE

1. **Outline the major shapes:** For a flying eagle, the first lines and shapes will start with a horizontal line to define the length, two oval shapes for the wings and a horizontal oval shape for the body. From there, you can start drawing the wings by breaking it into sections. Since the wings can be very detailed, evolve your sketch from larger shapes to smaller shapes instead of sketching the feathers right away. At the sketching stage, you only need to mark basic guidelines that will help you know where to draw the details later. Once your sketch is clear enough, outline the eagle with simple lines, and then draw the feathers on the wings. Notice that the feathers are positioned in rows, and that they are of different sizes. Make sure to sketch the lines for these rows beforehand to help you draw the pattern.

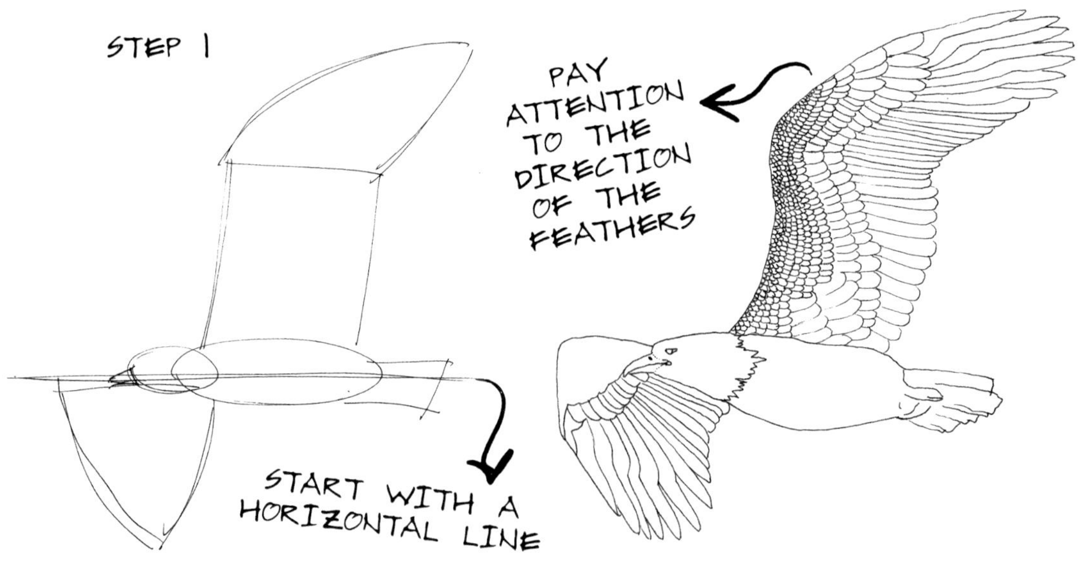

2. **Hatch to create darker values:** Since this outline is more straightforward and detailed, you can focus on adding ink on the feathers to create the right tones. The challenge here is to differentiate each feather since they are all dark and almost the same tone. To do that, start by simply hatching along each feather, leaving a thin white border on each of them. For the body of the eagle, you can draw some very light feathers that behave similar to scales. Since we don't want to see a clear, hard definition for each feather, use an old, thin pen for this step. Add a light hatching at the bottom or tip of each feather on the body, making some feathers slightly darker than others to create a little bit of texture. For the wings, keep hatching along each feather to make it darker, and slowly build darker tones at the tip of each one, leaving the areas right under other feathers slightly lighter. In nature, the color "black" is not exactly black, as light reflects on it. So, to represent black feathers accurately, there will still be lighter tones on it, which you can produce with hatching. An old pen can be your friend when creating lighter tones, as you will have more control over the amount of ink being released on the paper.

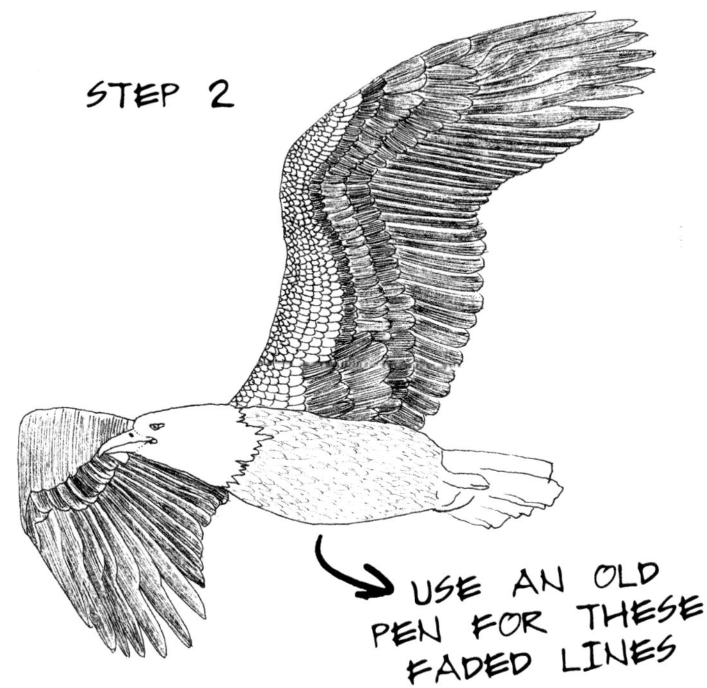

3. **Add final details:** When working on small details like these feathers, it's easy to stay too focused on small areas and lose perception of the whole, so make sure you stop once in a while to observe the bigger picture, keeping in mind the larger shapes of shadows you are trying to recreate. For example, on the top wing, each feather is very similar when it comes to the tones represented in each of them, but there is a slightly darker area closer to the body. There is also a darker spot on top of the wing, closer to the head. The bottom side of the body will also have a darker shadow that you can create with more hatching. At this final stage of the drawing, you want to define each shadow and create clear contrasts. For the claws, use hatching and stippling to create a lightly rough texture, and for the white feathers of the head, you can just hatch light faded lines, making the bottom a little bit darker than the top of the head.

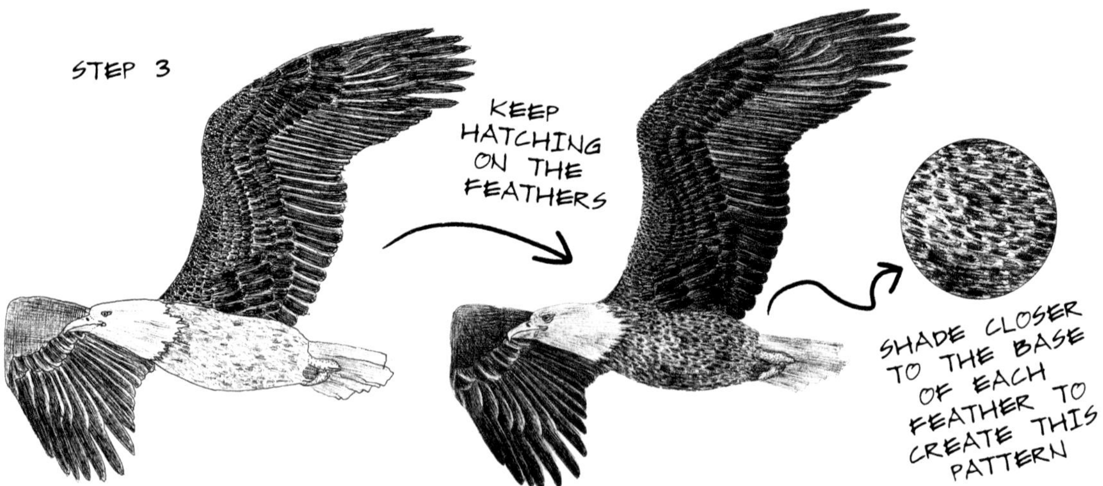

HOW TO DRAW A CARDINAL

1. **Outline the major shapes:** Now let's draw a bird from up close. Unlike for the eagle drawing, you will need to depict the feathers in more detail, but it is still your choice as to how much detail you want to portray. First, sketch the general oval shape of the cardinal, with a long oval shape at the bottom and a circle for the head. From these basic shapes, define more details like the eye, beak, leg, and two wings. For smaller feathers seen up close on a bird, the texture will behave similar to fur when it comes to drawing. So, for the general contour of the body of the bird, use hatching, like we did for the cat drawing, to define the outline. For the wings, in this case we are able to clearly see the definition of each feather, so feel free to outline those U shapes as well, overlapping them as demonstrated in the example.

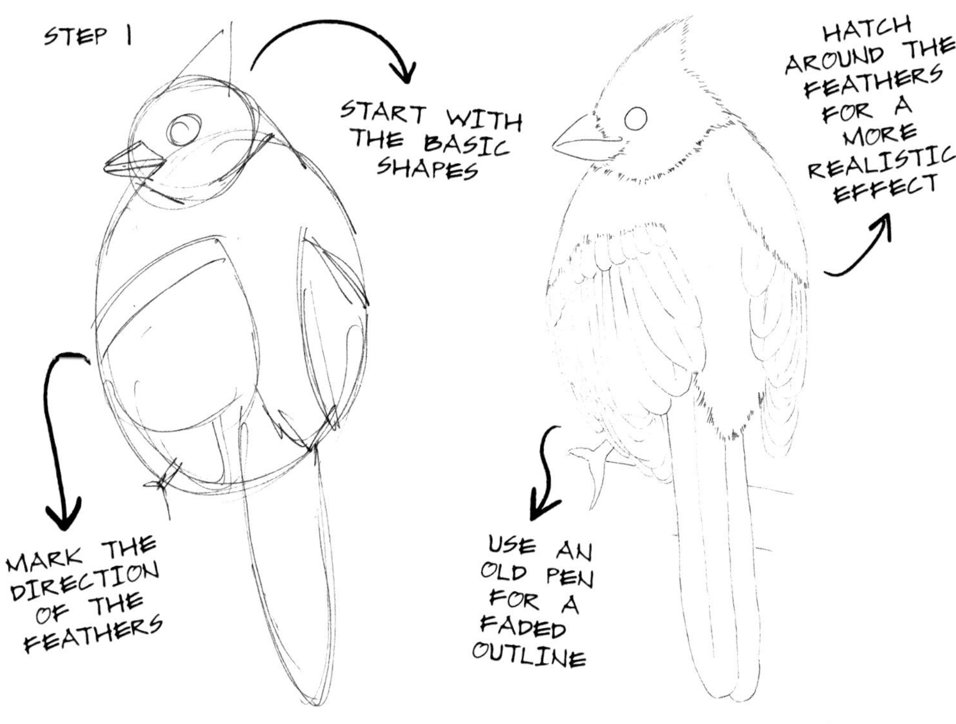

2. **Add texture:** Now that you have your out-line ready, start by defining the textures of the cardinal. Don't worry about shadows just yet—simply hatch short lines along the body to define the direction of the feather texture. Hatch these lines in a downward direction, following the curvature of the body. For the head, hatch as if the lines are coming from the beak and moving towards the back of the head and down towards the body. For the bottom feathers and the wings, you will need a thin, old pen to create very delicate lines. These work similarly to drawing leaves.

Each feather is divided in two by a vertical line in the middle, and the texture for each one can be created by light, faded hatching in an upside down "V" shape, as indicated. For the two long feathers at the bottom, hatch long, faded lines along them, keeping them clearly separated by two different tones, as the bottom one will be darker. When setting the pattern on your drawing, use the lightest tone as a measure for how much to hatch on each spot, as you won't be able to erase the ink later on.

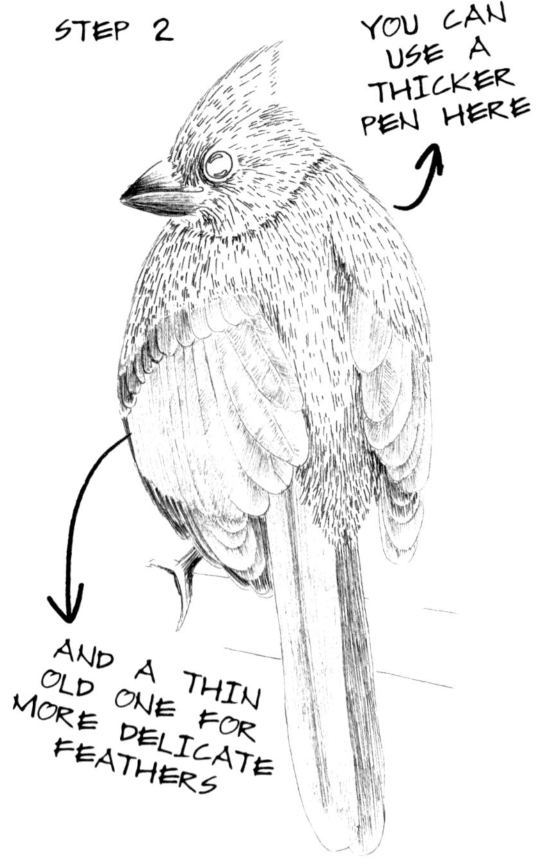

3. **Intensify shadows:** Once the pattern is clear, it's time to add shadows, increasing the contrast and depth in your drawing. Find the darker areas and hatch more in those areas, making sure the transition between light and dark is smooth to create the rounded, soft effect. Areas like the small, back feathers on the left wing, the lower area in between the two wings, the bottom feathers and the areas around the eyes, are generally darker and allow for more hatching. Make sure the hatching lines are positioned randomly, and not in clear rows and columns. This will help the final effect to look more natural. The eye is basically a black circle, but it's a good idea to leave a highlight on the top and bottom to add a reflective texture. Leave a white border in the immediate area around the eye instead of hatching around it. Don't forget to lightly hatch horizontal lines on the beak to create the texture, making the bottom darker.

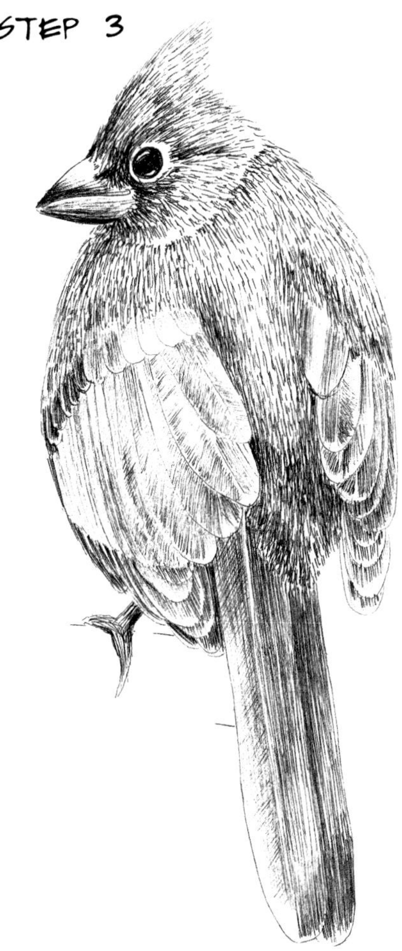

4. **Add final details:** To make your cardinal look more realistic, work on the transitions between shadows and general textures. Intensify the darker shadows and add fewer lines as they move towards the lighter areas. Also, between each feather on the wings, you can add a thin drop shadow to create contrast and depth. This can be done with a simple solid black line contouring the top feather, where it covers another feather. Drop shadows naturally happen in nature when elements are exposed to hard light sources. As the intensity of the light increases, so does the contrast between drop shadows and highlights. Drop shadows become more pronounced, while highlights become lighter. The light areas are just as important as the shadows, as that's where the attention of the viewer will be directed when first looking at your drawing. If you covered too much of the light, use white ink or a white gel pen to add extra highlights. Don't overdo this step as the white ink might become too visible if you are trying to cover a large area of black ink.

HOW TO DRAW A TURTLE

1. **Outline the major shapes:** To draw an aquatic turtle, start with an oval shape for the body and shell, add a small circle for the head, two longer oval shapes for the flippers, the front feet, and a circle for the back foot. Define the shell area, and sketch a simple pattern on the shell, as demonstrated in the example. Since turtles have hard and hairless textures, we can simply outline the contour of our pencil sketch with an ink pen. For the lines on the shell, try to contour right around the lines in order to leave them lighter than the remaining texture that we will build in the next steps.

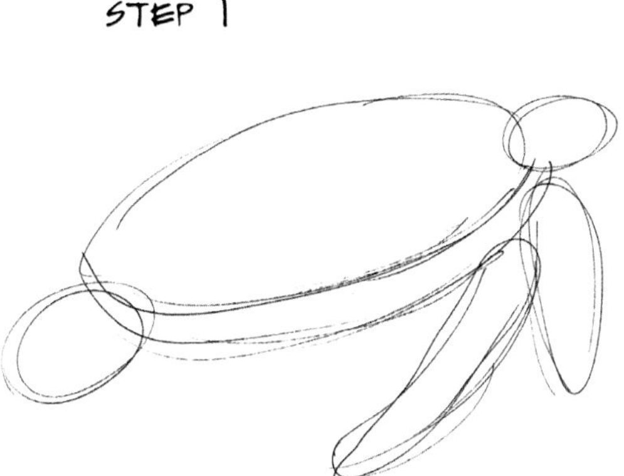

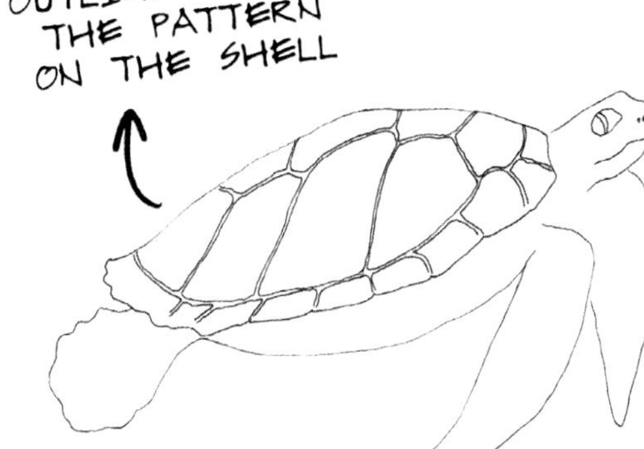

2. **Add stippling in the shadows:** Since turtles have very uneven skin, with many variations in tones and textures, stippling can be a great choice to best represent these details. Start covering the darker areas with dots. Don't rush the process, as your dots will turn into little dashes, and the final result won't look as clean and sharp.

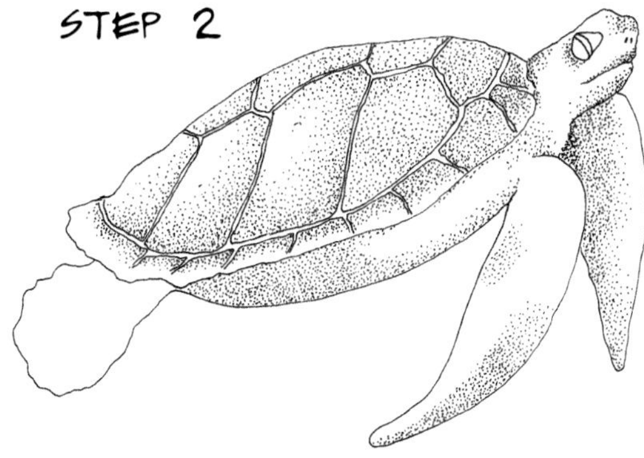

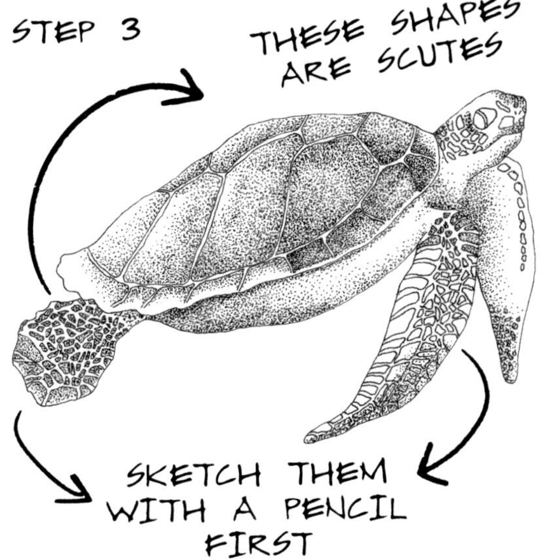

3. **Intensify shadows and draw scutes:** In this next step, keep adding dots in the darker areas, moving towards the lighter areas until the whole turtle is shaded. Next, outline the pattern on the flippers, also known as scutes. These shapes resemble hexagonal or diamond-shaped tiles arranged in overlapping rows, as in the example.

4. **Increase contrast and add the pattern details:** Combining stippling with covering specific areas with solid black, intensify the shading to give the drawing more depth and dimension, always considering the light source. Create darker tones inside the scutes, making most of them solid black shapes, and use stippling to create lighter tones for some of them. At the bottom of the turtle, add some solid, small black circles and round shapes to create the skin pattern.

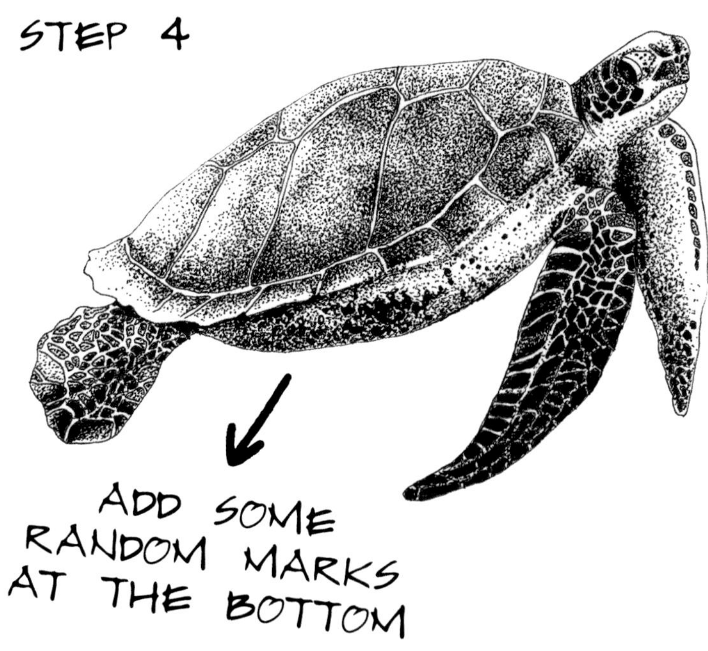

HOW TO DRAW A GOLDFISH

1. **Outline the major shapes:** When drawing fish, start with an oval shape, and then other geometrical shapes and lines to define the fins and other areas. Specifically for a goldfish, the fins can be longer, and they will flow and move with the water, so the fins can have a more fluid shape. Once you have your basic sketch and are ready to detail the contour of the fins, choose curved, fluid lines instead of hard, sharp lines. To outline this sketch, simply contour it with a thin line. Since the fins can have some transparency, a thinner line will help convey how delicate its texture is. Don't forget to also lightly outline the eye, mouth, and gill.

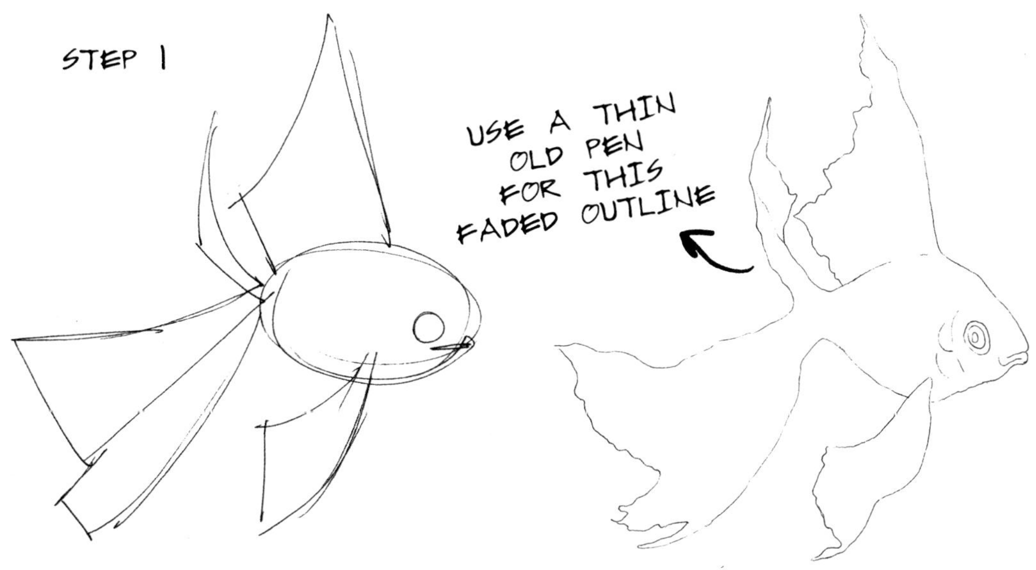

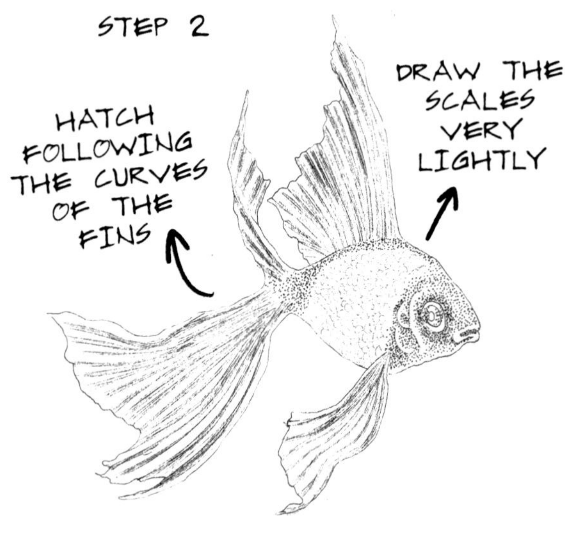

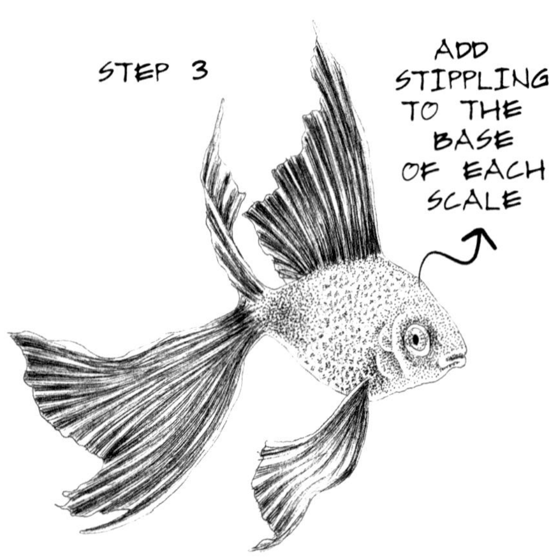

2. **Define the pattern styles:** For this fish, we will be working with two main textures—one for the body and another for the fins. Let's start with the body. First, with an old, thin pen, mark the scales around the body. As you can see in the example, the lines are very faded and almost hard to see. This is ideal, as thicker, darker lines would make the scales look unnatural. Fish scales usually have a reflective aspect to them, making the top of the curve of each scale reflect light and look white. To create a similar effect, use stippling to shade the base of each scale and the rest of the body. Start with the head and back part of the fish, as those are the darker areas of the body. For the fins, use an old pen to hatch long, faded lines along them, following the curvature and alternating between dark and light sections.

3. **Increase contrast and work on the scales:** At this stage, you can add more hatching on the fins, making the lines darker to create more movement. The areas closer to the body can be darker, as well as some areas at the outer edges. For the scales, keep stippling at the base of each scale, making the areas under other scales darker to create a more realistic effect. Don't worry if this process hides the scales a little bit as they don't need to be too clearly defined. As long as you leave white areas on each scale, you will be able to create the right effect. For the head and base of the body, intensify the stippling to create darker shadows. Make sure to leave highlight spots around the gills and mouth to create a slightly rounded effect.

4. **Add final details:** Using the same techniques as in the previous steps, add the final shadows, creating darker values. Use stippling to cover part of the scales, while leaving a lighter area where the scales are more visible in the center of the body. This helps create a more natural effect without using dark, unrealistic lines. Pay special attention to the eye, as the highlight spots on the sides will help create a slightly rounded effect and add more life and depth to your drawing.

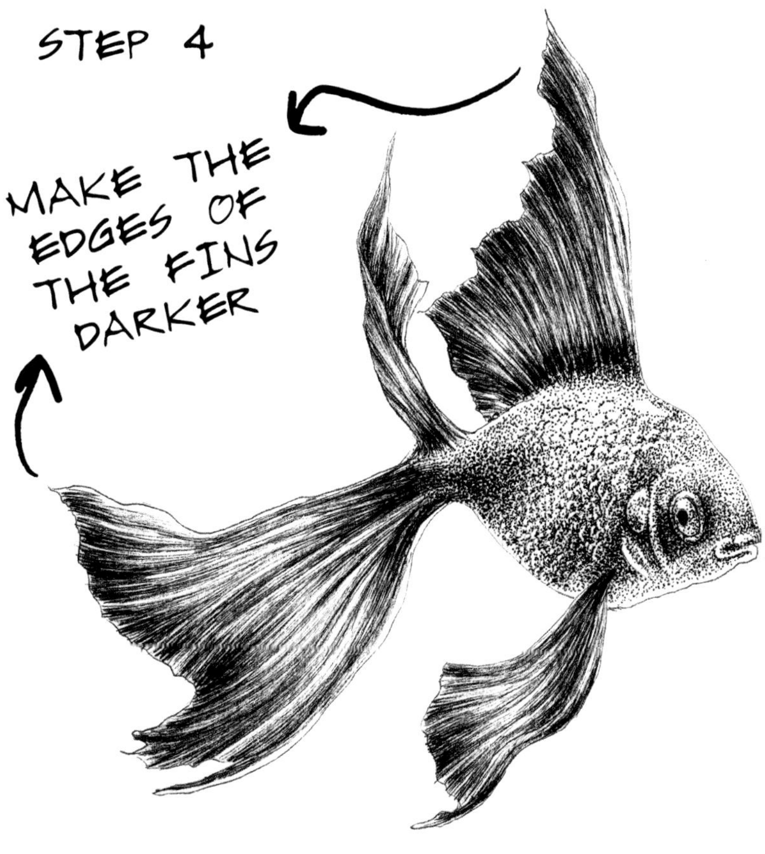

HOW TO DRAW A FROG

1. **Outline the major shapes:** When sketching a frog from the side, start with an oval shape or a rectangle for the main shape of the body, then add a circle for the head and angled lines for the arms and legs. Then add more details, like the eyes, mouth, and toes. As seen in previous examples, since frogs have rather smooth skin without fur or feathers, you can simply outline the sketch with continuous lines. Dark, well-defined wrinkles can also be outlined, while well-defined shadows and textures can be marked with dots at this stage.

2. **Choose a stroke style and start shading:** To create the textured skin of the frog, I chose stippling for this drawing. Start with the shadow areas by covering them with dots. The smaller the dots, the smoother the skin will look in the end. You can also combine two thicknesses of pens, adding slightly larger dots in the darker areas and smaller dots on the lighter areas. Focus on defining where your light source is and where the shadows are, leaving the remaining lighter spots white.

3. **Increase contrast and add more shading:** Still using stippling, intensify the shadows and spread the dots out towards the light spots. Frogs generally have a moist, slimy skin texture, which can be represented by sharper transitions between light and dark to create more well-defined highlights in different areas of the body.

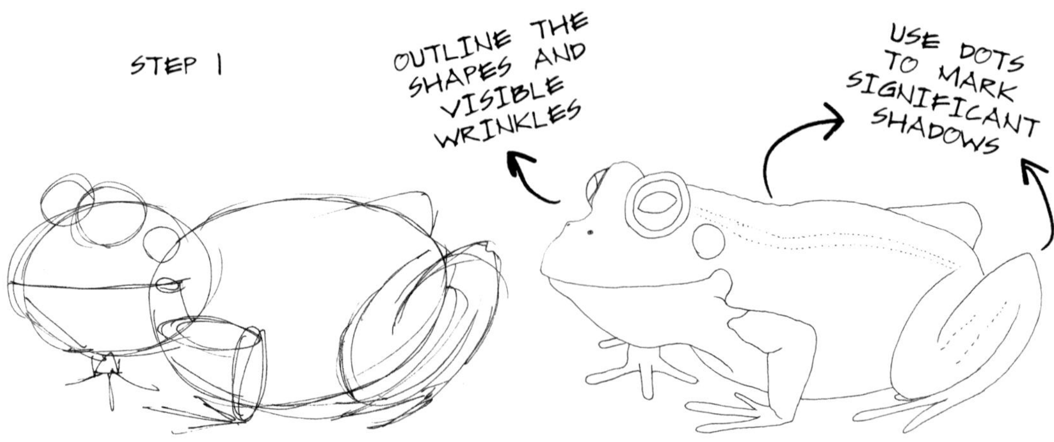

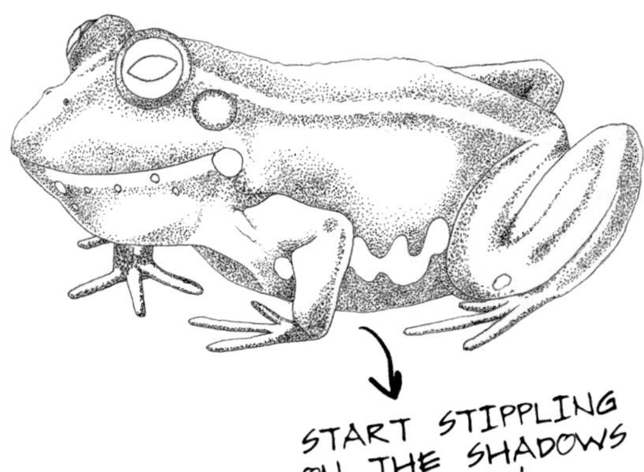

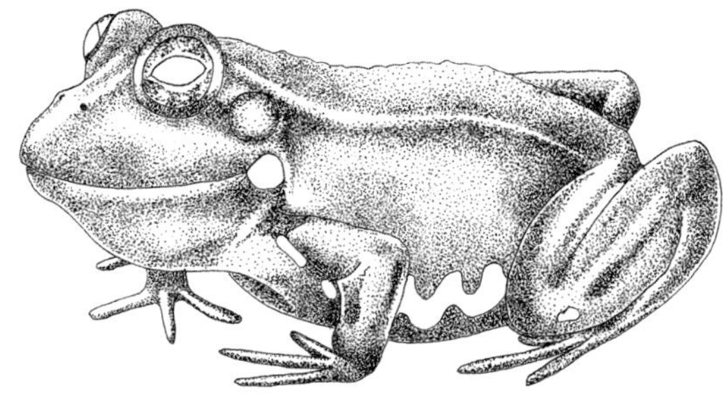

4. **Add final details:** To finish your drawing, use solid blacks to clearly define the darkest shadows, especially on the mouth, around the eyes, and on the wrinkles. The higher contrast will create more depth and make your drawing more three-dimensional. Some frogs have specific patterns on their skin defined only by change of color, which can be represented in a black-and-white drawing using the same stippling technique, combined with solid black. Simply add some round shapes in different areas of the body and make them darker by using both techniques.

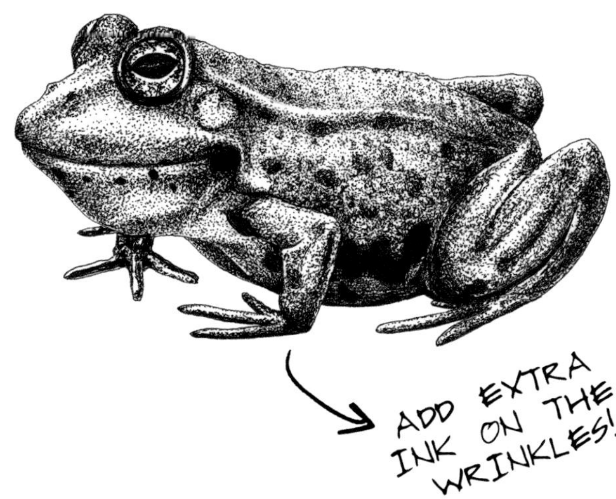

HOW TO DRAW A BUTTERFLY

1. **Outline the major shapes:** To draw a butterfly with open wings, we will use symmetry. Start with a vertical line that will be your symmetry line, then add three horizontal lines to define the top of the wings, the area in between wings, and the bottom of the wings. Next, mark small oval shapes to represent the body and head, and start shaping the wings, trying to reflect everything you do on one side on the other side. Still with the pencil, draw the veins of the wings as curved lines moving from the body of the butterfly towards the outside edge of each wing. Add a curve in a drop shape on each wing, following the curvature of the veins. When the sketch is well defined, outline it with the ink pen, making the edge of each section of the wings curved, and contouring the veins with thin, faded lines. We will add shading to the sections of the wings, leaving the veins white, so this is why we contour them instead of just drawing a simple line where they are positioned.

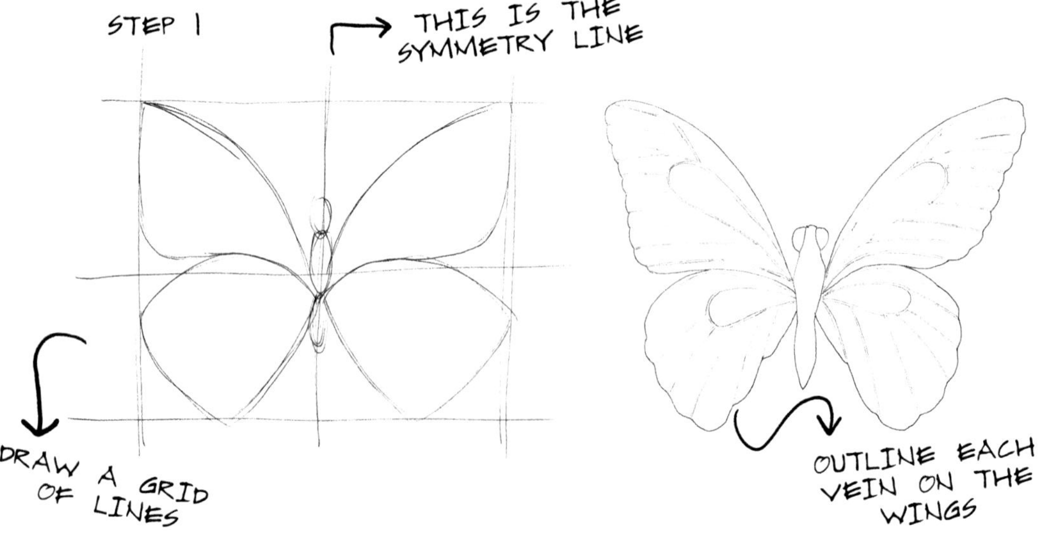

2. **Define the patterns:** There are so many possibilities for wing patterns, which means you can be creative in this step. Create a symmetrical pattern on the wings, considering that you will be able to play with different tones to differentiate shapes and colors. Always keep the veins white. Don't worry about shading or filling the shapes just yet. Simply use your creativity to draw shapes all over the wings to design a beautiful pattern. You can also create a simple pattern for the body of the butterfly.

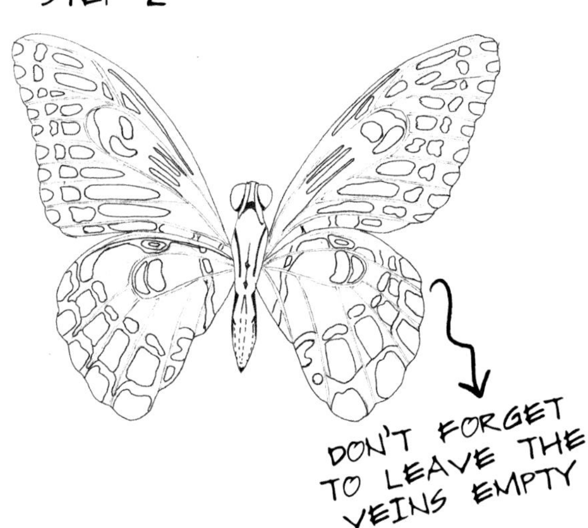

3. **Play with different values:** To allow the white veins to stand out, add darker tones to each wing section by filling the shapes of your pattern using the techniques and stroke styles of your choice. A simple way to get started is by filling some of these shapes with solid black. If you want the wings to look darker, fill more shapes with solid black. You can also hatch or stipple to create lighter tones on certain areas.

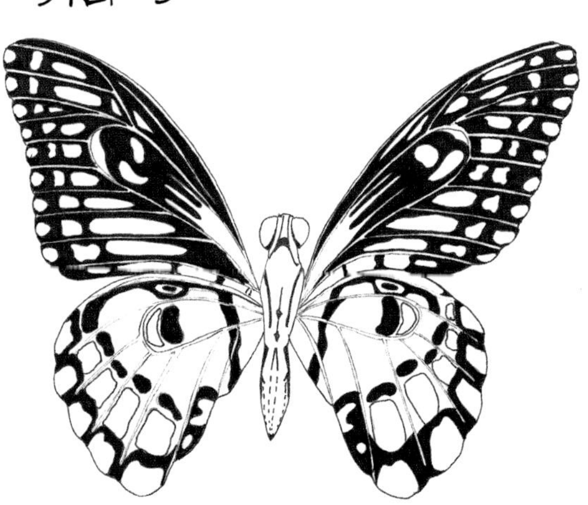

4. **Add shading and contrast:** To create depth and make your butterfly look more realistic, add a light hatching to make the wings slightly darker when closer to the body. The lines should be thin and faded, which can be done more easily with an old pen. Move the pen strokes from the body towards the outer edges of the wings. You can also hatch on the butterfly's body, making the sides darker than the center. For the eyes, leave a white highlight. Use stippling to create smooth shadows around it to create the rounded effect.

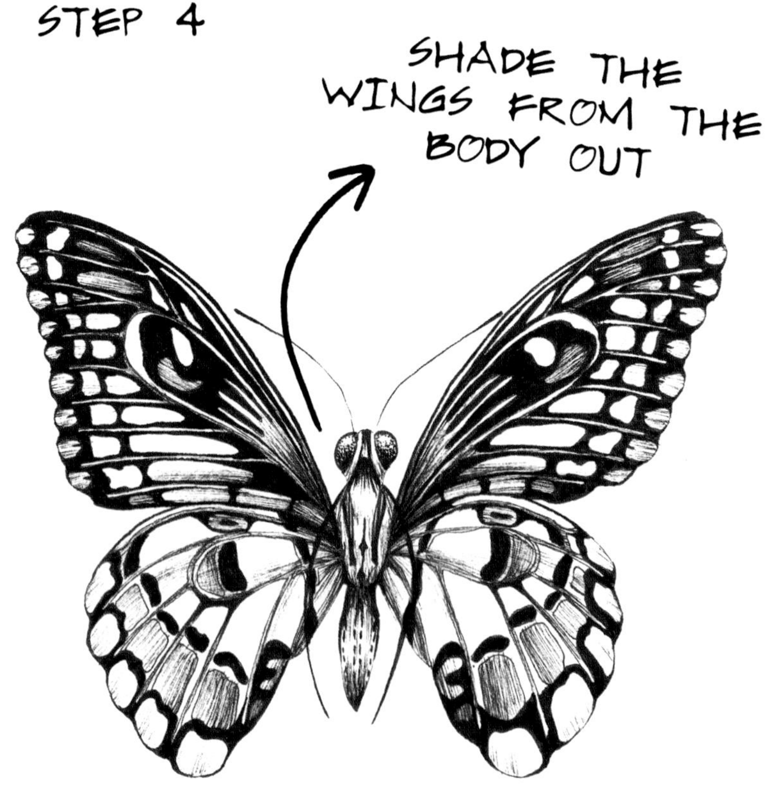

HOW TO DRAW A BUMBLEBEE

1. **Outline the major shapes:** To draw a bumblebee, start with an oval shape for the body and two symmetrically positioned triangles coming from the sides of the oval shape for the wings. Sketch some sectioned lines for the legs and antennas. Divide the oval shape into five sections that will represent the black-and-yellow pattern that bumblebees are commonly known for. Since their bodies are covered by hair-like structures that appear as a furry or fuzzy texture, to outline the sketch we will use the same hatching technique used for fur. Simply hatch short lines on the contour of the body, making sure that the direction of the lines is from the center of the body outwards, in all directions. The legs should be split into different sections each, as indicted in the example, and the sections that are closer to the body should also have the same fuzzy texture. Don't forget to outline two semicircles for the eyes and add the antennas. For the wings, use a thin pen as we want them to be delicate and portray a certain transparency. The wings are symmetrical and have a delicate network of fine lines, resembling the veins on a leaf. These veins move outwards from the base of the wings, branching and intersecting to form a grid-like pattern.

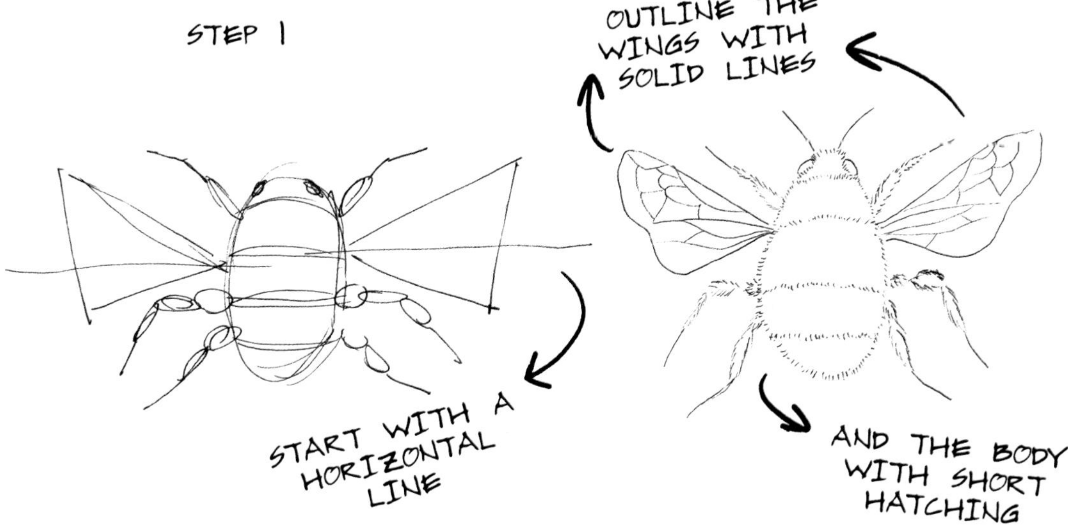

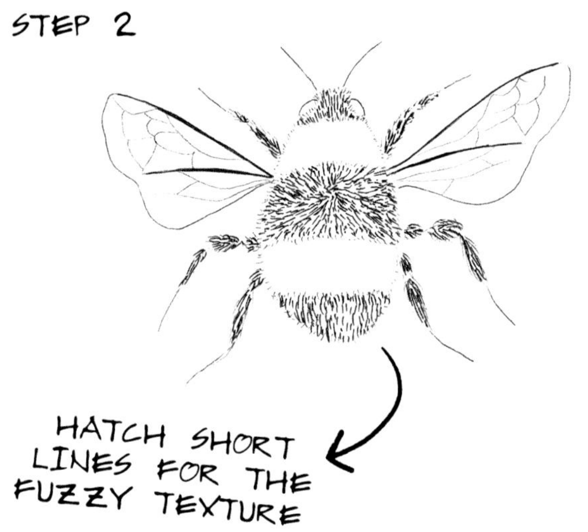

2. **Define the textures:** Start working on the fuzzy texture of your bumblebee, starting with the darker areas. In order to create the black-and-yellow pattern with the black ink, the black will be a darker tone while the yellow will be represented by a lighter one. Keep in mind the direction of the lines, always moving from the center of the body outwards. As the hairs are closer to the center, the lines will become shorter, closer to dots, creating the illusion that they are growing in the direction of the viewer. Don't forget to hatch on the legs to create a similar texture, and make the top lines of the wings darker.

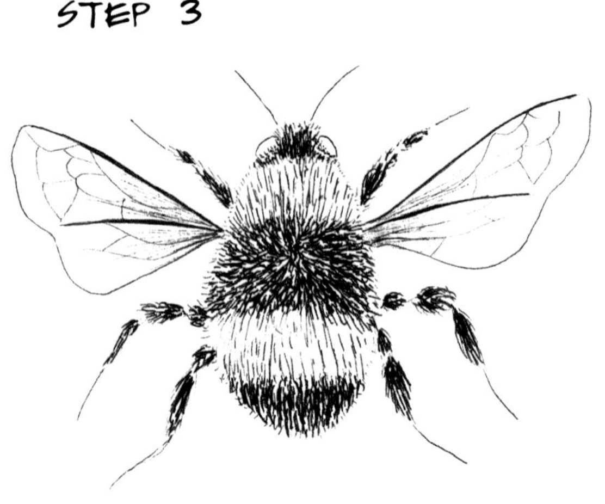

3. **Add shadows and depth:** Hatch more over the black, furry sections, making them even darker. Start lightly hatching on the remaining sections, following the same directions, from the center out. On the wings, use a thin, old pen to hatch faded lines from the base towards the outside edges. This will help make them look more three-dimensional and create the transparency effect. Lightly intensify the veins on the wings if necessary.

4. **Add final details:** To make the bumble-bee look more natural and realistic, make sure to add variation in tones on each section of the body. Also, hatch some faded lines on the wings in the opposite direction as we did in the previous step, now moving from the outer edge of the wings towards the base, leaving the middle lighter. You can also round up the connections between the veins on the wings and add extra details on the tips of each leg, as seen on the example. Use stippling to shade the eyes, always leaving a highlight spot.

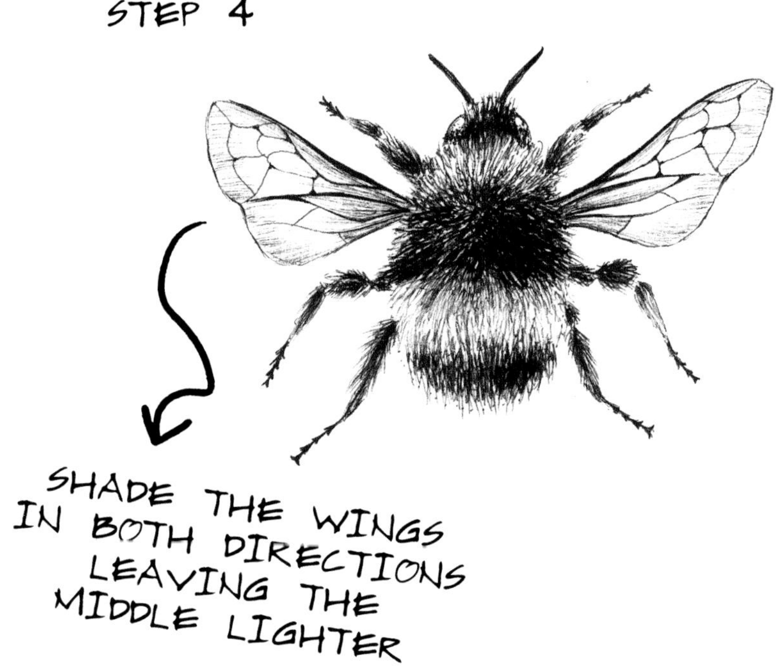

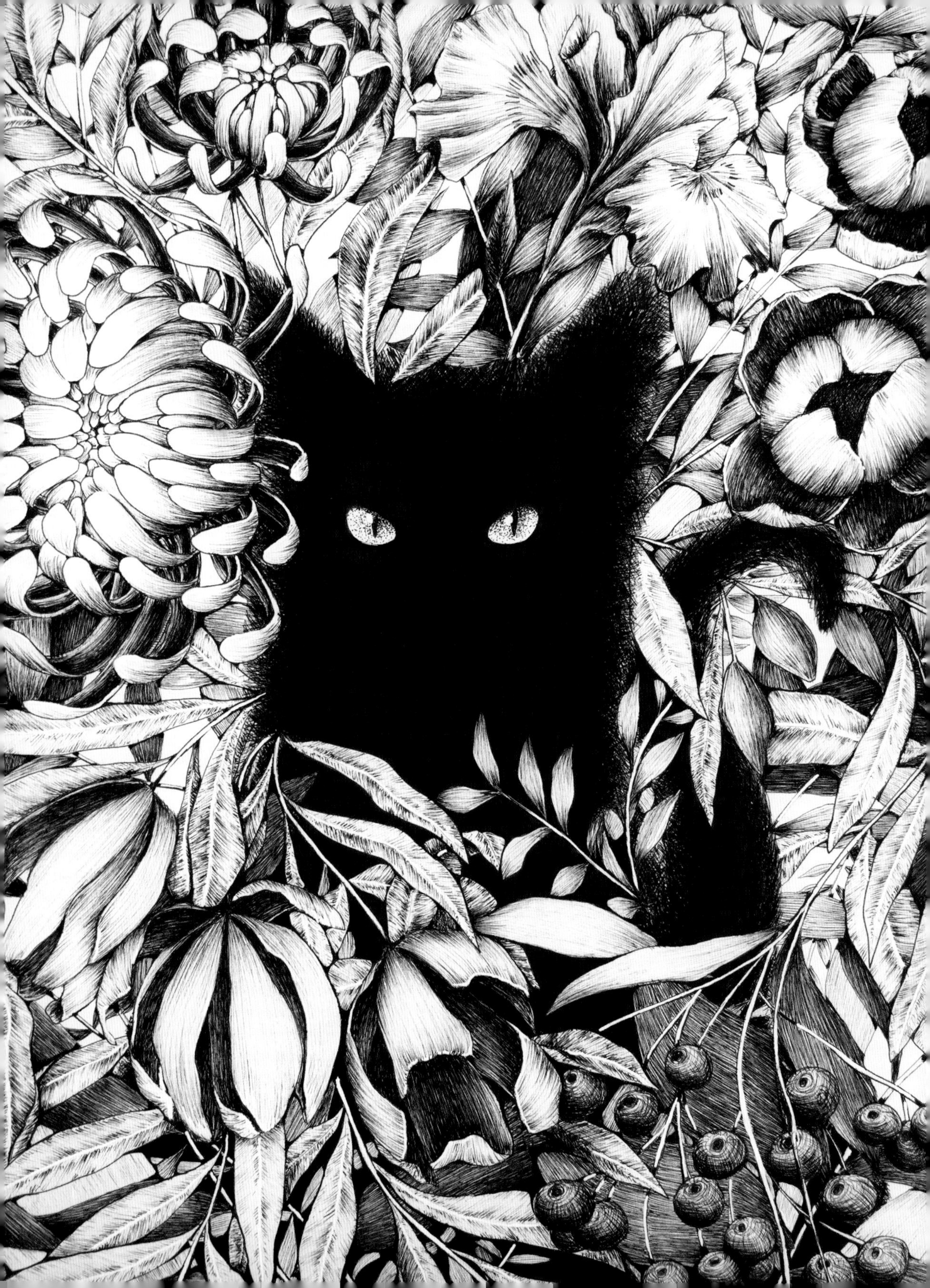

DRAWING PLANTS

In this chapter, we will explore the different techniques of drawing plants using ink pens. With the vast variety of leaves, flowers, trees, and other plants, it would be impossible to cover in detail how to draw all of them. Instead, you will learn how to apply the techniques learned in previous chapters to draw specific plants of your choice, from sketch to a final drawing. This guide is not intended to limit you to realism or the specific drawing techniques demonstrated in this chapter, but instead to serve as inspiration and future reference on your own art journey.

LEAVES

Leaves can be represented in drawing in many ways to achieve realistic results. When portrayed from afar, as see on trees, for example, they can be drawn as fast scribbles and random lines. In contrast, when drawn from up close, intricate details, textures, and patterns can be observed. In this section we will focus on different ways to draw leaves and all of their details from an up-close perspective.

If you are not familiar with botanical drawing, using reference pictures or even real leaves you find outside can be an excellent tool to help you study and understand them. In nature, each leaf, flower, and tree will be different, so it's important to observe how each plant interacts with the environment in order to draw them accurately.

Here are some general steps for drawing a simple leaf:

1. **Understand the leaf structure:** Start by observing and studying the leaf you want to draw, by using a real leaf you found on the ground or a picture as reference. Pay close attention to its shape, the pattern of its veins, the general texture, and any unique characteristics it may have. Observe how the shadows behave when the light hits it. This will help you define a good foundation for your drawing.

2. **Outline the shape:** Begin your sketch by drawing the outline of the leaf with a pen. If you are working with a more complex shape, feel free to start with a pencil draft first, breaking the leaf down into geometric shapes and angled lines, to help guide your ink outline. Try to capture the overall shape as accurately as possible. Don't worry about details at this stage.

3. **Draw the veins:** After you have the basic shape outlined, draw the main veins of the leaf. Usually, the veins will be lighter in color, so at this stage, simply define where the leaf vein should be positioned. These usually start from the base of the leaf and branch out towards the edges at a diagonal angle. The pattern of veins varies among different types of leaves, so I recommend that you use a reference when starting out.

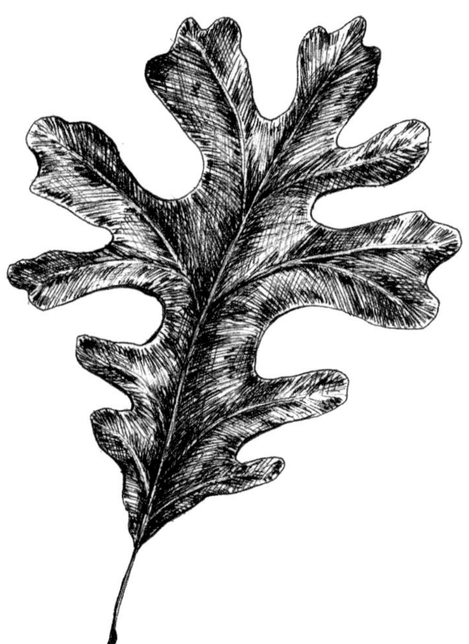

4. **Define the texture:** Next, add texture to your leaf. You can use different techniques and stroke styles such as hatching, crosshatching, or stippling to represent the texture of the leaf surface, always leaving a white stripe next to your vein lines. Since this is a simple leaf where the veins have a clear direction, the hatching technique is a great choice to portray the curvature of the leaf. When adding texture, be mindful of the light source and slightly curved shape of the leaf. Start slow by inking in the directions of the veins, which is usually slightly diagonal and symmetrical on both sides. Hatch or stipple from the outside inwards on each side, stopping halfway towards the main vein. Then repeat the same motion, now moving from the vein outwards, always in the same diagonal direction, stopping halfway in order to leave a white, highlighted area on each side.

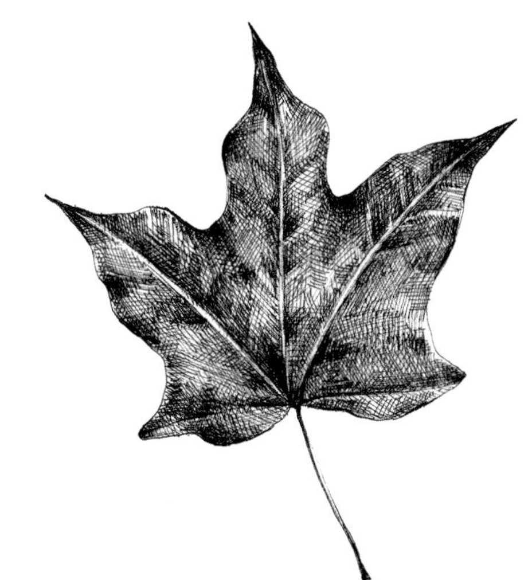

5. **Start shading:** After you have defined the pattern and chosen a stroke style to create the leaf texture, it's time to add shading to give your drawing depth and dimension. Observe where the light and shadows fall on the leaf, and try to reproduce the same contrast in your drawing. Finally, look over your drawing and add any final touches, which might include deepening some of the shadows, refining the shape, or adding more details to the texture.

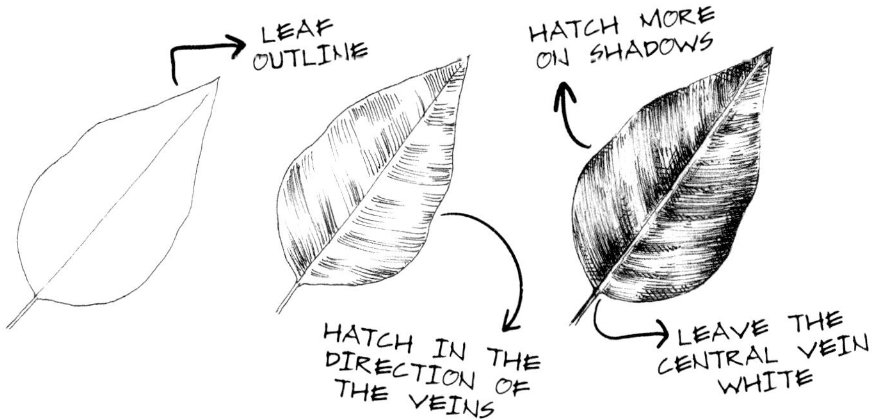

This guide isn't the only way to draw leaves, by any means. It's meant to be a helpful starting point for beginners. I encourage you to explore beyond these instructions to create your own textures and styles.

Next, let's work with a larger, more complex example, like the Monstera deliciosa leaf. Its broad, heart-shaped structure has prominent splits and holes. The leaf's surface is smooth, with a glossy, firm texture, and has several pronounced veins running through its length.

1. **Understand the leaf structure:** As usual, start by observing and studying the leaf by using a real example or a picture as reference. Pay close attention to its shape, the pattern of its veins, the general texture, and any unique characteristics it may have. Observe how the shadows behave when the light hits it. Start with a pencil sketch of the general shape of the leaf, which in this case can be a circle. Define the direction of the main central vein and sketch the veins branching out from the first one. Pay attention to their angles and lengths. Now, shape the outside contour of the leaf, and then add the openings in between each leaf section of the secondary veins. Finally, sketch any holes or fenestrations the leaf might have.

2. **Outline the shape:** Outline your sketch with a thin-line ink pen. In this case, since the veins are clearly defined, outline around them instead of sketching just simple lines to indicate their position. This will help you to keep the veins white. Also notice how they fade as they get closer to the outer edges of the leaf, so

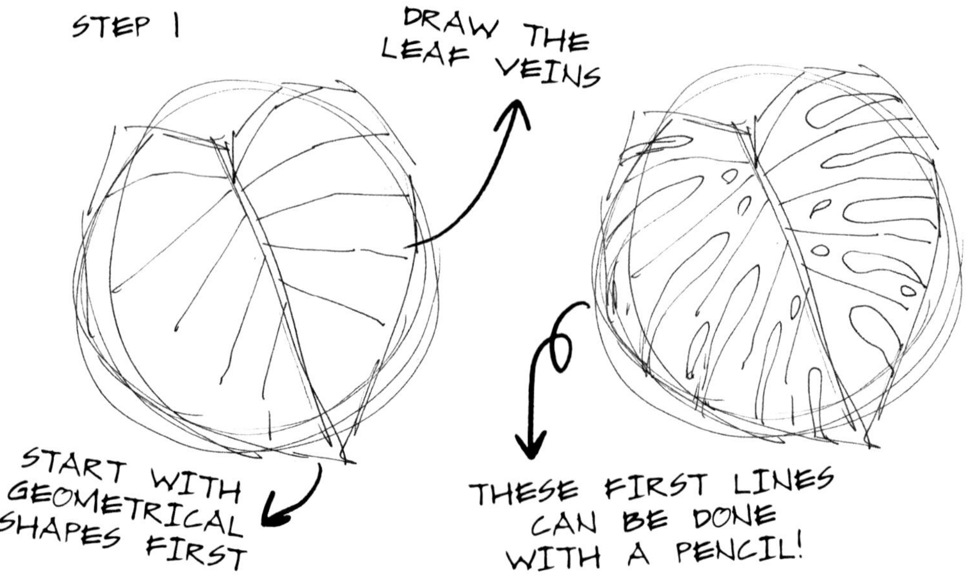

make sure to portray that aspect by stopping the veins before the end of the leaf, as seen in the example.

3. **Define the texture:** There are many ways to create the texture on this leaf. Since this example has a firm, glossy texture, we will experiment with crosshatching to create all the intricate shadows in the next step. First, start hatching in one direction, being mindful of the lights and shadows in your reference. Make sure to keep the light areas lighter, and feel free to hatch more where the shadows are in order to start building those values. Also, try to follow the curvature and position of the leaf by adjusting the hatching direction according to the direction of the main vein and outer edges of the leaf. Follow by hatching in the opposite direction, along the secondary veins. Slowly, layer by layer, start building the different tones for each area of the leaf.

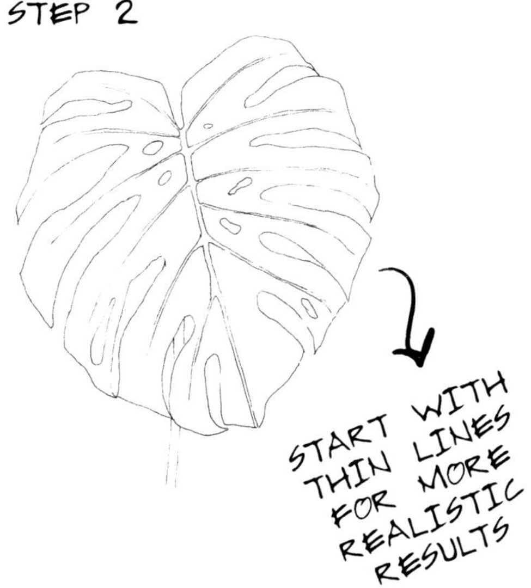

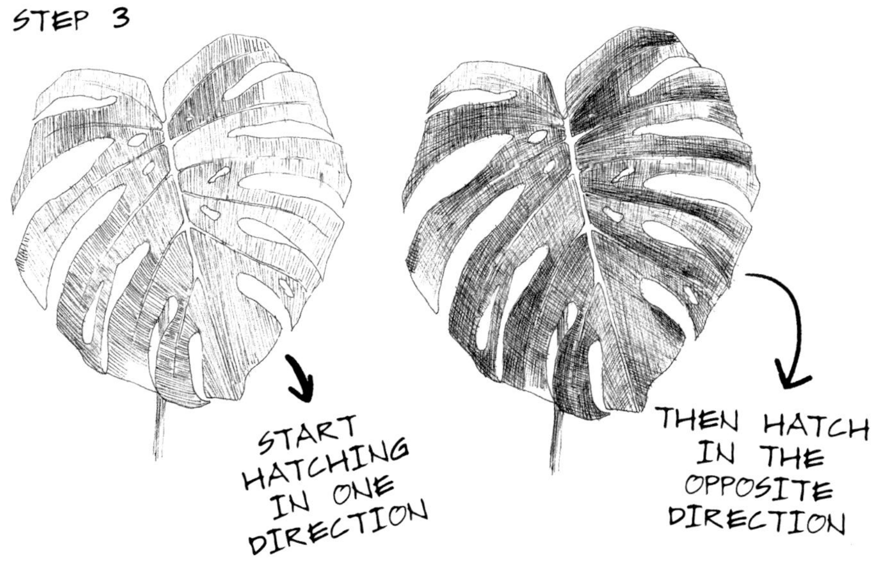

4. **Keep building the shadows:** Add more layers of hatching as needed to create more contrast and depth. Don't be afraid to add solid blacks on small areas to intensify the darker areas. Finish by adding a solid dark shadow along the shadow side of the main vein and the secondary veins, to create that three-dimensional effect. If your drawing includes the stem, make sure to add a drop shadow right under the lower edge of the leaf. This will increase the contrast and make the leaf stand out.

Notice that crosshatching can create a rougher, more stylized texture in a leaf drawing. It's a great way to play with the ink to create a realistic shadow scheme while studying the shape of a subject. Observing the curvature of each section of a complex leaf will help you define the best directions in which to hatch each layer of lines. Use parts of your outline as a directional reference and you will be able to create very interesting effects.

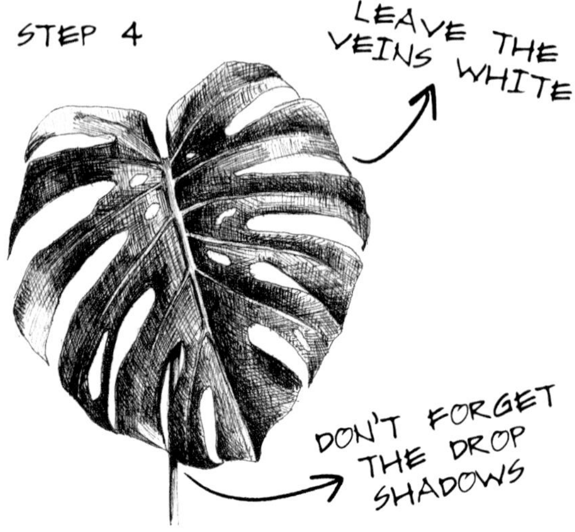

Composition

When drawing a more complex arrangements of leaves, keep the composition in mind. Before you start, think about how to position your elements in the frame, considering the rule of thirds and making sure it has a balanced visual weight. If elements occupy mostly one side of the page, leaving the rest of the space empty, this will cause visual discomfort, making the composition unbalanced. This doesn't mean the arrangement needs to be centralized and symmetrical. Simply sketch a rough draft on paper before you start a final piece in order to observe and correct the composition beforehand. Feel free to add other elements, such as a vase or other objects to compose your illustration.

When drawing a branch of leaves, if you want to achieve a realistic result, note how each leaf interacts with the others and how they vary in positions, shapes, and lighting.

In the example below, two branches of leaves overlap with each other, with leaves in several unique positions, where some leaves are folded and curved, and they all have different shapes and shadows. To create a complex composition with many leaves together, each leaf should be worked on individually. If all leaves have the same or very similar shapes, shadows, textures, and positions, the drawing will seem unnatural. In nature, leaves are alive, moving, and interacting with the environment. Keep that in mind when creating botanical illustrations, and study different reference pictures to create visual memory and build confidence in your drawing style.

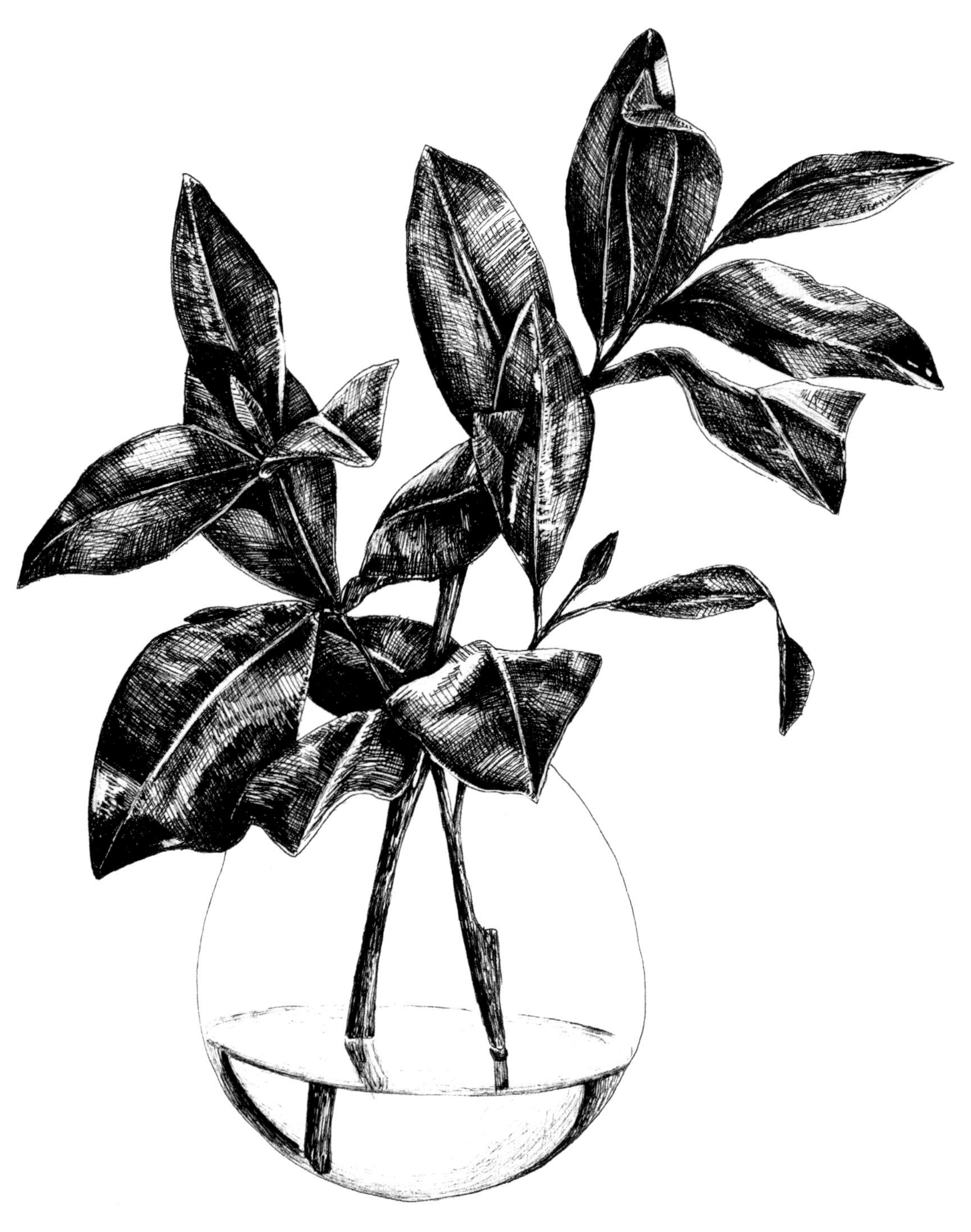

FLOWERS

With a multitude of shapes, textures, and types, flowers offer many possibilities for designing and representing them with ink. Even though all the techniques learned in previous chapters will be helpful when drawing different flowers, we will now study real examples of flower drawings using different stroke styles, and we will see how they differ from drawing leaves.

Let's start by studying the basics of flower anatomy, using a few examples that represent common flower shapes seen in nature. This will help you understand the structure and form of various types of flowers. We will then move on to techniques for capturing the delicate petals, the detailed centers, and the subtle shading that gives flowers their depth and realism.

The step-by-step instructions will make the process easy for beginners, while also providing advanced techniques for seasoned artists. We will cover everything from sketching the basic shape to adding the final touches that bring your flower to life.

Finally, we explore ways to add creativity and personal style to your flower drawings. I encourage you to experiment with different styles and techniques to create flower drawings that reflect your personal artistic style.

Let's start with some step-by-step examples.

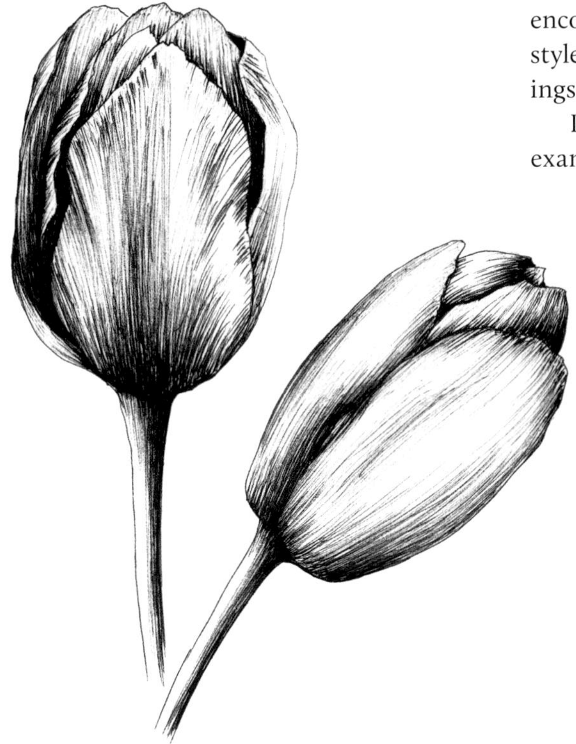

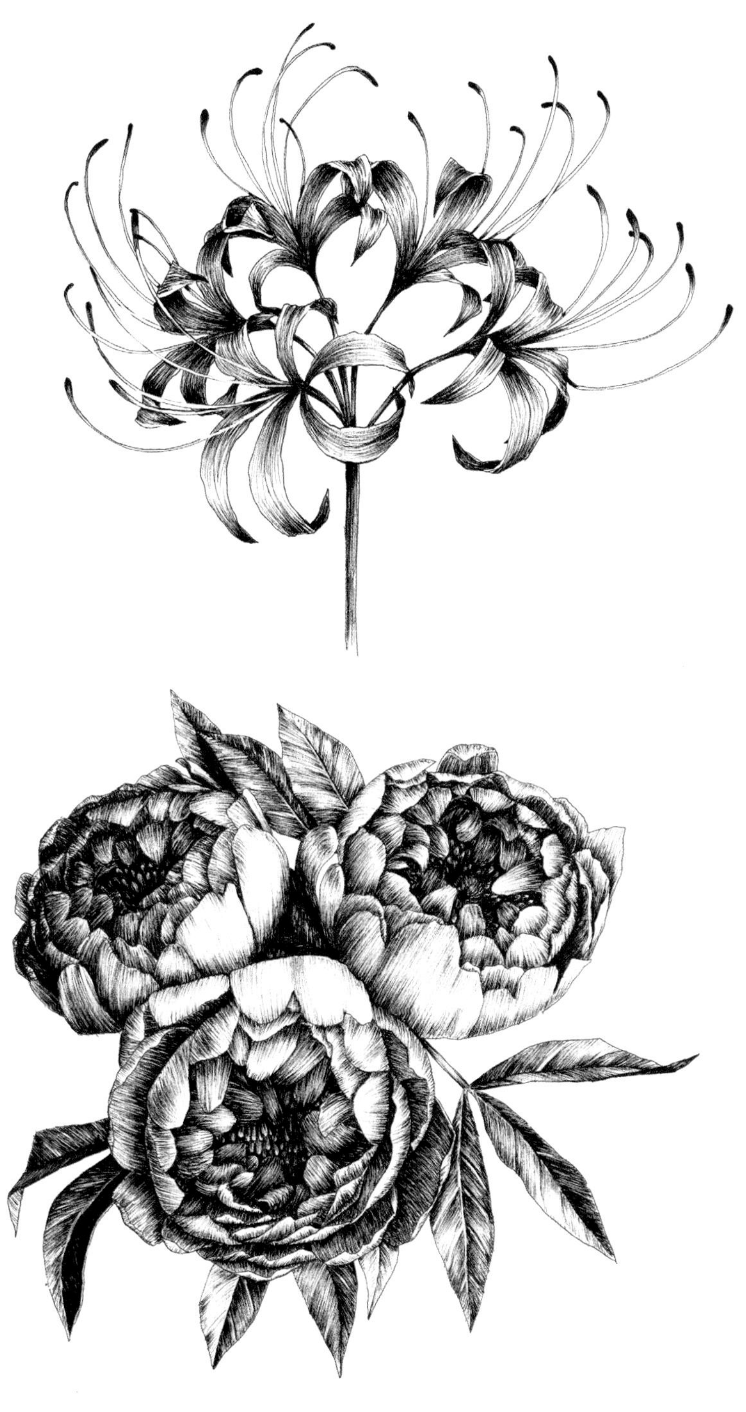

How to Draw a Daisy

1. **Understand the flower structure:** Start by observing and understanding the basic structure of the flower you are going to draw, in this case, a daisy. Decide if you are going to include the stem and leaves, or focus on the flower itself. For the sake of this exercise, let's focus on the flower only. If using a reference to draw, observe the position of the flower. Notice that its three-dimensional shape is close to a round, flat disk. When sketching with a pencil first, its simplest representation starts with two circles, one defining the perimeter of the petals and another one defining the center of the flower. If seen from the side, the drawing will start with an oval shape. Begin your sketch by drawing the basic shapes of the flower in the position of your choice, and then start adding the petals coming from the center. Notice the petals are positioned randomly and not perfectly side by side. The distances between petals changes from one to the next, and by overlapping some petals, slightly grouping them randomly, you will create a more realistic shape. When outlining with an ink pen, keep the details in mind, like the small dents on the tips of the petals. They will help guide the texture and shadows in the next steps. The center area or flower head can be sketched with a slightly dashed line.

2. **Define the texture:** Once your outline is ready, use a thin, old ink pen to hatch along the petals to create the texture and start building values. Each petal will have two sections of hatching lines to create

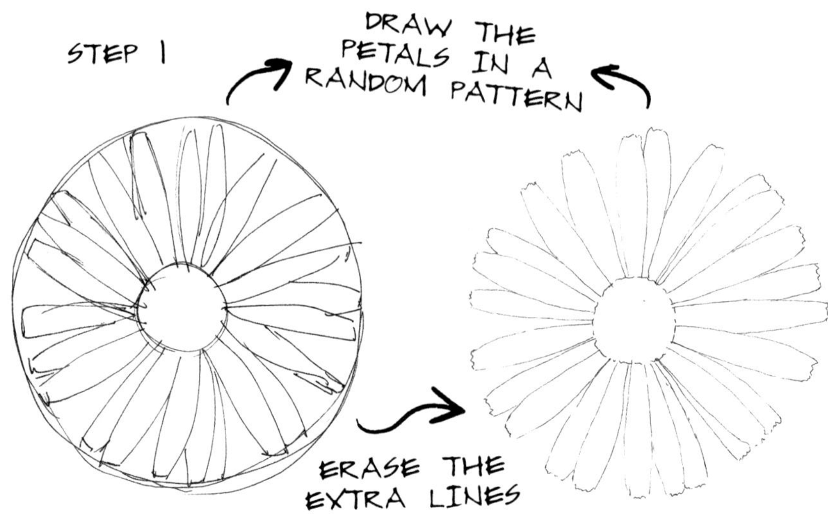

the uneven surface. Hatch in both directions, moving from the tips of each petal towards the center, and from the center towards the tip, leaving the middle of each petal lighter. This will help create a light curved effect on the petals. On the overlapping petals, make the underlying petals, the ones behind the front petals, darker to create the illusion of depth. For the center or head of the flower, mark some light, faded small circles, leaving a white highlight on the upper left side.

3. **Add shading and contrast:** Shading adds depth to your drawing, making it look more three-dimensional. Identify where the light source is positioned and what sides will be your shadow sides. In this case, the light is coming from the upper left corner, creating more intense shadows on the lower right side of the flower. The lights are just as important as the shadows, so make sure to leave enough white space as the highlights of the petals. Even though in nature these petals might be white, for the purpose of drawing they won't really be white. To represent the color white realistically, we can focus on adding darker values on the shadow areas, leaving enough highlights to indicate the light tonality of the original color. For the center of the flower, use more ink to contour the right side of the outside circles, and hatch more on the petals, moving from the center towards the right lower side to create a light casting shadow. A little solid black contouring on certain lines and corners goes a long way to make your drawing look more polished and finalized. Add some drop shadows on the underlying petals and make the immediate areas closest to the center darker than the rest of the petals.

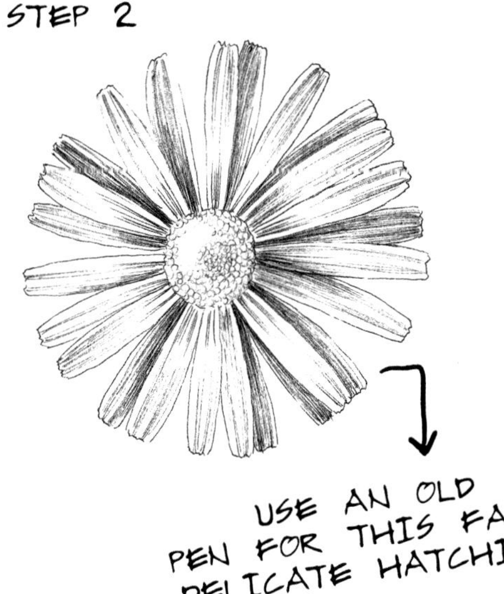

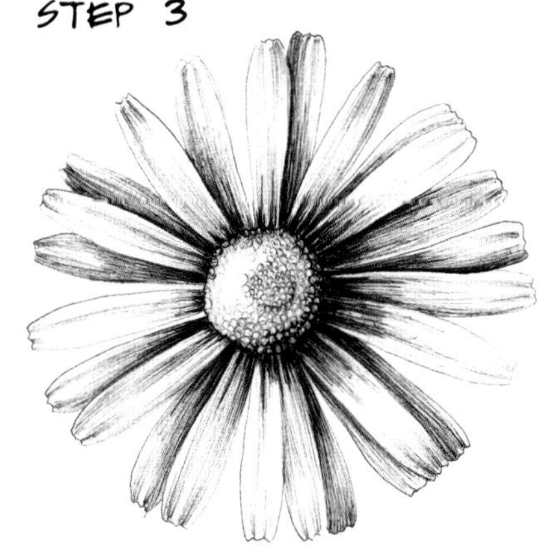

Let's look at one more example for a more complex flower, the chrysanthemum. Start by observing and studying the structure of the flower you're drawing, in this case, a composition with two flowers with its leaves. Start your sketch by drafting the general circular shapes of the flowers next to each other, then define the center of the flower heads and the general shapes of the leaves. Add the petals to each flower, remembering that they're not perfectly aligned. In this case, the flower has a rounded shape and it's not flat like daisies. The petals are thin and curved, so to get their shapes correctly, use a pencil to sketch the curved lines beforehand, as seen in the example. The petals curve as if they are hugging the flower head. Follow by adding extra petals opening all around the flower, making sure we see the inside and outside of each petal, as they fold backwards in the direction of the center. For the leaves, start with their general shape, sketch the central vein, and add the openings on the sides, following the diagonal direction as seen in the first leaf exercise of this chapter. Vary the distances between the leaves and overlap some for a natural look if you wish. Use an ink pen for outlining, paying attention to the details like small notches on petal tips. Sketch the flower heads with dashed lines.

Once the outlines are done, you can use a thin ink pen to hatch faded curved lines along the petals, creating texture. Start with the insides of the petals, where visible, as they will be darker. Hatch in both directions, from the tips of the petals towards

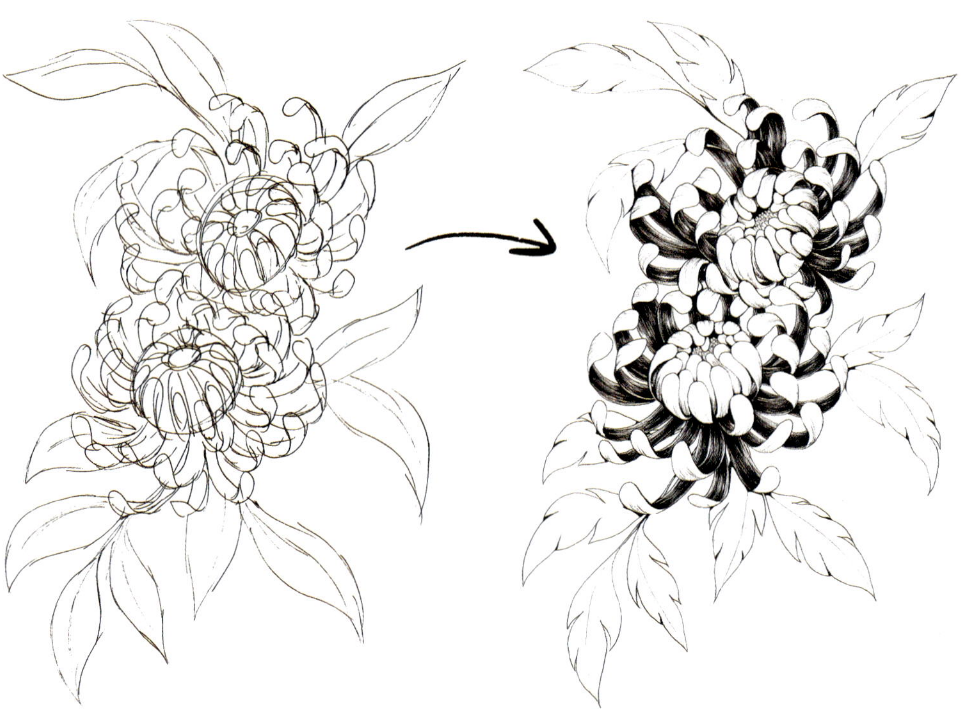

the center of the flower, and from the center out, along the length of each petal. Darken the underlying petals where they overlap for depth. A lighter hatching can be done on the outsides of the petals, but this time, only in the direction from the center or bottom of the petals upwards, towards the tips. Make sure to leave highlight areas on the tips of the petals. You can create an interesting, high-contrast effect by shading the insides of the petals much darker, leaving the outsides with almost no shading. For the leaves, hatch along the secondary veins on each side of each leaf, leaving highlighted areas to start

building values, or leave them white for a stylized effect.

Finish by adding darker values to the shadow areas, leaving empty spaces for the highlights. Use solid blacks to create drop shadows in between petals and on the leaves, right underneath the flowers. Pay attention to details like leaf veins and texture. If the insides of the flowers are visible, add some florets—the small structures coming from the flower head—and shade the remaining visible area inside the flower with a darker tone.

TREES

In this section, we will explore how to capture the beauty and character of trees using simple inking techniques. Drawing trees can seem daunting and challenging, but with a simplified approach, anyone can create stunning tree illustrations.

First, it's important to understand the form and structure of the tree you want to draw, as they come in many different shapes and textures. For the purpose of drawing, we don't need to go too deep into the anatomy of trees, but simply observe and study the general shapes and positions of the main elements. Usually, the potential visible elements are roots, trunk, branches, foliage, leaves, and sometimes fruits or flowers.

The amount of detail you want to add to a tree in an ink drawing is up to you. In a

complex composition with many trees, as in landscape or perspective drawing, the trees that are in the foreground will be larger, allowing for more details and textures. The trees further back need fewer lines and details. It all depends on your composition, how much space you have available to work with, and how realistic you want the final result to be.

As in previous chapters, you can use a pencil to sketch the first lines and shapes using one of the methods suggested in Chapter 2. Sketching beforehand can be helpful to build the confidence to start with inking.

Let's work with some real step-by-step examples, starting from the ink outline.

How to Draw an Oak Tree

Oak trees have an archetypical shape and can serve as a great study subject when learning the most useful techniques to draw trees. Here's the drawing process:

1. **Outline the shapes:** After sketching the general shapes of the tree, the ink outline will consist of two major parts: the trunk and the foliage. This is a simple tree, so the trunk can be done simply with two parallel lines perpendicular to the ground that branch up and outwards into smaller sections. These branches will hold the foliage. To start the foliage, just define the general shape using an uneven abstract pattern, similar to scribbling. Add some openings where parts of the tree branches can be visible, being mindful of the base and where they are coming from. The branches shouldn't be randomly positioned, as we want to represent their natural growth. The lines that define them should be directed up and outwards, as seen in the example. The foliage openings on the other hand should be random and not similarly spaced or shaped. Each opening can have its own shape, and the distances between them should vary.

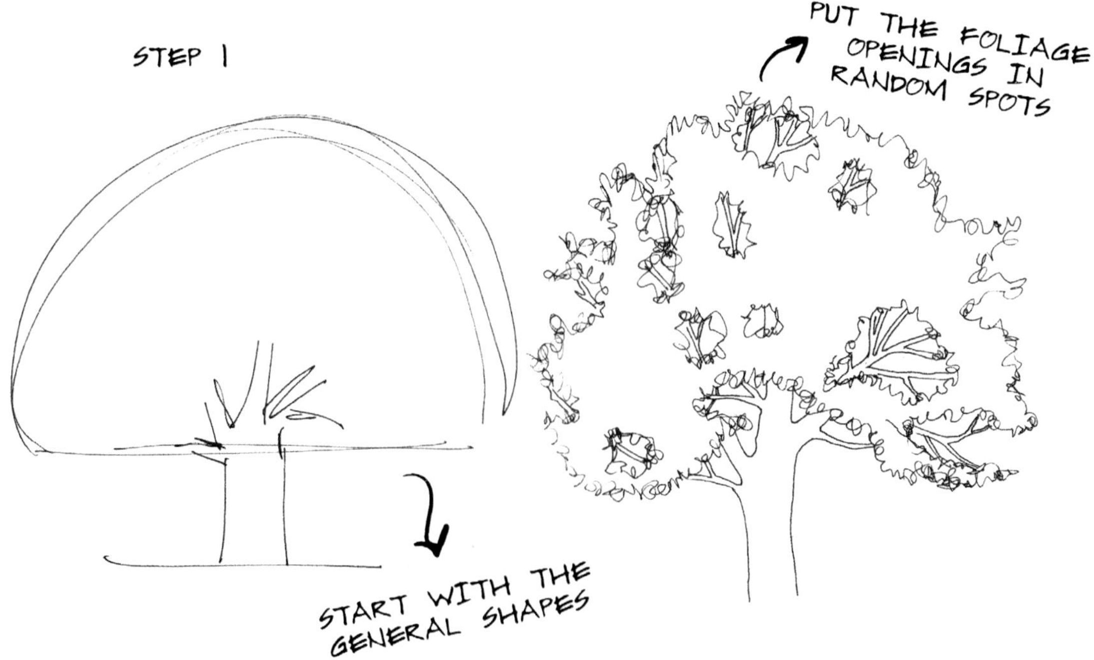

2. **Define the foliage texture:** Next, start filling the foliage area with an abstract or scribbling pattern, starting with the shadow areas. In order to know where to position the shadows, define where the light source is and your shadow side will be in the opposite direction. In this example, the light source is coming from the upper right corner, so leave the lower left side of any element in shadow. Start adding ink on the left side of the tree and on the areas right above the foliage openings. This will add depth to your tree. Add more ink in other empty areas, always keeping the light source in mind by leaving the right, upper side of the tree lighter.

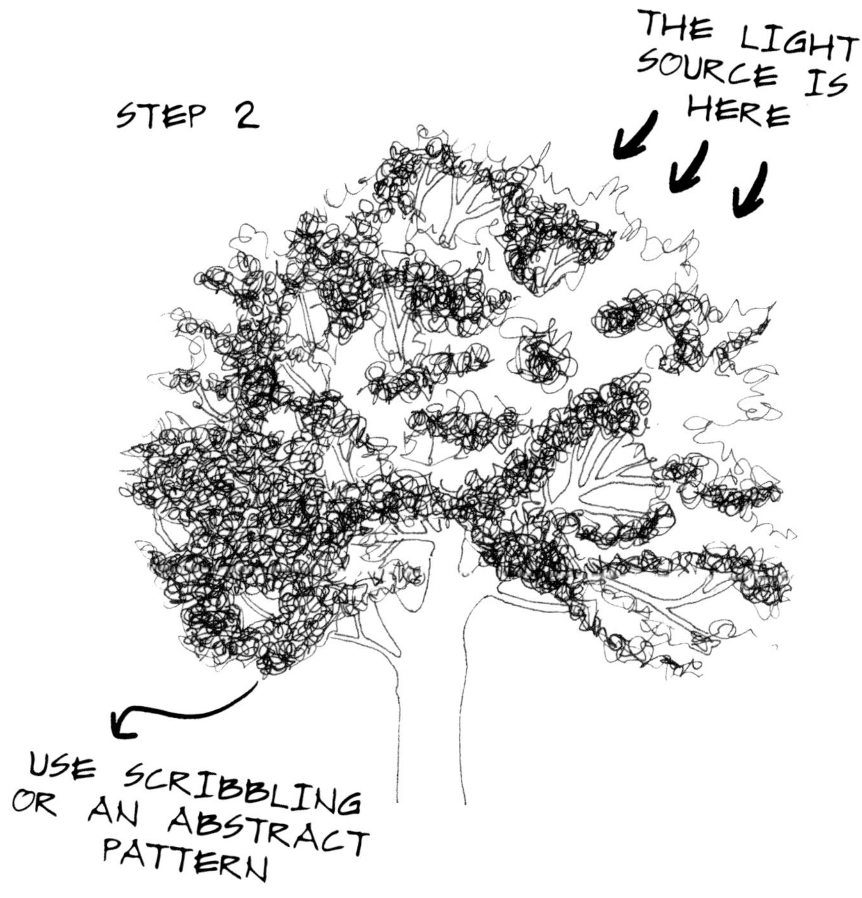

3. **Add shading:** Follow by increasing the darkness of the shadow areas with more layers of the same pattern, spreading them out towards the lighter spots. The whole tree should be filled with this abstract pattern, but the shadow spots should be darker and transition smoothly towards the light. Start the first layer of hatching for the trunk and branches by simply hatching long, slightly faded lines along their length. For the ground, start with a series of short, vertical dashes around the base of the trunk.

4. **Add final details:** To finish this drawing, intensify the shadows to create more contrast and depth, and hatch darker lines on the left and lower side of the trunk and branches. Make sure to add extra shadows on the branches right under the foliage. The visible parts of the branches seen through the foliage openings can be filled with solid black as they would receive little to no light being in the inner parts of the tree. To make your drawing look more polished and realistic, add tiny leaf branches all around the tree

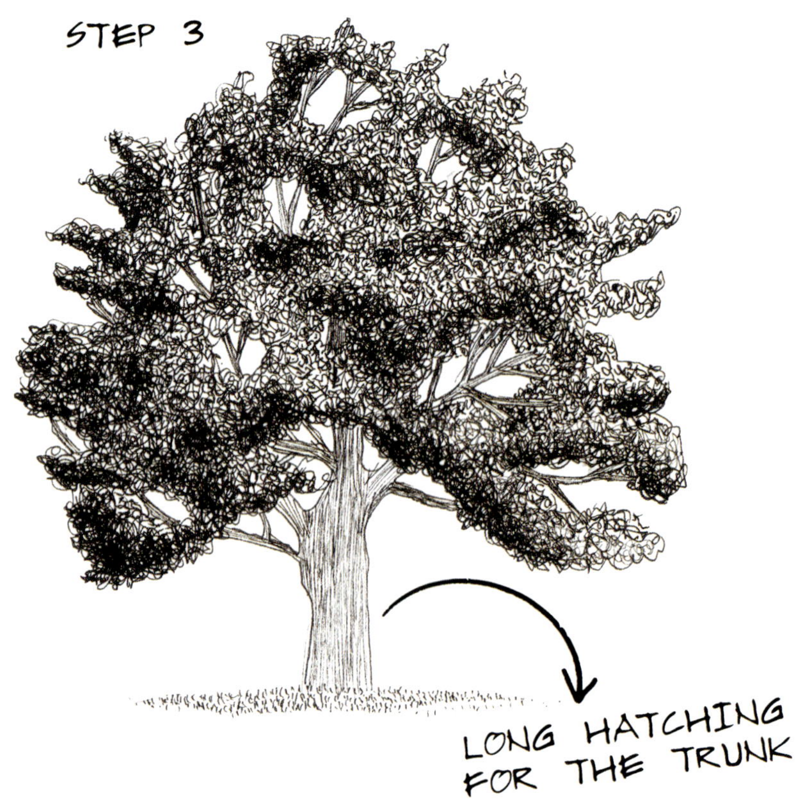

foliage. There's no need to be too perfectionist with this step—just make sure the small leaves are proportional in size to the whole tree. This will create the illusion that the entire mass of foliage consists of tiny leaves instead of the abstract pattern that is much easier and faster to draw. On the ground, add extra dashes of ink on the left side of the trunk to create a cast shadow, making sure that it transitions smoothly towards the lighter areas.

Use this simple process as a first step to adding realistic trees to your illustrations.

Feel free to simplify this process to create more stylized trees, or even make it more detailed by creating a more realistic foliage. This can be achieved by drawing the small leaf branches, as done in the last step of the oak tree example, all over the foliage instead of using the abstract pattern for the main part. If you want to attempt this more detailed style, work on a larger scale in order to have enough space to draw the leaves. This will be much more time consuming than the method described above, so take your time and enjoy the process!

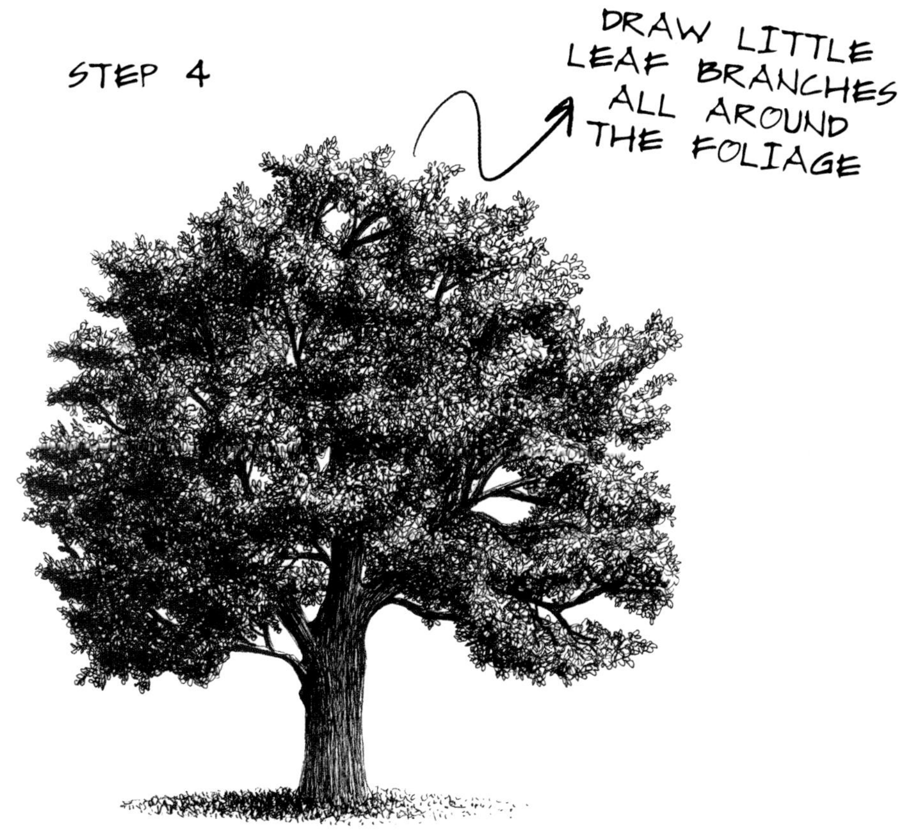

How to Draw a Pine Tree

Pine trees require a different drawing process than oak trees, and we will be able to experiment with another technique. These trees typically have a triangular shape, and their foliage and branches are organized in rows.

1. **Build the structure of the tree:** This drawing starts from a simple tall triangular shape and two short lines under the base of the triangle to represent the trunk. Draw several diagonal lines, slightly curved upwards along the sides of the triangle, to help you create the foliage rows. For the sake of brevity, I will refer to these lines as "rows" from now on. Follow by hatching several short lines along each row, mostly downwards, as seen in the example.

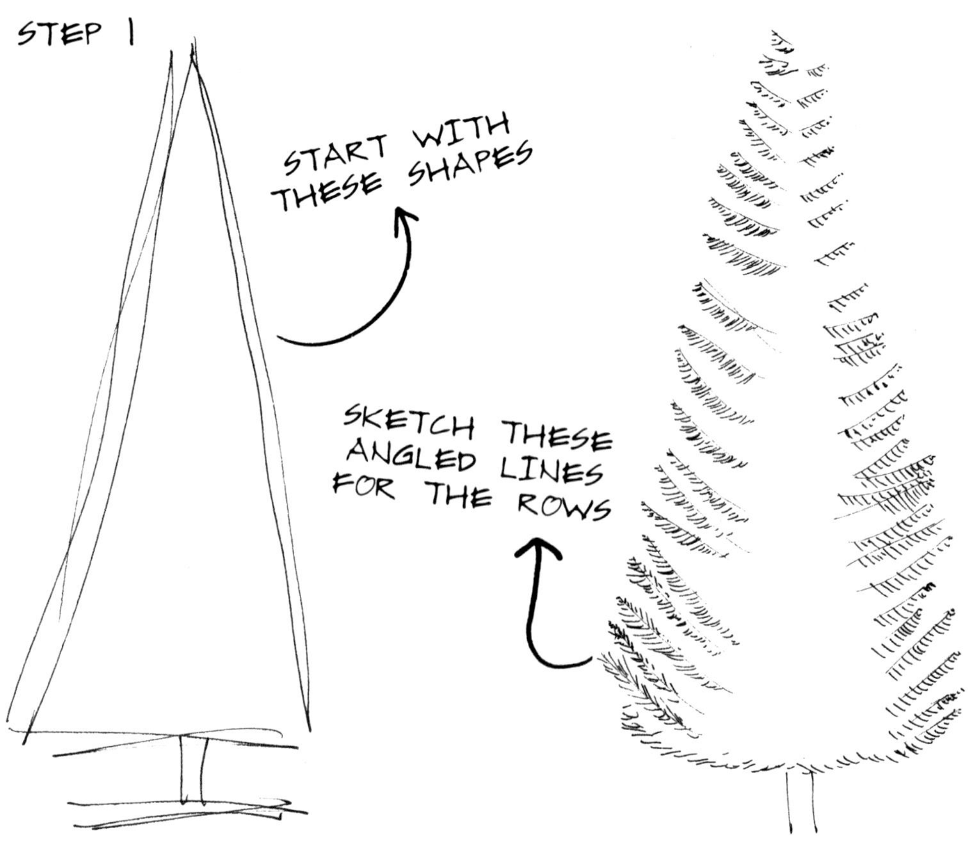

2. **Define the foliage pattern:** For this tree we will use a simple short hatching technique to portray the foliage. Simply hatch short lines randomly inside the triangle and in between the base of the rows, leaving their tips poking out of the tree. Hatch fast lines along the trunk, and draw the pattern of the grass as short dashes all around the base of the trunk.

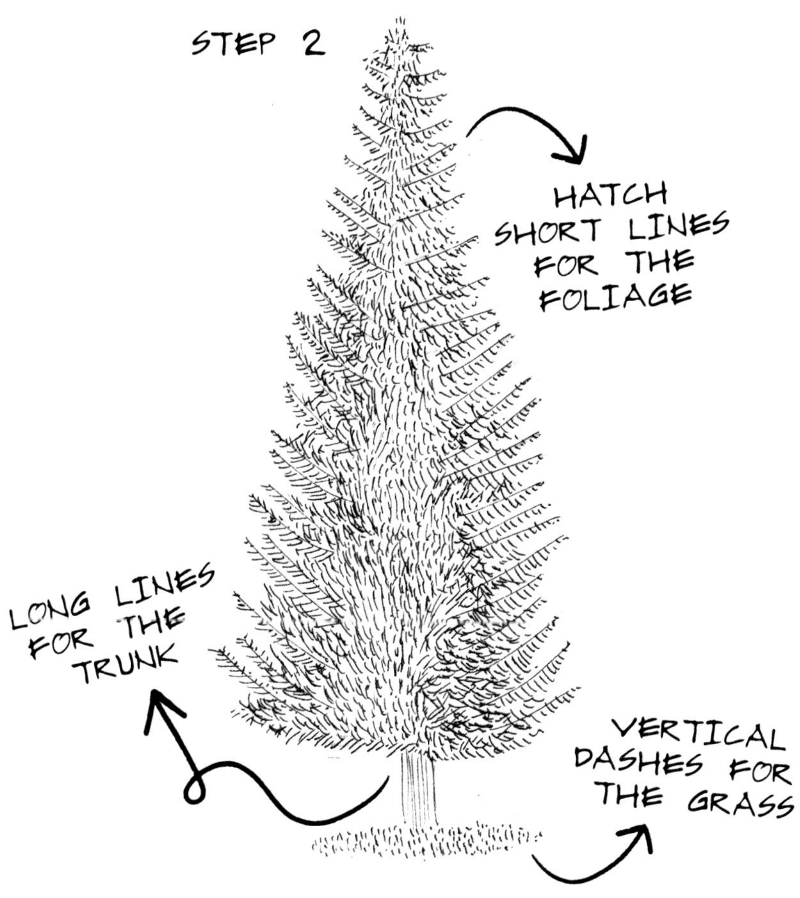

3. **Start shading:** Create the shadows with the same hatching technique, simply layering more lines where you want to make it darker. Generally, the shadows will be under each row and in the center of the tree. Remember that in real life, a pine tree is not shaped as a two-dimensional triangle, but as a three-dimensional cone. This means that, just as the rows branch to the sides of the tree, it also branches towards the front and back. This effect can be achieved by creating shadows on one side of these central branches. In this example, I chose the left side. Notice that there are shadows on both sides, but they are slightly darker on the left. These shadows are not necessarily being created by the light source that comes from above. They simply demonstrate the depth of the tree—the areas that are further back inside the tree behind branches that are receiving light.

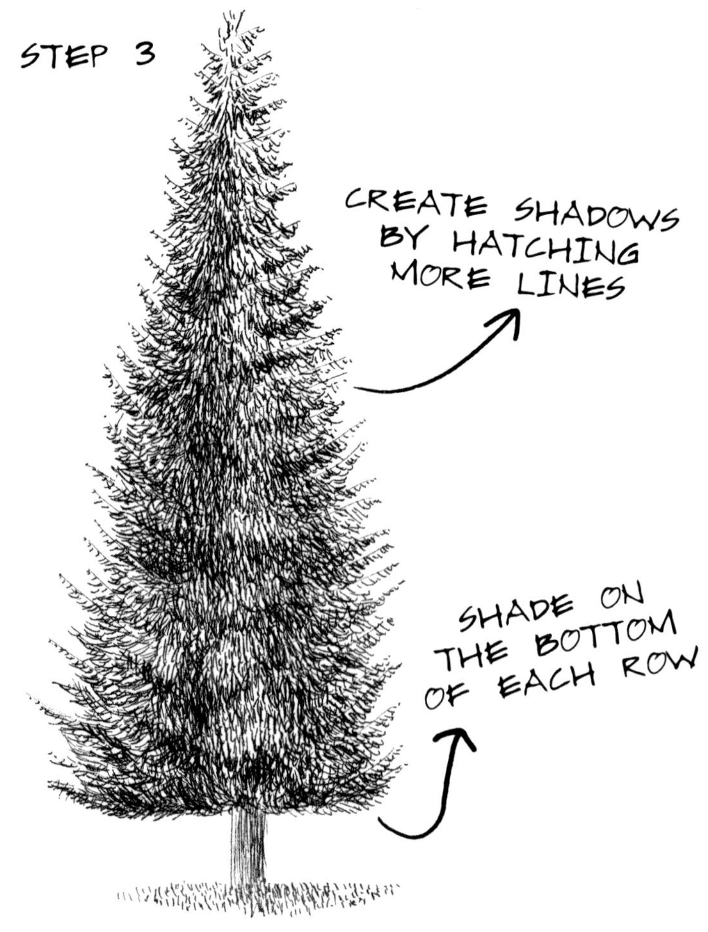

4. **Add final details:** Finish by darkening the shadows to intensify contrast and depth. You will notice that a little solid black on the deeper areas of the tree goes a long way to creating a more three-dimensional effect. Follow by hatching darker lines on the tree trunk, especially right under the foliage. To improve the realistic illusion even more, add a cast shadow on the same side you added the shadows on the trunk. In this case, the light source is coming almost directly from above, creating a shadow slightly to the right side, but mostly under the base of the tree.

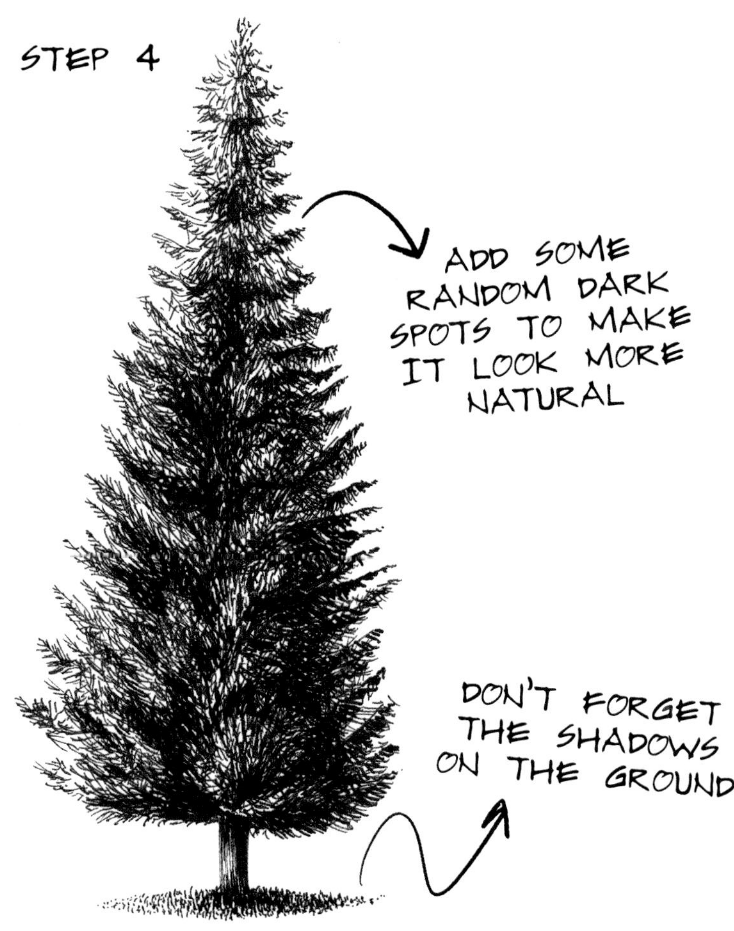

CREATING YOUR OWN BOTANICAL COMPOSITIONS

Drawing more complex botanical compositions involves understanding the basic structure of plants and learning to observe subtle changes in shape, position, and texture. It also requires a good grasp of perspective and shading. With this understanding, you can develop compositions in which different plants interact with each other

In this section, we explore ways to stylize your plant drawings using ink pens. Stylizing is all about adding your unique touch and personality to your artwork, so these are not the only ways to approach botanical art. Use these ideas to get inspired. Remember, there is no right or wrong way to stylize your drawings. What matters is expressing your creativity and making the artwork truly yours.

- ✧ **Find inspiration in nature:** One way to create unique illustrations is to find inspiration in the real world. Go for a walk in nature and find elements that inspire you. Without harming the environment, you can take small samples home to use as reference, or simply take pictures with your phone or camera to use in your practice later. Even better, bring your sketchbook to a beautiful place in nature and take some time to illustrate what you see. This can be a beautiful practice that will allow you to express yourself in your drawings from a unique, genuine perspective.

- ✧ **Use multiple references:** As seen in previous chapters, references are great tools for enhancing your creativity while improving your drawing skills at the same time. Simply plan a botanical illustration from imagination, and look for references to support your idea, as opposed to choosing one reference picture to draw from. In this case, since you are combining multiple references for all the elements in your composition, you can confidently say this is a drawing you created from your mind, and simply used references for research and study.

- ✧ **Combine non-botanical elements:** To make your botanical illustrations more creative, you can add other elements to complement the composition. It could be elements that make sense in the botanical context, like bugs or birds, or you can really get creative and let your imagination take over.

- ✧ **Experiment with line quality:** Line quality refers to the thickness or thinness of a line. By varying your line quality, you can add depth and interest to your plant drawings. For instance, you might use thin lines to suggest delicate features like flower petals and thicker lines to depict sturdier elements like tree trunks.

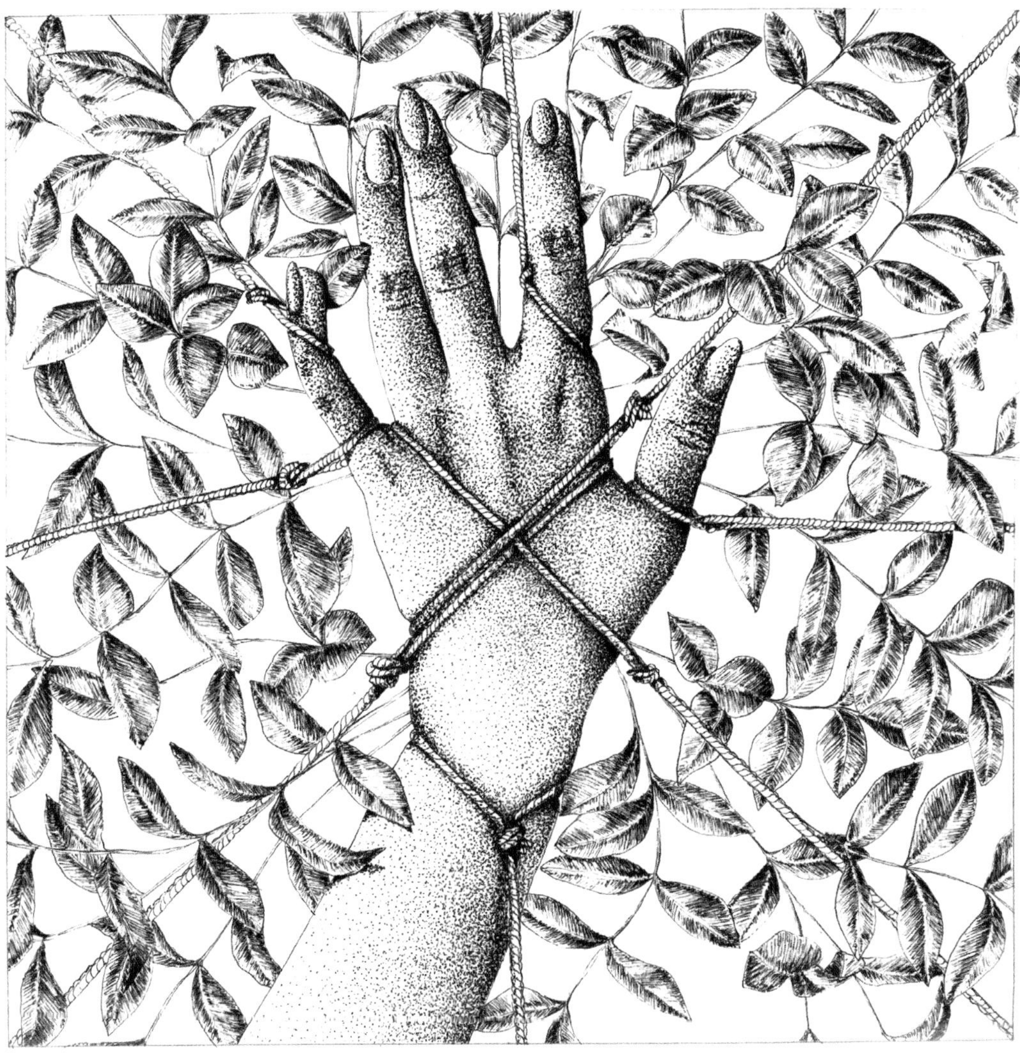

- ⬧ **Play with textures:** Textures can greatly enhance the realism of your plant drawings. Use a variety of pen strokes to suggest different textures. For example, short, quick strokes can be used to depict the rough texture of tree bark, while smooth, flowing lines can suggest the glossy surface of a leaf.

- ⬧ **Consider the negative space:** Negative space is the space around the subject of your drawing. By carefully considering your negative space, you can create a sense of balance and composition in your artwork. For instance, you might leave a part of your paper untouched to suggest a light source or draw attention to a particular element.

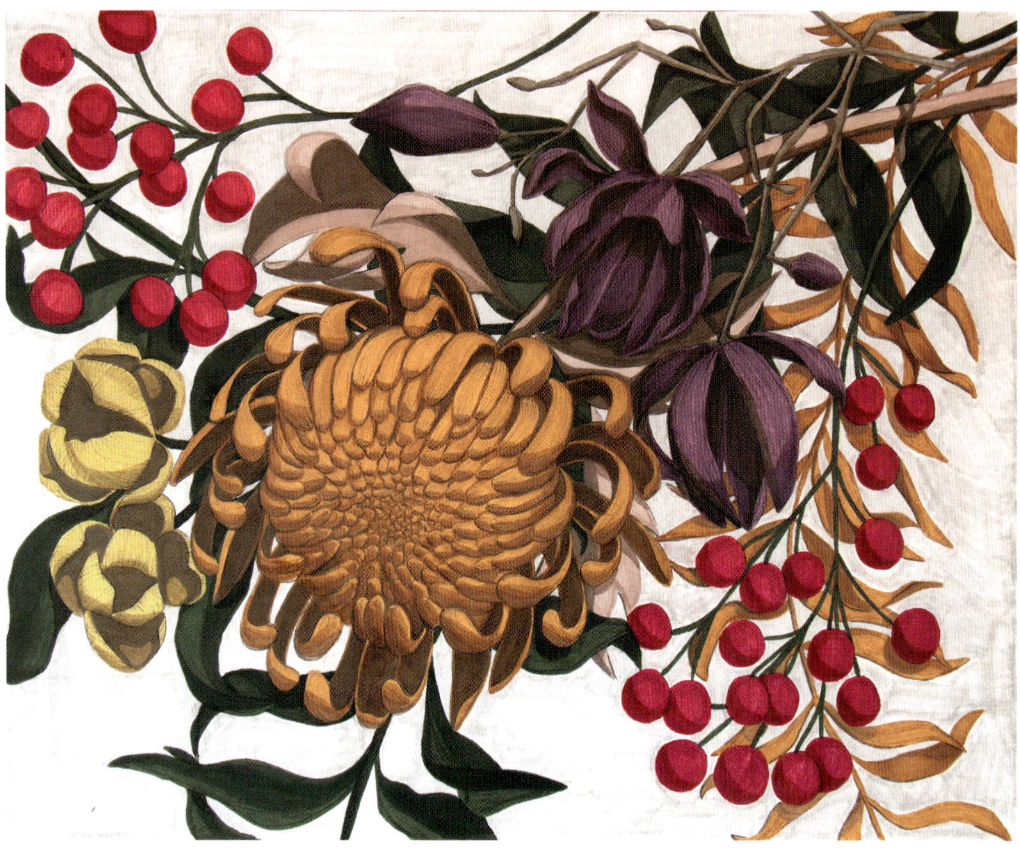

⋄ **Add color:** While this guide focuses on ink pen drawings, don't hesitate to add a dash of color to your art. You can use colored ink pens, watercolors, pastels, markers, or any other medium of your choice to add vibrancy to your plant drawings. In this botanical illustration, the color was added with alcohol markers, followed by the details and shading with fineline ink pens.

⋄ **Experiment with mixed media:** Don't feel limited to stay within the ink pen world. Try combining ink with other mediums, like gouache, watercolors, colored pencils, collages, or any other method you would like to try. See what materials mesh well with the ink and which ones do not. You might discover styles or aspects of combining different mediums that make your art more unique and authentic to you.

Stylizing your plant drawings is a personal journey. Feel free to experiment, make mistakes, and discover your unique style.

FINAL THOUGHTS

As we come to the end of this book, it's important to remember that anyone can be creative, and this is a skill that should be nurtured with love. Don't worry if things don't always turn out perfectly—sometimes what you see as a mistake can lead to amazing discoveries! Drawing with ink pens is a slow and intricate process, and it is all about expressing yourself with calm and patience. Let the ink calm your mind, and allow yourself to enjoy this journey.

If you don't know what to draw, just draw anything. Scribble, doodle, draw something different, something new. What matters is that you keep this creative spark alive.

Thank you for reading this book, and I genuinely hope that it pushed you further in your artistic journey and helped you reach your goals. Happy drawing!

ACKNOWLEDGEMENTS

Creating this book has been a truly rewarding journey for me as an artist, and it wouldn't have been possible without the incredible support of so many people. I'm deeply grateful to each one of you.

A special shoutout to my husband, Justin, for his unwavering belief in me—sometimes even more than I believed in myself. His encouragement has been a game-changer, and I really couldn't have done it without him.

I'm also incredibly thankful to Kelly Reed and the entire team at Rocky Nook for this fantastic opportunity and for their assistance in turning my vision into reality.

A big thank you goes out to the amazing community of artists and illustrators who were generous enough to share their expertise and wisdom with me. Your inspiration was essential to this project.

And to all the artists who've inspired my creativity with their incredible work, even though I can't name everyone, please know your influence has been a constant motivator for me to get where I am today as an artist.

Lastly, to you, the reader, thank you for embarking on this adventure with me. Whether you're experienced or just starting out, I hope this book ignites a spark of creativity in you.

Thank you to everyone who played a part in bringing this book to life. You've all been essential in making this dream a reality, and I couldn't be more grateful for this experience.

ABOUT THE AUTHOR

Giovana Vescovi is an artist and designer who finds in her drawing practice a source of joy and peace. After many years experimenting with different styles and mediums, Giovana has developed a distinctive style characterized by intricate ink drawings that blend surreal elements in dream-like scenarios, inspired by the whimsical beauty of nature.

Her love for drawing developed into her passion for teaching and motivating other artists, and she now provides art classes to students all over the world. Each class is designed to offer students not only methods and techniques to improve their skills, but also to inspire them to explore the depths and particularities of their own creativity. Giovana's passion for teaching reflects her belief in art as a universal language and a tool for connection and personal growth.

To learn more about Giovana's teaching, visit www.artsygio.com or connect with her on social media:

Website: www.giovescovi.com
Instagram: gio_vescovi
YouTube: gio_vescovi
TikTok: gio_vescovi

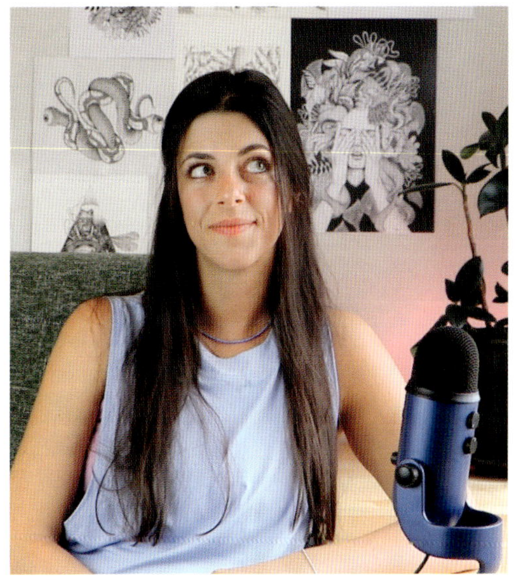

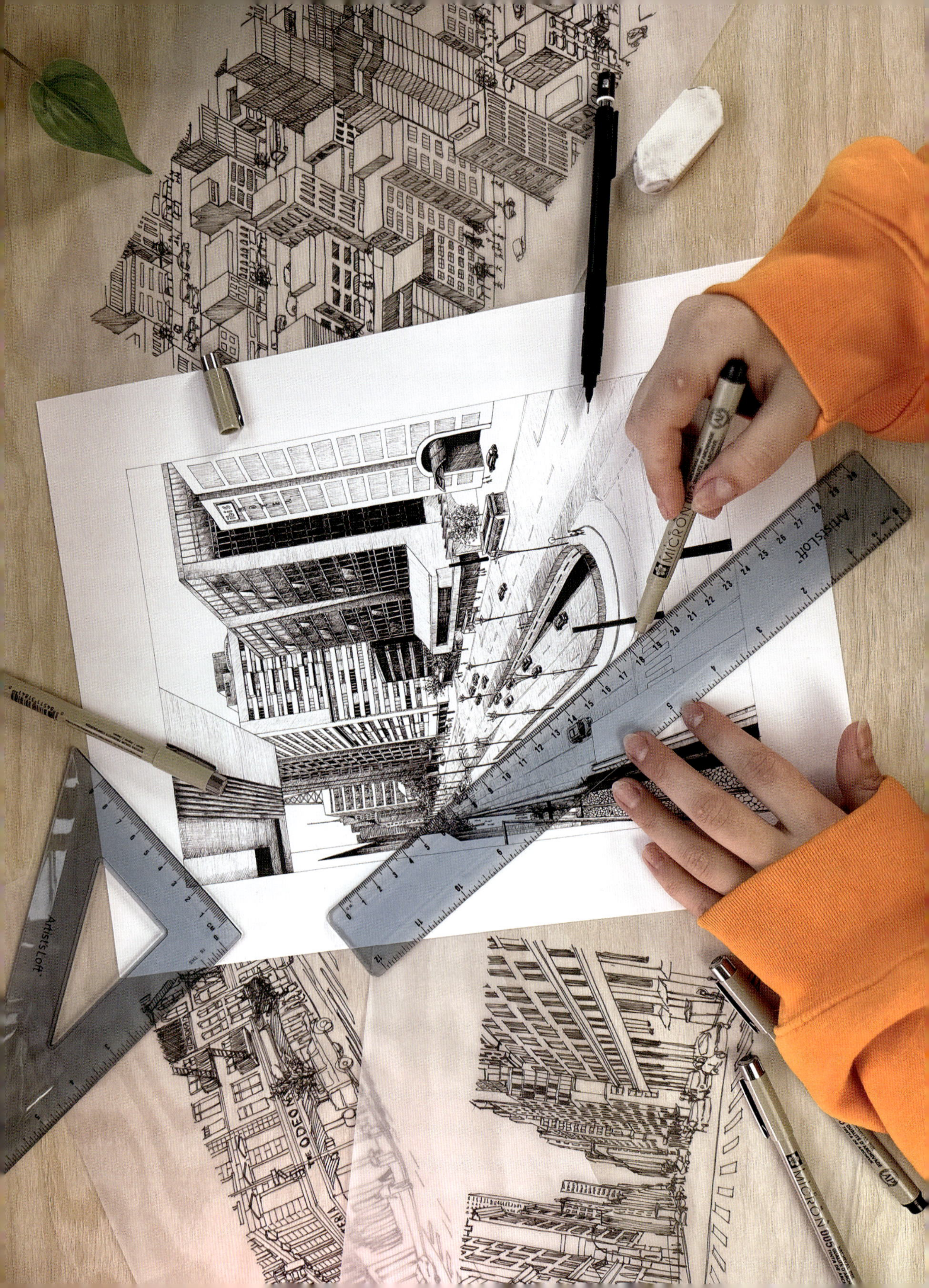

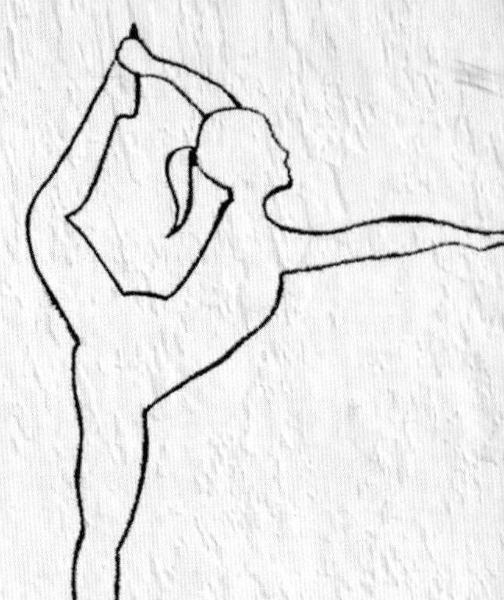

Don't Close The Book On Us!

Sign up today to receive a copy of The Introduction to Morpho Anatomy Drawing Basics ebook

Plus access to:
- Discounts
- Free Online Events
- Exclusive Content
- And More!

www.rockynook.com/drawing-newsletter